Women Vendors in Urban Informal Sector

Women Vendors in Urban Informal Sector

S. Bhanu Baba Saheb

AKANSHA PUBLISHING HOUSE
NEW DELHI • GUWAHATI • VISAKHAPATNAM

AKANSHA PUBLISHING HOUSE
4649-B/21, Ansari Road
Daryaganj, New Delhi-110002
Phones: 23268193, 09435116718
Email: ektabooks@yahoo.com
visit us: www.akanshapublishinghouse.com

Women Vendors in Urban Informal Sector

First Published 2011

ISBN 978-81-8370-277-5

PRINTED IN INDIA

Published by Akansha Publishing House, New Delhi-110002 and printed at Harmain Offset Printers, Delhi.

Contents

Acknowledgements

I would like to gratefully acknowledge my enthusiastic research director Prof. Mrs. P. Tara Kumari for her immense help in planning and executing the works in time. Her company and assurance at the time of crisis would be remembered lifelong.

On the other hand, profound knowledge and timely help came as a blessing under the guidance of Prof. V. Gandhi Babu and Mrs. Gandhi Babu for the help extended to me when I approached him and the valuable discussion that I had with him during the course of my research.

My sincere thanks are due to Prof. R. Sudarshan Rao, Head, Department of Economics for his constant encouragement. I am also thankful to Prof. G. Rama Chandrudu, Chairman, Board of Studies of Economics, Department of Economics, Andhra University, for his cooperation and support. I specially thank late Prof. C. Ratnam for his valuable suggestions during the course of my work which are greatly acknowledged. He would have been much more delighted, more than anyone, had he been in our midst today.

Special acknowledgements are due to Prof. K. Siva Prasad, Prof. Mrs. K. Rani Gopal, Prof. K. Ravi Babu, Prof. K. Srirama Murthy, Prof. S.K.V. Suryanarayana Raju, Prof. T. Koteshwara Rao, Prof. L. K. Mohana Rao, Prof. D. Pulla Rao, Prof. M. Sundar Rao, Prof. M. Bhavani Shankar, Dr. M. Prasada Rao, Prof. E. Naga Bhushnam, Prof. S. Ramesh Babu, Prof. R. Rama Krishna, Prof. N. Bhaskar Reddy, Dr. V. Seshagiri Rao, Mrs. Y. Ravini., of Department of Economics, Andhra University.

The episode of acknowledgement would not be complete without the mentioning of my parents sri M. Krupa Varan (father), Mrs. M.S. Sakunthala (mother), who taught me the value of hard work by their own example. I would like to share this moment of happiness with my wife Mrs. Shalima, my son, my brother Mr. Jam Babu, Mrs. Sunitha (sister) and Ravi Kumar (brother-in-law) and their son Mr. Rishi and daughter Sresta who rendered enormous support during the whole tenure of my research.

I am forever indebted to my uncles Mr. I. D. Raju, B. Ajay Kumar, Dr. N. Vijayanand Peter and N. Sri Nagesh for their moral support and endless encouragement when it was most required.

I wish to express gratitude to my beloved friend G. Stevenson and my fellow research scholars for their encouragement to pursue my research studies.

At the outset, I am ever indebted all my life to my Almighty God for keeping me in good health and spirits all through the course of my work which would otherwise have been left out as an unaccomplished task.

Last but not least I am thankful to Mr. H.K. Misra and Mr. M.P. Misra, Akansha Publishing House, New Delhi for undertaking publication of this book.

S. Bhanu Baba Saheb

List of Tables

1

Introduction

Women in any nation constitute nearly half of its population. But their contribution to the economic development throughout the world is meager they were kept away from the mainstream of the economic development. The position and status of women in any society is an index of the socioeconomic and cultural achievements of the society. It significantly varies from urban to rural, educated to uneducated, employed to unemployed, privileged class to underprivileged class and upper economic strata to lower economic strata of women.[1]

There have been some changes in the position of women in India over the years but these changes are not uniform. Though the position of women in India is not unique when compared to the women in other developing countries, it still presents certain distinct features due to traditions, backwardness and history of exploitation of women in various aspects of Indian social life. The reasons for the low status and position of women belonging to lower strata are one and the same in all the ages irrespective of changes that have occurred in society. Although women now work in diversified and occupy positions of importance, official statistics itself indicate that six decades of development has not been very kind to women workers in general. This is especially so in regard to the women participation in the unorganized sector. Mazumdar[2] points out that the urban poor but the same as those in rural areas–both laying at the bottom of the social structure and suffering from cumulative inequalities.

Women's contribution played a vital role in the economies at family and society level. Women refer to persons of the female (above) fifteen years older, whether or not they were already married.[3] In the early stage of societal development, agriculture was the main economic activity. In shifting agriculture, men do little work, while women do the most. In somewhat more densely populated regions where agriculture is of extensive plough cultivation, women do little work and men do much more. In regions of intensive cultivation of irrigated land, both men and women certainty put in more hard work. In that way women are put to hard work to meet the economic ends. Since India's economy is primarily oriented and rural based, all women tend to work. In recent years rapid industrialization contributed to the growth of urban centers. Location of industries, expansion of government administration, literacy institutions etc. are playing a major role in the urbanization process. Employment and income earning opportunities in these centers attract migrants from the nearby rural areas. This coincides with increase in the population pressure on agricultural land and mechanized agriculture. The women workforce engage in traditional sector in the rural areas is now slowly shifting to the urban areas. Consequent to this trend, a large majority of women are employed in various categories of work in the unorganized sector and it is more so in the urban areas. Important reasons for this situation include unemployed husband, with children to be taken care of, women separated from their spouses.

Petty Trade in Informal Sector

In the Informal sector, an enterprise is defined to include an economic unit engaged in production of goods and services whether it employs only one person (the proprietor) or more, whether or not it uses fixed capital, whether or not it has a fixed location for conducting business.[4] In this connection a construction worker, a Rickshaw driver, a shoes shine boy, petty shop keeper etc. or all treated as constituting an enterprises even though they hire no employees own a little or no capital and do not own any business premises. They also do not have any fixed location of business.

The small unregulated establishment or enterprises conducting business with low capital may be treated as petty trade. The petty trade is a small scale sole trading business run by a single individual, with or without any assistance of paid workers or family members. The profit or loss borne by the trader himself and is in no way responsible to any higher authorities in conducting the business. Petty trade may deal in many varieties ranging from the small item like pan shops, Kirana shops, fruit, fish, vegetable vending, sweet shops, laundries , hair cutting saloons etc., to more expensive fancy goods, cosmetics etc., and in general, there vendors are called as retailers. This retailing business is done on low level and there by catering the needs of the local people. Retailer is an independent merchant middleman–stand between the producer, whole sale dealer and the consumer. He acts as consumers purchasing agent. Retail trading is a broad word, which includes "all those business activities associated with the selling of goods and services to an ultimate consumer or final user for personal consumption.

In the retail business, there are many types depending upon the working capital, for example, large retail business, small retail business and medium retail business etc., Petty trade comes under the group of small retail business. These retailers desire to operate a small business and be independent to take quick decision, since they need not wait for the orders of the superiors. Hence the element of flexibility is an unmatched boon to the small retailer they are generally sole vendors who run the business by themselves with or without the help of paid workers and some time with the help of the family members. Though the Asian countries have witnessed an increase in street vendors, their governments are by and large indifferent to the specific needs of this sector. Street vendors perform an important role in providing services to the urban population, especially the poor. Their contributions are unfortunately hardly ever recognized by the governments. Instead, the governments are more often than not hostile to them. This is a result of a broader issue concerning the informal sector as a whole. In most Asian countries the informal sector is very large and it constitutes the mainstay of the economy. Instead of protecting this sector and ensuring that its workers get their minimum dues, the governments are indifferent to their existence. Street vendors are an important parts of the informal sector not only because of their numbers but because of the crucial roles the play in preserving this sector. The goods sold by street vendors are usually consumed by those in the informal sector, as they are cheap. Moreover, a significant amount of goods produced by small industrial units in the informal sector is marketed through them. In fact we have a situation where one section of the urban poor (street vendor) helps the other sections of the urban poor by providing them low priced goods and by marketing their products.

Women in the Informal Sector – International Scenario

Women supply visible and invisible labor in street vending activities. Street vending is one of the few readily accessible avenues of employment open to women who need to earn a living. The low cost of entry into many types of hawking and vending as well as schedule flexibility is an attractive factor for some women. In addition, in certain situations, women actually inherit their vendor status. For some women, vending and hawking are the only occupations they know, while for others they are occupations of last resort. With limited literacy and mechanical skills, poor women have few alternatives. Table 1 illustrates the importance of the informal sector, and of women in this sector, in selected countries of Africa and Asia.

Many of the Population Censuses and Labour Force Surveys collect data on place of work, sub-categories of occupations. Based on the available statistical data, Table- 2 gives the size of street vendors in ten developing countries, their share in non-agricultural employment and the proportion of women in the street vendors which was compiled by Jocques Charmes in the year 2002 for International Labour Organisation. In 10 developing countries, the estimated share of street vendors in total non-agricultural employment ranges from less than 2 per cent (in Costa Rica in 1997) to 9 per cent (in Guatemala in 2000) and is 4 per cent or more in six of the countries (Tunisia, Benin, Kenya, Guatemala, Mexico, and Venezuela).

One of the important features of the street vending activity is flexibility. Measuring the magnitude of street vendors in the total informal sector is very difficult, particularly great variance exists in the activity they undertake because some sellers sell only few hours during the day time, may be morning or evening. Some sellers conduct their activity only in the weekends. Sellers change the activity based on the seasons. One study conducted in Mexico City in the mid-1990s estimated that there were roughly 185,000 regular street vendors and an additional 90,000 occasional street vendors in Mexico City.[5]

Table -1.1: Informal Sector activities as a percent of total employment and GDP, and female informal traders' share of informal employment and informal GDP in selected countries of Africa and Asia

Countries	*Informal sector as a percentage of*		*Female informal traders as a percentage of*	
	Total trade employment	*Total trade GDP*	*Total informal trade employment*	*Total informal trade GDP*
Africa				
Benin	99.1	69.8	92.2	64.3
Burkina Faso	94.7	45.7	65.9	30.1
Chad	99.2	66.7	61.8	41.2
Kenya	84.9	61.5	50.2	27.3
Mali	98.1	56.7	81.3	46.1
Tunisia	87.6	55.6	7.9	4.4
Asia				
India	96.4	90.0	12.4	11.2
Indonesia	93.0	77.2	49.3	38.0
Philippines	73.1	52.3	72.0	21.6

Source: "Women as Street Vendors: Where, Why, and How?", *Seeds*, No. 20, 2000. p. 2.

A 1997 census on street vendors in Durban, South Africa, counted 19,000 street traders: 57 percent of these were in the central business district (CBD) and 30 per cent were in high-density but non-central areas (such as Umlazi Township). Sixty-one per cent of the street traders were women; 39 per cent were men. This survey counted both street traders who sold goods (78 per cent of the total) and street workers who provided services

Table -1.2: Street Vendors in Ten Developing Countries: Estimated Number, Share of Non-agricultural Employment, Proportion of Women

Countries	*Number of Street Vendors*	*Percent of non-agricultural labourforce*	*Percent Women*
Tunisia (1997)	125,619	6	2
Benin (1992)	45,591	5	81
Kenya (1999)	416,294	8	33
India (1999-2000)	3,881,700	3	14
Turkey (2000) urban	255,000	2	3
Brazil (1991)	1,445,806	3	30
Costa Rica (1997)	13,085	1	18
Guatemala (2000)	259,203	9	55
Mexico (2000)	1,286,287	4	44
Venezuela (1997)	318,598	4	32

Source: Jocques Charmes (2002): "Is asking for 'place of work' a pertinent and efficient way to better measure and understand the category of home-workers, and more generally, outworkers in the labour force?" in ILO, *On Measuring Place of Work*, Geneva.

(21 per cent of the total). Of those who sold goods, seven out of ten sold food stuffs (fruits, vegetables, meat, and poultry); some sold new and used clothing; and less than 1 per cent sold traditional medicines. Those who sold fresh produce were mainly self-employed, while those who sold clothes were most often employed by someone else. Nearly half sold only one type of product, one quarter sold two types of products, and one quarter sold three or more types of products. Only a few (3 per cent) sold goods or foods produced by themselves. The Durban study found some important gender differences in street trading. Although few vendors overall hired other people, slightly more men (13 per cent) than women (10 per cent) did. Among those hired, there were nearly twice as many women as men. Nearly all of the women, but only two-third of the men, were vendors only. More men (61 per cent) than women

(54 per cent) purchase from a large wholesale dealer, rather than from a small retail shop. About six out of ten of the immigrant street traders were men.[6]

Bellagio International Declaration of Street Vendors[7]

In 1995, representatives from street vendor associations and activists, lawyers, and researchers working with street vendors from 11 cities around the world met in Bellagio, Italy to form an international alliance (now called StreetNet) of street vendor associations and of organizations working with street vendors. The founders of the network drafted the Bellagio International Declaration of Street Vendors.

The Bellagio Declaration identifies the following common problems of street vendors around the world:

- No Legal Status, No Right to Vend
- Lack of Space or Poor Location
- Restrictions on Licensing, Costs of Regulation
- Harassment, Bribes, Confiscation, and Evictions
- Lack of Services and Infrastructure
- Lack of Representation or Voice.

The Declaration urges national governments to incorporate street vendors in economic policies relating to trade, financial policies relating to micro-entrepreneurs, and social policies relating to the working poor. The Declaration also urges city governments to incorporate street vendors in urban planning processes and urban policies and to promote institutional mechanisms for street vendor associations to voice grievances, make demands, and resolve disputes with other urban stakeholders.

Street Vending in India

Street vending as a profession has been in existence in India since time immemorial. However, their number has increased manifold in the recent years. According to one study, Mumbai has the largest number of street vendors numbering around 250,000, while Delhi has around 200,000. Calcutta has more than 150,000 street vendors and Ahmedabad has around 100,000[8]. Women constitute a large number of street vendors in almost every city. Some studies estimate that street vendors constitute approximately 2% of the population of a metropolis. The total number of street vendors in the country is estimated at around 1 crore. Urban vending is not only a source of employment but provide 'affordable' services to the majority of urban population. The role played by the hawkers in the economy as also in the society needs to be given due credit but they are considered as unlawful entities and are subjected to continuous harassment by civic authorities. This is reported to be continuing even after the ruling of the Supreme Court that "if properly regulated according to the exigency of the circumstances, the small traders on the side walks can considerably add to the comfort and convenience of the general public, by making available ordinary articles of everyday use for a comparatively lesser price. An ordinary person, not very affluent, while hurrying towards his home after a day's work can pick up these articles without going out of his way to find a regular market. The right to carry on trade or business mentioned in Article 19(1)G of the Constitution, on street pavements, if properly regulated cannot be denied on the ground that the streets are meant exclusively for passing or re-passing and no other use." Street vendors provide valuable services to the urban population while trying to earn a livelihood and it is the duty of the State to protect the right of this segment of population to earn their livelihood. This policy tries to ensure that this important section of the urban population finds recognition for its contribution to society, and is conceived of as a major initiative for urban poverty alleviation.

1. Definition of a Street Vendor

A street vendor is broadly defined as a person who offers goods for sale to the public without having a permanent built up structure but with a temporary static structure or mobile stall (or headload). Street vendors may be stationary by occupying space on the pavements or other public/private areas, or may be mobile in the sense that they move from place to place carrying their wares on push carts or in cycles or baskets on their heads, or may sell their wares in moving trains, bus etc. In this policy document, the term urban vendor is inclusive of both traders and service providers, stationary as well as mobile vendors and incorporates all other local/region specific terms used to describe them, such as, hawker, pheriwalla, rehri-patri walla, footpath dukandars, sidewalk traders, etc.

2. National Policy on Street Vendors

Government of India appointed a National Task Force on Street Vendors. The task force prepared a "Draft National Policy on Street Vendors" and submitted it to the Ministry of Urban Development and Poverty Alleviation in the year 2004. The main objective of this Draft on National Policy is to provide and promote a supportive environment for earning livelihoods to the Street vendors, as well as ensure absence of congestion and maintenance of hygiene in public spaces and streets.

The policy calls for a paradigm shift in the perception of the role of street vendors and appeals for 'regulation' instead of 'prohibition'. It estimates that about 10 million of working force is constituted by street vendors. Various factors of street vending are covered by Supreme Court Judgments, Articles of Constitution, definition, objective of the policy, Planning norms, Regulatory Committee at Town and Ward level, Weekly Markets, Regulatory Process, Registration System, Relocation and Rehabilitation, Municipal and Police laws, Access to Credit, Insurance, Social Security, Training and Skill Upgradation, Self Regulation.

3. National Association of Street Vendors of India (NASVI)

It was initiated by SEWA in September 1998 to bring together the street vendor organisations of India so as to collectively struggle for macro-level changes which had become imminent to support the livelihood of around 10 million vendors which stood severely threatened due to outdated laws and changing policies, practices and attitudes of the powers that be. Last one and half decade had seen considerable increase in the momentum and intensity of attack on the livelihood of urban poor particularly street vendors. Reasons and the manifestation of the attack are many. NASVI is a coalition of trade unions and voluntary organisations working for street vendors spread all over India. NASVI, based in Patna, started off as a networking organisation of street vendors. Nidan,a leading Non Governmental Organisation of Bihar was given the responsibility to co-ordinate NASVI. However, as NASVI grew in terms of recognition, membership, activities and created a niche for itself, the need for a separate legal identity of NASVI was felt. A constitution was prepared through a consultative process and NASVI was registered in November 2003. 276 organisations representing 1,68,278 street vendors from 20 states of India have taken the formal membership contributing membership fee. Ever since its inception, the strategy of NASVI has been to:

- Build a strong grassroots movement of street vendors of India.
- Look for lasting and sustainable solution to the problem faced by street vendors.
- Dialogue with all decision-makers and stake holders in finding solutions.
- Make available information about good practices, initiatives, methods of struggle.
- Maintain continuous communication with and between street vendor organization and also with other stakeholders.
- Strengthen street vendor organization and support them in their endeavor to ensure livelihood of street vendors.

Need for the Study

From the beginning the role of women in Indian economic system is minimal. However, their participation is gradually increasing in the recent decades. Their participation in the beginning was restricted only to the labour activities in agriculture, agro based, cottage industries and in construction workers. The women employment in the above mentioned unorganized sector is associated with petty trading like fruit, fish, vegetable, milk and milk products, tailoring, home made eatables, domestic servants. Unorganized sector consists of unregistered economic activities in both urban and rural areas. These economic activities vary from household manufacturing to agricultural processing, to construction, transport, trade and other kinds of services in urban areas.

Of late, large majority of women are employed in various categories of work in the unorganized sector. It is more so in the petty trade in the urban areas. No clear estimate is available regarding the actual number of women engaged in the unorganized sector. About 90% of the total women workforce is expected to be working in the unorganized sector.[9]

Considering the above factors several studies were undertaken to understand the role and status of women in the Indian context. However, these studies analyzed only the integrated picture of total women workforce. But studies pertaining to the economic contribution either at family or society level are limited. Research studies on women workers especially on petty business women are still fewer. A large number of women workers, especially in urban areas, are self employed, vending fruits, fish and vegetable. Generally they are perpetually indebted to money lenders or to wholesale suppliers. They are losing much of their meager earnings in paying exorbitant weekly interest charges. Generally they often suffer the indignities of sexual harassment and lack of access to public water and toilet facilities. In this context, an attempt is made to analyze the socio-economic conditions and the working environment of women petty traders of the unorganized sector in Visakhapatnam city.

Petty trading has been one of the most rapidly growing economic activities in Indian urban economy during the last two decades. This is neither unexpected nor surprising for it is a trend observed in nearly all major third world cities in the post-independence period. The growth of such small scale activities in these cities is generally attributed to the dynamism of the urban centers and its ability to attract capital and labour. While the capital finds lucrative working capital in capital intensive activities, the excess labour moves into labour intensive low productivity and low income activities like petty trade or business.[10]

Petty trade consists of many activities like fruit vending, vegetable vending, fish vending, sweets shops, pan shops, kirana shops, laundries, hair cutting saloons, plastic wear shops etc. This petty trade also includes pavement vendors, street hawkers, allied services etc. Until very recent times, there was no information about the women petty trade with respect to its origin and its problem. Generally the studies on petty trade are very few, even the available studies also concentrate on the problems of petty vendors with respect to legal, space, credit and social problems. Studies relating to the economic aspects of these petty traders, particularly with respect to their earning or profits are very scanty. Therefore, there is a need to conduct microeconomic research into the determinants of profits of these petty traders. A study with primary level field survey will be better suited in order to assess this aspect.

In petty trade also variations in level of trade exists based on the volume of trade and mode of operation of the trade. Some traders will have fixed space with proper shelter for conducting their trade which in turn allows them to invest more. Some traders will conduct the trade at a fixed space but without proper shelter. Some others will carry their activity moving around the streets either carrying head-loads or by using a push cart. Therefore, based on the nature of their activity the petty traders can be categorized as 'Street Vendors', 'Small Petty Vendors', and 'Petty Vendors'.

Hence, the present study aims at analyzing women petty traders belong to these three categories in two different types namely 'Fish Vending', and 'Vegetable Vending', in Visakhapatnam city to fill this gap, with a view to offer policy prescription for the empowerment of women in this sector.

Objectives

The main objective of the study is to analyze the profits earned by women vendors with respect to seasonal variations and the determining factors with reference to fish and vegetable vendors. The specific objectives of the study are:

(1) To examine the socioeconomic conditions of women fish and vegetable vendors in the informal sector in Visakhapatnam city.

(2) To analyze the impact of migration on the women fish

and vegetable vendors in the informal sector of Visakhapatnam city.

(3) To evaluate the seasonal variations in the profits of women fish and vegetable vendors.

(4) To study the determinants of profits of the women fish and vegetable vendors in the informal sector of Visakhapatnam city.

(5) To analyse the working conditions of these women vendors.

(6) To suggest the policy implications arising out of the study.

Methodology

The methodology used in this study, has been presented under three heads, namely, selection of the sample, method of data collection and techniques of analysis.

1. Selection of the Sample

The study followed a purposive stratified random sampling method. Being one of the fastest growing cities in the world, the city of Visakhapatnam was purposively selected for conducting the survey. The existence of huge informal sector is the major characteristic of the city as it has been growing fast. The total vending activity in the city is around five clusters known as five markets namely, Poorna Market, M.V.P. Colony Market, Pedawaltair Market, Harbor Market and Seethammadhara Market. Two trades, namely, fish vending and vegetable vending were purposively selected for the study which are prone to seasonal fluctuations. All the five clusters were covered to identify the sample women vendors. Again, in each trade, vendors are stratified into three categories, street vendors, small petty vendors, and petty vendors. From each strata, 60 women vendors were selected randomly for each trade. It means, for each trade, 180 sample vendors comprising street vendors, small petty vendors, petty vendors in the ratio 1:1:1 were selected. Therefore, a total of 360 sample women traders were considered for the study. 12 women traders were considered for the indepth study. They are presented in the manner of case studies. These case studies presents the whole background of these traders for better understanding of their life style, and trading activities.

Table: 1.3: Composition of Sample Women Vendors

Trade	*Level of Vendors*			
	Street Vendors	*Small petty Vendors*	*Petty Vendors*	*Total*
Fish	60	60	60	180
Vegetable	60	60	60	180
Total Vendors	360			

2. Method of data collection

The primary data were collected through well-designed and pre-tested schedules. The tools employed for the collection of the primary data were direct personal interview method. The Survey was conducted during the period from 1st August 2007 to 31st July 2008. All the selected 360 sample women traders were visited monthly once during the whole year. The monthly average profits, working capital values were collected during the visit.

3. Techniques of analysis

In the study, different statistical techniques are used apart from tabular analysis. To begin with, tabular analysis with averages and percentages are used to explain the general profile of the sample women traders as well as the issues regarding to migration. The total year was divided into three seasons as following:

1st Season: 1st April – 31st July

2nd Season: 1st August – 30th November

3rd season: 1st December – 31st March.

Simple and multiple regression techniques were employed to find out the seasonal variations and determinants of profits. The simple linear forms of the functions are used in the study.

The analysis was carried out both at aggregated level and disaggregate level.

Organization of the Study

In view of the objectives already mentioned, the Study has been organized into ten chapters. The introductory Chapter presents the background for the study, the objectives, methodology, techniques of analysis, and organization of the study. A review of the earlier studies on women in the urban informal sector in general and on petty and small vendors in particular is presented in Chapter -2. The socioeconomic profile of the study area has been presented in the third chapter. Socioeconomic characteristics of the sample households are discussed in the fourth chapter. The fifth chapter explains the migration pattern of employment. Seasonal variations in the profits of women vendors were analysed in the sixth chapter. In the seventh chapter the influence of the working capital on the profits of the women vendors during the three seasons is analysed. In the eight chapter the factors influencing the profits of the women vendors under the Human Capital Approach were analysed. The ninth chapter presents the case studies. The major findings of the study and their implications are highlighted in the tenth chapter.

REFERENCES

1. Tara Kumari. P (1999): *Women in Urban India,* Chugh Publications, Allahabad, p. 31.
2. Muzumdar, Vina (1975): Women in the Unorganised Sector, paper presented at the seminar on optimum utilization of women power for development, New Delhi.
3. Nye I Ivan and Hoffmen, I M (1963): *The Employed Mother in America,* Chicago, Rand Mcnally and Company.
4. S.V. Sethuraman (1976): *op. cit.,* p. 81.
5. John C. Cross, (1998). *Informal Politics: Street Vendors and the State in Mexico City,* Stanford, California, Stanford University Press.
6. Francie Lund (1998): *Women Street Traders in Urban South Africa: A Synthesis of Selected Research Findings,* Centre for Social and Development Studies, Research Report No. 15.

7. *Bellagio International Declaration of Street Vendors* drafted by founding members from 11 countries of the international alliance of street vendors, Street Net, at a meeting in Bellagio, Italy, 1995.
8. Jeemol Unni (2005): Urban Informal Sector: Size and Income Generation Processes in Gujarat: Parts I and II (National Council of Applied Economic Research, Reports # 2 and 3, Delhi.
9. Lalitha Devi (1982): *Status, Employment of Women in India*, B.R. Publishing Company, Delhi, p. 8
10. Manohar Murali.K (1983): *Socio-Economic Status of Indian Women*, ALWC, Seema, Delhi.

2

Review of Literature

A brief review of literature pertaining to the topic is presented in this chapter. The studies relating to unorganised sector are outlined first then, the studies relating to women in the unorganised sector are discussed. The studies on problems facing by women in the unorganised sector and Government policies are presented in the third section. The specific studies on women workers in petty trade are highlighted in the fourth section. Emerging issues from the earlier studies are presented in the last section.

Evolution of the Unorganised Sector

The unorganised sector is arising largely out of excessive controls in the formal sector, attributable to the policies of the government. The liberalization strategies initiated in recent times at the instance of multilateral agencies seek to make the formal sector less controlled. The recently announced exit policy for the industrial sector by the government laid controls in the formal sector as growth retarding, while the informal sector is growth inducing. Marxists and neo-Marxists Schools identified unorganised sector as the outcome of government controls, and petty commodity production. Evolution of the unorganised sector as structural is the outcome of an incomplete transition to capitalist development. The other reasons like limited size of home market, inward and outward looking orientation policy etc. are also playing important role.

Studies on Unorganised Sector

The formal and informal sector classification is the latest to arrive on the scene and has a wide publicity since half a decade. It is described by writers in many ways. Clifford Geertz[1] referred to these two as firm centered economy and bazaar type of economy' respectively. According to ILO[2] unorganised sector consists of small scale units engaged in production and distribution of goods and services with the primary objective of generating employment and income to their participants notwithstanding the constraints on capital, both physical and human and know how. It is thus, clear that it includes not only traditional artisans, services and petty vendors but also small units in manufacturing construction, trade and commerce, transport and service sectors engaged in the production of goods and services which operate on a very small scale and have no formal business organizations. Thus the various elements of the definitions of the unorganised sector indicate a broad spectrum of heterogeneous activities of urban poor households, rising from employment in small scale industries to self employment, skilled and unskilled, including street vendors and petty vendors with low and irregular incomes.[3]

Of late the unorganised sector is very frequently referred to as Informal sector. The term first used by Keith Hart[4] in 1973 in the study of urban Ghana. One significant aspect of this is it highlighted the existence of variety of new income generation activities in trade and service categories in an urban economy. The study also observed that, most of these activities are also concentrated in the unorganised sector and as they are not covered by the existing data collecting machinery they fall into the unremunerated sector.

Keith Hart[5] broadly divided this sector into two types viz. legitimate and illegitimate, depending upon the income opportunities. Legitimate informal income opportunities include the following activities. Primary and secondary activities: Farming, marketing, gardening, building contracts, self-employed artisans, like shoe makers, tailors etc. Tertiary enterprises with relatively large capital inputs, such as housing, transport, utilities, commodity speculation, renter activities etc; Small scale distribution such as market operations, petty trade, street hawkers, caterers in food and drink, commission agents etc. Other services, such as musicians, laundries, shoe shiners, barbers, photographers, vehicle repair and maintenance workers etc.

Illegitimate informal income opportunities include the following: services such as hustlers and spiders in general, receivers of stolen goods, pawn brokers, drug purchasers, prostitution, smuggling etc; Transfers such as petty thefts, larceny, speculation, gamblers, confidence tricksters etc.

Guy Standing[6] in his article refers to this sector and says that it should be broken down into two sub-sectors based on the regularity income flow and the economic activity, as follows: An irregular sector constituting a variety of legitimate, low status fringe activities, such as begging, various forms of casual labor, vegetable gardening, car washing etc. The unorganised sector consisting of small scale economic activities, commonly non-wage and carried on by family concerns etc.

All developing countries in Asia, Africa and Latin America have a large scattered and over-whelming dominating unorganised sector. Its sphere in total employment is significantly large. In the case of Africa, it is a sort of survival sector since two out of three city dwellers already earn their living in survival sector.[7]

According to Kenneth King [8] unorganized sector is transient sector (working place for short time only), characterized by subsistence principle and self-employment, but leading to grow into modern capitalist sector.

According to Harold Lubell[9] the informal sector constitutes the residual labour market of the last report characterized by self-employment and low income producers of marginal goods and services for lack of any other means of earning a livelihood.

According to John Weeks[10] the distinction is based on the organizational characteristic of exchange relationship and the position of economic activities vis-a-vis the state.

Papola[11] opines that the distinction between the organized and unorganised sector employment can be made on the basis of registration of the manufacturing enterprises under the factories Act. Under the act, registration is obligatory once the employment size of enterprise reaches 10 working with use of power and 20 workers without the use of power.

Heather and Vijaya Joshi[12] have distinguished, organized and unorganized sectors in Bombay under three major heads: market structure, technology and relationship with government. They defined unorganized sector as those engaged in economic activity that are not identifiably performing for the organized sector.

P.R. Souza and V.E. Tokman[13] defined this sector as comprising all those engaged in domestic service, casual labour, the self-employed and employees of white collar, blue collar and family workers in enterprises with a total not more than four persons. This sector contains "a mass of the working poor, whose productivity is much lower than in the modern urban sector from which most of there people are excluded.[14]

To identify the unorganised sector clearly with regard to the number of persons employed, nature of business, structure etc. S.V. Sethuraman[15] has given a list which is most helpful for the identification. Suggested criteria for identifying unorganised sector enterprises:

A manufacturing enterprise may be included in the informal sector if it satisfies one or more of the following conditions. It employs 10 persons or less (including part time and casual workers). It operates on an illegal basis, contrary to government regulations. Members of the household of the head of the enterprise work in it. It does not observe fixed hours/days of operation. It operates in semi-permanent or temporary premises or in a shifting location. It does not use any electricity in the manufacturing process. It does not depend on formal financial institutions for its credit needs. Its output is normally distributed to the financial consumers. Almost all those working in it have six years or fewer than six years of formal schooling.

A construction enterprise may be included in the informal sector if it satisfies one or more of the following conditions. It is engaged in the construction of semi-permanent or temporary building only. An enterprise providing services related to transport, storage and communications may be included in the formal sector if it is satisfied one or more of the conditions. A trading enterprise may be included in the informal sector if it satisfies one or more of the conditions. A services enterprise may be included in the formal sector if it satisfies one or more of the conditions.

The term informal sector has been adopted by the ILO-UNDP[16] employment mission for analyzing the employment situation for working out a strategy for employment. The report also distinguished the organized and unorganised sectors in terms of government favors.

According to ILO/UNDP employment missions report on Kenya[17], unorganised sector has the following characteristics: The unorganised sector is one where free entry to new enterprises exists. Enterprises in this sector rely on indigenous and are family owned. The size of operation is small in unorganised sector. Smallness may be differing in different situations. Most of the management is supervisory and some times some of the production function is performed by the proprietor himself. Unorganised units are labour intensive, using predominantly manual labour. Most of the products produced by these units cater to the low and middle income groups of consumers. Unorganised sector has no access to public infrastructure like bank credit, advantage of capital market, foreign technology, electricity water etc. Labour market in the unorganised sector is unregulated and highly competitive on the supply side, with also lute freedom to entry. In the unorganised sector, wage rates get set not only on the basis of labour market conditions, but also to clear the market, lower than legal minimum wages. Unorganised sector worker includes a person who is working in an unorganised sector work place or is self-employed including a home-based worker or a person who works under no clear employment contract. It also includes workers who are not covered by ESI and P.F Act[18].

Heather and Joshi[19] taking mode of production or service into account observes that the informal sector is very often having a heterogeneous bunch of activities, such as own account workers, unpaid family workers, household industries, home servant maids, domestic servants, employees of small unregulated establishments, casual wage labor employed on day to day basis or family established etc.

Heather and Joshi[20] defined the informal sector enterprises as those, engaged in economic activity, which are not indenting performing it for the formal sector. This sector is just covering a considerable range of economic activities, which bear frequently marshaled under the term "self-employment".

Till recently, unorganised sector was not given much importance in the literature as well as in statistics. But it is estimated that over 60 percent of the employment in Nairobi and Kunasi, 50 percent in Jakarta, and 95 percent in Calcutta, Mumbai and Ahmedabad is to be found in this sector and it seem to have been increasing rather than declining[21]. At the same time the sector was treated as traditional, in the sense that it is having inefficient man-power and using labor intensive technology resulting in low wage rates. It was also viewed that this sector was lacking dynamism but using the labor-intensive technology of production. But as this sector has been steadily growing in production of goods and services, which are helpful to the main sector, slowly the gloomy view is vanishing.

According to Renana Jhabvala[22] studied a uniform two-pronged change of policies is needed to strengthen the unorganised sector. Firstly, a review and revision of constraining policies, and secondly, a change in the method of implementing schemes intended to strengthen the poor. The resources for these schemes need to be handed over to people's own organizations, with the government and NGOs playing a supportive role of strengthening and helping such organizations at the grass-roots.

S.L.Shetty[23], who studied the relative flow of institutional credit into the unorganised sector in recent years, found that the organized private corporate sector has been able to exercise command over significantly larger amounts of resources. The share of the unorganised sector in total institutional credit has suffered a setback.

Nirmala Banerjee[24] studied the methods currently used by the Central Statistical Organisation for assessing the contribution made by these unorganised workers are incapable of capturing precisely those qualities dynamism and potential for growth that the latter have exhibited in a remarkable degree. It seems that these results can be achieved better through a worker-oriented approach. Rather than try to locate enterprises work out their frequently changing GUA, the Indian official data systems would be better if they focus on the workers themselves because the latter are the only ones to possess full information about exactly what they do and how and of what worth is that work.

Ratan Khasnabis and Pranab Nag[25] in their paper attempted to study the features of the labour process in a transition situation, on the basis of a field survey in the informal handloom weaving sector in Nadia district. The study concluded that the features of labour process in a transitional situation studied here have some similarities with what had been outlined by Marx and Braverman in their studies on labour process in the context of west European and North American society. At the same time, there exist some other features which are new and different. The deskilling tendency in the labour process associated with the tied or bondage relation between the direct producer and merchant lender known as 'mahajan,, a separation between conception and execution in multi loom though technology remains simple and at the same time a unity of conception and execution in the labour process in some cases, are features that describe the labour process in a transitional situation with respect to a region in a third world country.

Louise Waite[26] in his study provided an opportunity for a closer examination of the pathways from work to well-being through a case study of the head loaders sector of the informal labour market in Kerala. The paper has shown that the energy intensive work of the head loaders in Kerala can take a significant toll on bodily well-being and the differential body capital of workers produces varying economic returns due to the predominant piece-rate methods of payment. Further, caste stratifications amongst the workers mean certain groups secure the more profitable pools of the head load work and thus receive greater economic returns. However, the interventions in the head loaders sector do seem to ameliorate some of the more negative consequences of effort-intensive work. Symbolic capital has arguably been enhanced for the Kerala head loaders as unionization and organization has conferred a certain social recognition to being a head loaders. The interventions have also provided the opportunity for organizational capacity to be developed amongst workers therefore enhancing social capital, although it must be acknowledged that internal stratifications amongst the head loaders make such transformations uneven.

Nirpendra K. Mishra and Ravi S. Srivastava[27] in their study begins by examining the changes in the composition of work force and trends in employment generation in Kanpur. Secondly, though a lot is known about workers of other textile centres of India and workers of organized mill sector of Kanpur, very little is known about workers of informal textile industry of Kanpur. This study aims to present a profile of these workers to understand how the workers of a traditional industry of a decaying industrial city (as is the case in Kanpur) have responded to this change of time and how these changes have affected their life. Secondly, labour issues like wages, labour processes, job security, job content, skill content, specialization, family labour vs. wage labour, are examined in the context of informal textile sector of Kanpur. An attempt has been made to study these issues in a comparative framework so that the differences between handloom and powerloom sectors are adequately captured. The study of workers of informal textile industry of Kanpur reveals that majority of workers are either from Hindu lower caste or from Muslim lower caste. Women are conspicuous by their absence in weaving but female labour, especially family labour, is a very significant part of the work force. Generally migrant workers are found in preparatory work. A significant part of the male work force, particularly weavers in power loom sector, is erstwhile mill workers. The incidence of family labour is higher in handloom than in power loom and is higher in manufacturing than in job-work in both sector. Piece rate mode of wage payment is preponderant. While wages of weaver are higher than preparatory labour it is higher in handloom weaving than in power loom weaving and higher in power loom preparation to skill content of job and consequent specialization determines the degree of job security. A part from factors intrinsic to textile industry of Kanpur, the general deterioration of industrial sector and shift in the industrial structure of Kanpur are driving the workers to destitution and deprivation. Various editions of the textile policy have failed to have any substantial impact on the informal textile industry of Kanpur and particularly on the work force, as these policies have not addressed labour issues directly.

Vinod Anand[28] – the purpose of this paper is three-fold. It firstly looks at the various connotations of the informal sector by putting together all the different ways in which informal sector is understood and distinguished from its counter-part, called the formal sector. It then attempts to look at the characteristics of informal sector and then finally at its enormous potentials essentially in the context of development issues. The would-be entrepreneurs of micro and small enterprises are invariably peasants prior to entering the urban setting, and hence they are normally guided not by profit maximization, but by effective utilization of household labour and that they are also risk averse. The small size limits the scope for specialization and realizing economies of scale. The activities of micro and small enterprises, no matter what they are; focus more on non-tradable than tradable, and, hence, they only take advantage of the existing demands but do not serve as the source of expanding new demands. This implies that increased output invariably means a lower price in the sense that there is a downward shift along the market's demand curve. There is likely a threshold involved in the high costs of shifting to formal work arrangements and to the protection required for an expanding formal activity.

K. Pushpangadan and N. Shanta[29] in their study tries to fill this gap using non-parametric methods. To behaviour of growth rates of the informal sector during the post-reform period. To provide the estimates on production efficiency of the non-agricultural informal sector using data envelopment analysis. To provide a distribution-free test for independence of growth and efficiency in the informal sector. Production efficiency is estimated using data envelopment analysis for the two sets of data, one in 1999/2000 on informal sector and the other in 2001/02 exclusively on unorganised service sector enterprises. The technical efficiency estimated from the two surveys separately and combined shows that many activities within the service sector have the maximum efficiency and the manufacturing sector, the least. The efficiency scores of the sectors were then tested for their relationship with the corresponding growth rates. The large sample approximation of the Hoeffding's Statistics, the distribution free test for independence, is then used for this purpose. All the three tests do not provide any evidence to reject the null hypothesis of independence of growth and production efficiency. In other words this analysis clearly shows that the growth of the informal sector in the post-reform period is not due to any efficiency in input use. Rather, growth seems to have occurred as a result of increased use of inputs. This can have serious implications for the competitiveness of this sector, particularly in the context of globalization.

Mohd. Hedayat Ullah Chowdhury[30] analyzed the informal sector within a general equilibrium framework. From the comparative static the study found that and increase in formal sector interest rate reduces the formal sector capital employment and at same time it reduces the prices of intermediate product. The effect of formal sector interest rate on both labour and capital employment in the intermediate sector and also on output of intermediate product is positive. The effect of formal sector interest sector and on the intermediate sector interest rate is ambiguous. An increase in interest rate has no effect on labour employment and wage level in both formal and rural sector. It is observed that on increase in formal sector wage level has positive impact on formal sector capital employment and on intermediate product but it has negative impact on price of intermediate product and capital employment in the intermediate sector. Increase in formal sector wage level has no effect on labour employment in both the formal and the rural sector and also on rural wage. The model found that an increase in price of consumer goods produces by the intermediate sector has positive impact on interest rate of the intermediate sector. An increase in rural interest rate has negative impact on capital and labour employment in the formal sector. Intermediate output, and wage level in both the intermediate and the rural sector. On the other hand, the effect of increase in rural interest rate on capital employment in the intermediate sector and labour employment in the rural sector is positive. An increase in price of rural goods has positive effect on capital and labour employment in the formal sector. Wage level in both intermediate and rural sector and intermediate output. It has negative impact on capital employment in the intermediate sector and labour employment in the rural sector. An increase in rural capital employment leads to a fall in informal sector capital employment. Formal sector labour employment, output of the intermediate product and wage level in both intermediate and rural sector. But increase in rural capital employment has positive impact on both capital and labour employment in the intermediate sector.

Jayoti Gupta[31] studied two brick kiln operations in northern India. His study focuses on the employment, and working condition of workers in the brick kiln industry, terms of trade of an industry of such a scale, living condition of this floating working population, nature of tenure of this large workforce, the rural-urban linkages that persist within this work force, the direction of rural to urban and rural to rural migration, and the implication that this linkage for the relationship between formal and informal sector, and the direction of industrial growth of India, social and economic security or lack of it for a registered / visible labour force of roughly five million. The study suggested interventions that are required in an industry which is one of the largest employer of migrant workers, one that guarantees no security to the workers except tying them down in ways such as debt bondage (ensuring reverse guarantee of labour force to the owners), and also to plan interventions based on the structure of the industry (the owners view point is taken into consideration too) in relation to larger policy that needs to be adopted for the brick kiln industry as a major sector next in scale and importance to agriculture perhaps.

For the brick kiln workers the main concern is increase in wage rates and better living conditions. The workers stated that they preferred to work in the kilns on a piece-rate rather than on a daily wage rate as they could take time off as they wished and work as much as they felt like. There is no such opportunity in daily wage work. They also pointed out though that if they were to get employment in the village they would not choose to work in the kilns. Perhaps if the kilns were given the status of industry then a large section of the rural surplus labour force couldbe permanently shifted from agriculture to the industry. If the kilns were recognized as industries, the owners could venture into large-scale working capital to mechanize the process of moulding (there is one such experiment in Punjab).

Studies on Women in the Unorganised Sector

Women are predominant in this sector due to the only work that they can find is informal in nature and their incomes are at poverty level. There are no entry barriers and any person who has some entrepreneur's skills or talent can enter this sector. Many of the women in this sector do not out of choice, and many of them have been working all through their lives.[32]

In the year 1960, Sen Gupta Padmini[33] conducted a study on women workers in India, in which she mwntioned about the women in unorganized sector. She opened that, the unorganised sector is broad and varied. Rural women are much more likely to feel the effects of structural adjustment on agriculture while urban women are more likely to face challenges around establishing and maintaining small and petty business. The informal sector in which women are working is highly heterogeneous and they take up a variety of activities in self-employment, home-based production small vendors and vendors and producers of services.

David and Alice Thorner[34] studied the occupational classification of women workers in 1961. He categorized women workers in the unorganised sector into three groups. They are: Agricultural workers and those engaged in traditional menial services. This group is the largest and very poor. Their counterparts in urban areas are construction labour, migrant workers, domestic servants and self-employed women in unorganised sector. The second category mostly comprises of women who work in offices is professionals. They can be called the blue -collar women workers. The third groups are those who are better educated and enjoy economic security but small in number women from this category work for improving their living standard and for self-actualization.

In his study in the year 1968, Kamal Nath[35] observed that the great majority of women are engaged either in agriculture or industrial rural or urban industrial or in services. More rural than urban women work as hired workers, paid household workers, and unpaid household workers. Four- fifths economically active women are involved in agriculture and the bulk of these are concentrated in rural areas women in agriculture in terms of farming practices, wages, quality of employment and access to foodgrains and land. On the other hand, women in small or petty trade or business or micro enterprises especially in urban areas are more in number. For example worldwide, women run about 70% of informal sector micro enterprises. These are predominantly based around home-based industries and agriculture.

Ranade, S. N. and Ramamohanchandra[36] conducted a study in the year 1970 in two cities viz., Delhi and Bombay. They found that in the face of decline informal sector opportunities, women increasingly initiate their own small business or micro enterprises, especially in urban areas. Worldwide, women run about 70 percent of informal sector micro enterprises. These are predominately based around home-based industries and agriculture. Surveys in India show that a number of women would like to take on extra income-generation projects at home. 30 percent of women and adolescents aged 15 and above in rural areas and 27 percent in urban areas are interested in such opportunities. Married women are willing to start business ion dairying petty trade and unmarried rural women are willing to start tailoring business. Unmarried and married urban women are also interested in Tailoring and petty trade. The amount of time that women have to devote to these opportunities varies. 63 to 68 percent have only partial time to devote to them, while 27 to 33 percent have full time, this indirectly reflects the amount of under-and unemployed women experience after domestic unpaid work has been considered.

According to Shram Shakti (1986) report[37] about 94 percent of Indian women are in the unorganised sector. This means that the majority of women are involved in employment which is insecure and therefore more vulnerable to exploitative relationship between themselves and employers, suppliers or others in who have more power than they do. The sector includes women who work outside the home for wages, women who work inside the home for wages and women who receive no remuneration for their work in either private or public spheres.

According to NSS report No. 443 (1998)[38] on small trading units in India and their basic characteristics, out of total of 44 lakh hired workers, only 2.4 percent are women, while, in other areas of unorganised work, women constitutes 18.1% percent. In the urban sector out of 14.46 Lakh of hired workers are women. A higher number of hired women workers live in kerala, Tamil Nadu, Andhra Pradesh and Karnataka.

Women's experiences of unorganised labour are sharply divided along rural urban lines. Women in rural areas are more involved in occupations that rely on natural resources and either very large or very small manufacturing enterprises. Urban women, on the other hand work more in occupation that rely on middle men, whole sales and suppliers and in small /petty trade.[39]

Women in rural areas are involved more in gathering or free collection, agriculture, dairying, small animal husbandry , fishing, social and agro-forestry, Khadi and village industries, sericulture hand looming and handicraft production. In 2001, 42.24 percent of women workers were engaged in agriculture and one third were cultivators. Women in the urban unorganised sector are predominantly involved in retail and whole sale trade (93.6 percent of women in the sector over all – 2001 census), services and household industries.[40]

The latest official vital statistics shows that States differ in their concentration of urban and rural women workers.[41] Orissa, Uttar Pradesh and Madhya Pradesh have the most women working in the rural sector and Tamil Nadu and Maharashtra have more working in urban areas. Urban-rural divides are also evidenced in the manufacturing sector. More urban women than rural women work in small, household run manufacturing enterprises, but more rural women work in manufacturing over all. 378 women per 1000 work in rural manufacturing but 175 women per 1000 work in urban manufacturing.

Out of the total number of women employed in the unorganised sector, 10% or 10 lakh work in direct manufacturing establishments (DMEs), 68% of which are located in rural areas, 4% work or 4 lakhs in non-direct manufacturing establishments (NDMEs), 59% of which are in urban areas and the rest, or 89 lakh work in manufacturing establishments, the bulk of which are in rural areas.[42]

Mridul Eapen[43] emphasized that though statistics reveal that increase in women's employment in Kerala's informal sector, this employment is more in the nature of casual and irregular, contractual labour. Moreover, though women's earnings contribute substantially to the household, this is more often than not denigrated. Women, especially in the lower classes and the lower castes, not only have to cope with physical hardships that impact their health; they continue to be paid much lower wages than men in the same category. His analysis has cast doubts on the veracity of the decline observed in informal sector employment for women in Kerala based on official organized sector statistics.

Renana Jhabvala and Shalini Sinha[44] in their article looks at the micro sector – the world of the unorganised woman worker and analyses the varied impact that liberalization and globalization has had on her working conditions. In this article they have attempted to look at the effects of liberalization by examining the micro, rather than the macro picture. Women workers continue to be at the receiving end of policies, often getting victimized in the process. They have no say in the formulation of the policies as they have no voice in economic affairs. Perhaps the most important action is to help these women to organize and to help their organizations, in turn, get representation to policy-making forums. In organizations of women workers, but they tend to work against many odds. It is necessary to recognize that these organizations exist to help them to grow and to give them a voice.

Supriya Rao Chowdhury's[45] study look at women employed in the garment manufacturing industry in Bangalore, and at an activist group engaged in articulating the interests of these women. In the current context, where capital is located beyond national boundaries, and therefore far more inaccessible, where states are powerless against internationalized capital, the battle lines have changed irrevocably. The focus on influencing the opinion of retailers and consumers may therefore mean little in a context where the debate on international labour standards remains unresolved. Where the impact of international organizations such as the ILO in implementing labour rights it arguably inadequate (Brown 2001), and where the broader ideological environment now clearly prioritizes profits over welfare. In such a context, there may in fact be no alternative to waging micro battles in order to raise wages and working conditions at the factory level, and at the same time to pressurize the state to turn away from economic policies that pitch international capital against domestic workers.

Studies on Problems of Women in the Unorganised Sector and Government Policies

Padmini Sen Gupta[46] explains that women were so far largely employed in unskilled jobs because of their backwardness and because of rigid distinction between the work available to women and the work reserved for men, religious and traditional conditions of women, illiteracy and cultural factors. Women in the unorganised sector face many problems like: the women labour force in the unorganised sector is characterized by a high incidence of casual labour mostly intermediary jobs at externally low wages or are doing their own account work very uneconomical returns.

This informal sector is also referred to as the unprotected sector by Dipek Mazumdar[47]. This sector is termed as unprotected because it is not having any type of protection either through government laws or through any trade union activity or both. This sector is also not protected by minimum wages legislation and nor technically registered under shops and establishment Act. In this sector there is no protection for job security, work situation etc. as the firms in this sector are not registered in the government records.

Every worker in the unorganised sector should be given an official identity card so as to provide a definite legal entity and recognition. According to NCL, social security must certain at least health care; child care, shelter and old age support that strengthening the productivity. As per the recommendation of the National Commission on Labour, a series of studies were launched by the Labour Bureau of the Government of India on unorganised sector.[48] The first report of the Bureau considered the working and living conditions of workers in the building construction industry in Delhi. A series of studies aimed at collection of data on employment, wages, working and living conditions etc. of manual employees at different places of the country are proposed by the Labour Bureau. They include the one on jar industry at Surat, Matches and firework industry in Sivakasi, metalware industry in Karnataka and graphite crucible industry in Andhra Pradesh. The growth of employment, manpower requirement, trading and literacy facilities etc were studied by a team of experts with reference to Visakhapatnam. It is evident that the unorganised sector has been playing a major role in absorbing labour and generating income for the poor particular women.

Cultural Social Welfare Board has started socioeconomic programme for women in 1958. Andhiappan in his study[49] "public policy and six discrimination in employment in India" concluded that the protective legislation has adversely affected female employees in two ways: restricting the type of work and increasing the cost of female employment.

Rekha Sharan[50] made an attempt to study the working conditions and job satisfaction among women working in the organized as well as unorganised industries of Kanpur City. The study revealed that the women in the unorganised sector have received inadequate wage and other benefits.

Leela Gulati[51] narrated the life stories and problems of five women belonging into the bottom of the income pyramid. These women were chosen taking into account the broad occupational distribution of female working population of informal sector in Kerala state.

Despite all the limitations a working women is put forth, every women must be a worker, contributing to society in a large or small measure. Women have to psychologically prepare themselves to be more effective members of the society. Every woman who has the privilege of literacy must be willing if necessary, to share with men the task of shaping society. This alone will remove stigma of dependency attached to her and ensure respect and dignity and ultimately enhance the status of women. There is enough empirical evidence, problem and policies shows that unorganised labour particularly petty vendors cannot have the same bargaining power vis-à-vis employers as organized labour and would also not be enjoying the same degree of support from the government and public institution. All this is bound to impinge on it living and working conditions which compounded with other unfavorable factors characteristic of enterprises in the unorganised sector tend to keep it perpetually in low-wage /earning equilibrium.[52]

Margrate Biswas[53] detailed the struggle of women at work. Little attention to the contribution of women both at work and whom, poor working conditions, in qualities in wage payments, oppression by the males and inability to organize themselves, have led to the exploitation of women in the society.

Anuradha[54] et al. reported that the situation of women workers in the Beedi manufacturing units of Vellor, made them in bargaining position, as the existing trade union which are male dominated do not feel any responsibility for the betterment of women workers, and they are allowed to be exploited with out any legal protection. Most of the women work in the unorganized section is not out of choice but because of compulsions of survival, they also bear the burden of other domestic chosen, child rearing and cultural obligation.

Lal Das[55] discussed the nature and extent of perceived discrimination of respect of wages of the women workers in the unorganised sector. It revealed surprisingly that female workers in developed region were more discriminated against these those in under developed regions.

Sudha Kumari[56] in her paper explains the working conditions in unorganised sector in India. A large segment of women labour forms the part of unorganised sector, which results in exploitation of women. Unless, they are given literacy and training, their lot can never be improved, says the author.

Panigrahi N.P[57] in his paper "Gender in Quality in India", suggested some measures to improve women's status in the society. To over come the gender inequality in India, legal equality was granted to women which enabled them to improve their status in the society.

According to Ponna Vignaras[58] the sectors of the economy in which women remain a dominant section of the labour force are those, which demand low skills, repetitive functions and generate low returns. As such poor women function mainly in the unorganised sector, and have hither to not been organized. Even when belonging to trade unions, they are marginalized and invisible. Along side exploitation and invisibility in economic sphere, women face an atmosphere of violence within and outside the family.

Kusuma[59] explained the various forms of exploitation of females. Like unfavorable tend in the sex-ratio, female infanticide, dowry, sexual abuse, etc. One of the problems that effects women's participation in agriculture is the introduction of modern methods of cultivation, which is resulting in gradual displacement of women and shrinking of their activities. Lack of information and awareness of women about governmental and non-governmental schemes for loans or adopting modern technologies or mechanization in agriculture and other small scale industries, affects their growth and development.

Neeta Tapan[60] in her article, "women labour in unorganised sector: Needs Reappraisal of labour laws", explains the various labour laws to safeguard the women workers in unorganised sector. The effects of the increase in rural and industrial unemployment have party been hidden by the high visibility of employment for women in urban white collar jobs, professions and administration. But the contrast between the working conditions of the great majority in unorganised sector and those working in the small visible organized sector is striking.

The Labour Bureau in India[61] conduct some investigations in to the social conditions and terms of employment of women in jute mills, coal mines and cotton textile industry in Ahmedabad. According to this report, the organized sector takes advantages of this vulnerable position of labourforce in the unorganised sector. Large industries now find it advantages to decentralize their production units of larger registered units. For example the power loom industry is case in point where large segments of artisans and workers are not independent producers, but are either employed on piece-rate basis or working on substantive order for large industrial units. They face problems like low wages, long hours of work, insecurity regarding job and sexual harassment etc.

An article entitled "Women in India at 50-facts, figures and Analysis 1947-1997"[62] explains the positive steps that have been taken by the government to improve the socioeconomic status of women. Women themselves have become keenly aware of their rights and are spear heading movements across the court against social evils. This consciousness is largely due to insurance in women's literacy although there is still a long road to travel. The most significant milestone in this journey is the 1993 constitutional reservation of one-third scats for women in rural and urban local bodies. This not only bestowed a right of participation to women in the decision-making process on matters of direct concern to them but also helped to facilitate the emergence of a cadre of young and trained leadership for active participation in the political process at higher levels. Yet, a lot remains to be done to give women their rightful position in the social structure.

Poor women workers are unable to access even small sums or loans from formal financial institutions. The gap between availability of technology in agriculture and its utilisation by rural women should be narrowed. In the case of home-based production, lack of recognition of home-based work as work, and the consequent invisibility of much of women's work, deplorable working conditions and the non-availability of labour legislation.[63]

Self- employed women workers in retail trade and services, face problems such as access to credit, raw materials and lack of infrastructure. Wage employment in casual wage sector includes large section of women in activities such as construction and domestic services in urban areas and large number of women in rural areas employed as casual labour in agricultural sector. They face the problem like low wages and instability of employment in contract labour.[64]

The number of women in the unorganised sector is many times more than that in the organized sector because of their helplessness due to lack of employment opportunities, limited skills, illiteracy and restricted mobility. The unorganised sector is not governed by labour laws. Hence, it does not guarantee security of job or terminal benefits many of them are unpaid family workers.[65] In India there are laws such as Minimum Wages Act, the Contract Labour Act, the Equal Remuneration Act etc. but poor implementation and enforcement has often prevented women from benefiting these legal safeguards. National efforts have been made tremendously for the upliftment of women specially for granting equal and adequate opportunities for their works and employment.

In 1994 the National Commission for Women conducted a public enquiry on "Women in Unorganised Sector" realized the need for new mechanism for benefiting the women from legal safeguards.[66] Support to training and employment projects (STEP) to seeks to empower group of poor women in unorganised sector through training and employment in dairy, handloom handicrafts, sericulture and fisheries. Special schemes for women cooperative were established. NGO's and agencies are provided financial grants, aids etc. for creating the employment opportunities for women. The second term of references of the National commission on labour 2002[67] was to suggest an umbrella legislation for ensuring a minimum level of protection to the workers in the unorganised sector. The basic approach of this legislation is recognition and protection for all type of workers regardless of industry, occupation, work status and personal characteristics. Since these unorganised workers contribute 61% of GDP according to NAC 2001, they are also entitled to recognition and protection. The purpose of proposed umbrella legislation is removal of poverty of the working population through improving their productivity, quality of work, enhancing income earning abilities and increasing bargaining power. The National commission on labour beneficiating the steps to taken in this regard mentioned above. Workers in the unorganised sector recognized as workers and included in official survey.[68]

Studies on Women Workers in Petty Trade

In the year 1970, Prof. B. Sarveswara Rao[69] conducted a study on the entrepreneurship and the major characteristics of petty trade observed by him are as follows; low capital commitment, low turn over, absence of general sales tax and income tax liability, low level of literacy and skills, social and economic backwardness, reliance on money lenders for meeting financial requirements and individual or household operations.

Tara Kumari[70] conducted a study on women workers engaged in unorganised sector in the year 1999. She considered three categories of women workers namely construction workers, salaried women and vegetable vendors for analyzing the earnings of women workers. Particularly in case of vegetable vendors, her study found that education, age, experience, dependency ratio, caste, and marital status are not the important determinants of their income. But some of the selected explanatory variables are significant determinants in the other two categories. However, she followed human capital model in order to assess the incomes of women workers, which doesn't include the financial aspect of capital invested.

B. Ratna Kumari[71] conducted a study on self-employed women in Visakhapatnam City in the year 1994. Her study found that the investment and literacy, and age of the women are important determinants of the earnings of the self-employed women. The study covers self-employed women engaged in food processing, small business, tailoring etc. activities.

L. Rathakrishnan and B. Sellammalle[72] conducted a study on 400 women micro-entrepreneurs who are engaged in fish marketing in Kalupet of Pondicherry in the year 1999. The main objective of their study was to analyse the role of women in generating income through micro-entrepreneurial activities in the fishing community and also socioeconomic empowerment of women and fishing community. The study found that micro-women entrepreneurs generate more income than the male owing to dynamism of the women in selling the captured fish in the open market. The study also found that the participation of women micro entrepreneurs in uplifting the socio-economic status of the family is of paramount significance.

Beena and Sushma[73] conducted a study on women managing a petty business. The main objective of their study was to assess the motivational factors causing success of the petty business. They found that financial return was a very strong motive not only to start but also to carry on with the business. They also pointed out that there exist differences in the perception of the women about the degree of success.

Sharit K Bhowmik[74] conducted a survey on street vendors for NASVI in seven cities between April 1999 and March 2000. These cities were Mumbai, Ahmedabad, Kolkata, Imphal, Patna, Bhubaneswar and Bangalore. They were chosen because of their specific characteristics and their geographic locations. Mumbai, Ahmedabad, Kolkata, Bangalore and Patna have large populations of street vendors and are situated in different parts of the country. Mumbai and Ahmedabad are in western India, Kolkata and Patna in eastern India and Bangalore in Southern India. Imphal was chosen because it is in North-East India and more specifically because it presents a rare instance where street vendors, who are all women, have gained some legal rights to carry out their trade. Bhubaneswar was chosen because it is a planned city (after Chandigarh) and hence the position of street vendors needs to be studied in this environment. The main findings of the survey are noted below.

The laws relating to street vending in these cities varied. With the exception of Kolkata, all the above municipalities have provisions for providing licenses for street vending. A mention of Kolkata is necessary because of its unique position on street vendors. In 1997 the Government of West Bengal proposed an amendment to section 371 of the Kolkata Municipal Corporation Act. This section deals with street vending. The amended section made street vending illegal and anyone contravening or abetting in contravening this section, will be punished with rigorous imprisonment for a term extending up to three months or fined Rs. 250. In the Statement of Objects and Reasons, the act states in 2(ii) that in order to prevent encroachment in public places, "it has been decided to declare any such encroachment by the hawkers, stall holders and other organisations as cognisable and non-bailable offence." It is ironic that alleged rapists and murderers, in some cases, are granted bail, but a street vendor selling wares on the street is regarded as more dangerous criminals by the state government.

With respect to the problems of street vendors, Sharit K Bhowmik[75] emphasized that the street vendors across several Indian cities have generally been regarded as nuisance value, their presence seen as inimical to urban development. However, the range of goods and services they provide render them useful to other sections of the urban poor and thus they form an important segment of the informal economy. A draft national policy on street vendors argues that needs for this section is vital for urban planning purposes. Regulation of vendors and hawking zones and granting vendors a voice in civic administration need to become definitive elements of urban development policy.

Sharit K Bhowmik , in his paper attempts to examine recent research done on street vendors in Asia with the aim of assessing the magnitude of street vending in different countries and the composition of the vendors. Further, it collates information on the extent of unionisation of the vendors and other organisations, such as non-government organisations (NGOs), self-help organisations (SHOs), advocacy groups, etc, that work for their welfare.[76]

Jonathan Shapiro Anjaria[77] conducted a study in the year 2006 on street vendors of Mumbai. This article explores the essential presence of hawkers in a city, which requires a critical understanding of the functioning of public space. Street hawking is generally considered as a "menace" or an "eyesore" that prevents the development of Mumbai as a world-class city. The study states that the experiences of hawkers in Mumbai, as elsewhere in India, have taught them not to fear a regulatory state, but a predatory one, a state that constantly demands bribes and threatens demolition, against which a licence provides security.

Anuradha Kalhan[78] conducted a small sample survey to assess the impact of malls on small shops and hawkers in Mumbai in the year 2007. Her study points out that there is a decline in sales of groceries, fruits and vegetables, processed foods, garments, shoes, electronic and electrical goods in these retail outlets, ultimately threatening 50 per cent of them with closure or a major decline in business. Only 14 per cent of the sample of small shops and hawkers has so far been able to respond to the competitive threat of the malls with the institution of fresh sales promotion initiatives.

Emerging Issues from the Earlier Studies

From the review of earlier studies, it is clear cut there is no clear cut definition for the informal sector, but authors define informal sector depending upon the nature of their study. Many authors have considered the unorganised sector in various ways. But the above types give us the groups of various activities in unorganised sector. They clearly depict all the informal activities in the economy. Though there are different classifications in attempting to classify the informal sector, there seems to be no significant differences among them.

However, one should agree that informal sector is not a homogeneous category, but is spread over the entire economy in variety of forms. Workers in the informal sector may be an apprentice, casual, contract workers, home-based workers, service providers, self-employed persons engaged in any industry or trade or business.

Till recent times, the unorganised sector is viewed as on unproductive and a burden to the whole economy as it is not contributing anything to the direct production. But the concept of unorganised sector has gained considerable importance in the literature on development policy in general and employment planning in particular. In this context it is worth mentioning S.V. Sethuraman, who feels that unorganised sector will no longer be viewed as an endurable consequence of the development process but as an integral and valuable part of the urban economy.[79]

Worldwide the importance of the informal sector in proving employment and livelihood for the urban poor, as well as the importance of the petty vendors in growing needs of the urban population, particularly for the low and middle income people is well recognized. Their presence in the sale of small items, simple electronic goods, garments, food items, regularly used domestic items etc. nearby roadside pavements, mobile carts, head loads at cheaper rates than the costly items available at various shops made them more prominent. Most of the studies brought out the characteristics, problems and constraints of these pavement dwellers by conducting surveys in various cities. All these efforts, became fruitful in drawing international attention towards their issues. Bellagio International Declaration of Street Vendors, and the National Draft Policy on Street Vendors by the Government of India are the outcome of the efforts.

The studies conducted on the workers of informal sector, particularly on the earnings or incomes of these workers, generally followed the human capital approach where they tried to observe the influence of social or demographic characteristics of the workers on their incomes. These determinants are estimated on various categories like construction or casual workers, self-employed, manufacturing or processing activities, trade or business. The studies on single activity are very limited. The uniqueness of the petty business is, the problems differ from activity to activity, based on the nature of items sold (perishable or non-perishable items, necessary products or general products). In the similar manner, the way in which it is carried, the location of the activity etc, also differ from activity to activity, which in turn influences the earnings of the informal petty business activities. Not only that the time of conducting the activity, the duration of the activity etc. also differ from activity to activity. Therefore, the earlier studies conducted on categories provide an aggregated view about the informal activities. Any study, which aims at detailed analysis of a specific activity, can make the additional contribution for the existing literature for the better understanding of the functioning of the informal activity.

REFERENCES

1. Clifford Geertz (1963): *Peddlers and Princes: Social Change and Economic Modernization in Two Indonesian Towns*, Chapter-3, Chicago and London,University of Chicago Press.
2. International Labour Organization (1972): *Employment, Income and Equality: A Strategy for Increasing Productive, Unemployment in Kenya*, Geneva.
3. *Ibid.*
4. Keith Hart J (1973): "Informal Income Opportunities and Urban Employment in Ghana", *Journal of Modern African Studies*, London, pp. 61-89.
5. *Ibid.*
6. Guy Standing (1974): *A Dichotomy Model of Urban Labour Markets*, paper presented at the Research Conference on Urban Labour Markets, Geneva, September, International Institute for Labour Studies, Doc No. ULM/DP/12.
7. Louis Enmerji (1974): "A New look at some strategies for increasing productive employment in Africa", *International Labour Review*, Vol.110, No.3, September, p. 202.
8. Kenneth King (1974): "Keny's Informal Machine Markets: A study of small scale industry in Keny's employment Artisan Society", *World Development*, March, p. 30.
9. Harold Lubell (1974): *Urban Development and Employment, The Prospects for Calcutta*, Geneva, ILO.
10. John Week (1975): "Politics for expending informal urban sector of developing Economy", *International Labour Review*, Vol.111, No.1, January.
11. Papola, T.S (1976): "Wage determination in the unorganized sector in urban areas: A framework for Analysis", *Gujarat Economic Conference paper*, Gujarat Economic Association, Ahmedabad.
12. Heather and Vijaya Joshi (1976): "Prospects case study for

Employment of women in Indian cities," *Economic and Political Weekly,* Special number August.

13. Paulo R. Souza and victor E Tokman (1976): "The Informal Urban Section in Latin America", *International Labour Review,* Vol.114, Nov-Dec, p. 356.

14. Breman, J. (1976): "A Dualistic Economy", *Economic and Political Weekly,* p. 1871.

15. S.V. Sethuraman (1976): "The Urban Informal Sector: Concept, Measurement and Policy," *International Labour Review,* Vol. 114, No.1, July - August.

16. ILO/ UNDP (1977): *Employment Problem in the Rural and Informal Sector in Ghana,* Report of Mission Addis Ababa.

17. ILO / UNDP (1997): "Employment Mission Report on Kenya-referred to in S.V. Sethuraman's article, p. 71.

18. ILO/ UNDP (1977): *op. cit.*

19. Heather and Joshi (1980): The Informal Urban Economic and its Boundaries, *Economic and Political Weekly,* 29th March.

20. *Ibid*

21. T.S.Papola (1980): "Informal sector: Concept and Policy", *Economic and Political Weekly,* 3rd May, p. 817.

22. Renana Jhabvala (1997): "Policies Affecting the Unorganised Sector", *Margin special Issue,* Vol.30, No.1 (Oct-Dec. 1997). pp. 63-68.

23. Shetty, S.L. (1997): "Inadequacy of Domestic Saving and Other Macro-economic Issues: The Unorganised Sector", *Margin special Issue,* Vol.30, No.1, pp. 69-76.

24. Nirmala Banerjee (1997): "The National Accounts Statistics Methods of Assessing: The Unorganised Sector", *Margin special Issue,* Vol. 30, No.1, pp. 81- 87.

25. Ratan Khasnabis and Pranab Nag (2001): "Labour Process in the Informal Sector: A Handloom Industry in Nadia District", *Economic and Political Weekly,* Vol. XXXVI, No. 52, December 29, pp. 4836 – 4845.

26. Louise Waite (2001): "Kerala's Informal Labour Market Interventions: from Work to Well-Being?", *Economic and Political Weekly,* Vol. XXXVI, No. 26, June 30, pp. 2933 – 2397.

27. Nirpendra, K. Mishra and Ravi. S. Srivastava (2002): "Labour and Employment in the Informal Textile Industry in Knapur", *Labour and Development*, Vol. 8, No.1&2, pp. 27- 61.

28. Vinod Anand (2004): "Informal Sector: Connotations, Characteristics and Potentials", *Indian Journal of Economics*, part-2, Vol. LXXXV. pp. 211-236.

29. K. Pushpangadan and N. Shanta, (2004): "Growth and Efficiency of the Informal Sector in India: A Non- parametric Analysis", *Labour and Development*, Vol. 10, No.1, pp. 2-16.

30. Mohd. Hedayat Ullah Chowdhury (2007): "Development in the Presence of Informal Sector: A Three-Sector General Equilibrium Approach", *Indian Journal of Economics*, No. 348, Vol. LXXXVIII, July, pp.115-142.

31. Jayoti Gupta

32. Blood .R.O. and Wolfe R. I. (1958): "The Effects of wife's employment on the family power structure", *Social Forces*, 36.

33. Sen Gupta, Padmini (1960): *Women Workers in India*, Asia Publishing House, Bombay, p. 185.

34. Alice Thorner and Daniel (1961): "Occupation Classification of Women Workers", *Economic and Political Weekly*.

35. Kamal Nath (1968): "Women in the working force in India", *Economic and Political Weekly*, Aug 3.

36. Ranade, S.N. and Ramamohanchandra (1970): Women and Employment, Report of pilot studies conducted in Delhi and Bombay, Tata Institute of Social Science, Bombay, p. 61.

37. Shram Shakti (1984): Report on workshop on the unorganized sector, Ahmedabad, SEWA.

38. NSSO (1998): Unorganized Manufacturing in India's its size, Employment and some key estimates, Report No. 443.

39. *Ibid.*

40. *Ibid.*

41. GOI (2002): "Final Population totals" census 2001 paper, Register General of India.

42. *Ibid.*

43. Mridul Eapen (2001): "Women in Informal Sector in Kerala-Need for Reexamination", *Economic and Political Weekly*, Vol. XXXVI, No. 26, pp. 2390-2392.

44. Renana Jhabvala and Shalini Sinha (2002): "Liberalisation and the Women Worker", *Economic and Political Weekly*, Vol. XXXVII, No. 21, pp. 2390-2392.

45. Supriya Rao Chowdhury (2005): "Labour Activism and Women in the Unorganised Sector: Garment Export Industry in Bangalore", *Economic and Political Weekly*, Vol. XL, Nos. 22 and 23, pp. 2250-2255.

46. Sen Gupta, Padmini (1960): *Women Workers of India*, Asia Publishing House, Delhi, p. 7.

47. Dipak Mazumdar (1975): *The Urban Informal Sector*, World Bank Staff Working Paper, No. 211, Washington.

48. GOI (1976):National Employment Services: Area Level Survey, Visakhapatnam, Ministry of Labour, Directorate General of Employment and Training, New Delhi.

49. Andhiappan, P. (1978): "Public Police and Sex Discrimination Employment in India", *Indian Journal of Industrial Relation*, October, p. 395.

50. Rekha Sharan (1980): "Working condition and job satisfaction among industrial women workers a case study of Kanpur, *Indian Journal of Industrial relations*, April.

51. Leela Gulati (1981): *Profile in Female Poverty, A study of five poor Working Women in Kerala*, Hindusthan Publishing Corporation, New Delhi.

52. Bhatia, D. P (1981):"Raising wage rate gap between organized and Unorganized Sector", *Indian Association of Social Science Institution. First National Conference Social Science*, New Delhi, January, pp. 6-7.

53. Margrate Biswas (1983): "Women work and struggle", *Economic and Political Weakly*, 17th December.

54. Anuradha G.K. Eswar Prasad, K.V. Syed Kumar (1984): "Women Bidi Workers in Vallore", *Social Action*, January-December.

55. Lal Das, D.K. (1985): "Sex discrimination against female workers in unorganized sector", *Indian Journal of Industrial Relations*, October.

56. Sudha Kumari (1989) "Women Workers in Unorganized Sector in India", *Yojana*, July 1-15,1989

57. Panigrahi N.P (1989): "Gender Inequality in India", *Yojana*, Vol-33, No.12, July 15.

58. Vignara Ponna (1990): *Women Poverty and Resources*, Sage Publications, New Delhi.

59. Kusuma (1991): "Atrocities Against Women", *Yojana*, Vol. 35, No. 22, December.

60. Neeta Tapan (1995) : "Women Labour in Unorganized Sector: Needs Reappraisal of Labour laws", *Southern Economist* Vol. 34, No.12, Oct 15

61. GOI (1995): *Economic and Social Status of Women Working India*, Labour Bureau, Ministry of Labour, Publication No. 5, New Delhi, p. 6

62. Women in India at 50 (1997): *Facts, Figures and Analysis (1947-1997) - A Comprehensive Reference Volume*, Express Publications, Modhurai Ltd, Chennai.

63. *Ibid.*

64. *Ibid.*

65. *Ibid.*

66. Mridula Bhadareria (1997): *Women in India: Some Issues*, A.P.H. Publishing Corporation, New Delhi, pp.113-116.

67. GOI (2006): *Economic Survey* 2005-06.

68. *Ibid.*

69. Prof. B. Sarveswara Rao and others (1970): "A Study on Commercial Industrial Entrepreneurship in coastal Region Andhra Pradesh", Andhra University, Visakhapatnam.

70. Tara Kumari. P. (1999): *Women in Urban India*, Chugh Publications, Allahabad, pp. 109.

71. B. Ratna Kumari (1994): Self-employed Women in the Unorganised Sector in Visakhapatnam City, Project Report, Centre for Women Studies, Andhra University, Visakhapatnam.

72. L.Rathakrishnan and B.Sellammalle (2001): "Micro-Women Entrepreneurs and Socio-Economic Empowerment: A Study", Southern Economist, Vol. 40, No. 8, pp. 14-16

73. C. Been and B. sushma (2003): "Women Entreprenuers Managing a Petty Business: A study from Motivational Perspective", *Southern Economist*, May 15, pp. 5-8

74. http://www.nasvinet.org/articles/articles_1.htm

75. Sharit K Bhowmik (2003): "National Policy for street Vendors",

Economic Political Weekly, Vol. XXXVIII, No. 16, April 19-25, pp. 1543-1546.

76. Sharit K Bhowmik (2005): "Street Vendors in Asia: A Review", *Review of Labour*, Vol. 40, No. 22 and 23, May 28 - June 04.

77. Jonathan Shapiro Anjaria (2006):"Street Hawkers and Public Space in Mumbai" *Review of Labour*, Vol. 41 No. 21 May 27 - June 02.

78. Anuradha Kalhan (2007): "Shopping Malls: Social and Economic Issues, *Economic and Political Weekly*, Vol. 42 No. 22 June 02 - June 08.

79. S.V. Sethuraman (1976): *op. cit.* p. 81.

3

Profile of Sample Area

Introduction

In the context of rapidly growing population, the Indian towns and cities are constantly growing, while some have been growing at a moderate rate, others are expanding rapidly, and one such rapidly expanding city is Visakhapatnam. According to a study conducted by International Institute for Environment and Development, a UK based policy research non-governmental body; it is one of the fastest growing cities in the world.[1] The City of Visakhapatnam, the second largest city in the State of Andhra Pradesh next to Hyderabad, is located on the east coast of India, mid way between the metropolitan cities of Madras (Chennai) and Calcutta (Kolkata). According to the Census of India (2001) it had a population of over a million and half enjoying the rank of 21st among all the cities in the country in 2001. This chapter presents the socioeconomic profile of Visakhapatnam city in terms of the geographical features, people, economy, and informal sector.

Geographical Location and Size

Visakhapatnam City is situated on the East Coast of India in between 17⁰42' North latitude and 82⁰ 2' East longitudes, at a distance of 860 km, from Kolkata and 760 km, from Chennai. Visakhapatnam is one of the major ports in India. Besides this, the City has large public sector capital-intensive industries like Visakhapatnam Steel Plant (VSP), Hindustan Shipyard Limited (HSL), and Bharat Heavy Plate and Vessels Limited (BHPV) etc. Apart from this, Visakhapatnam is Headquarters of the Eastern Naval Command of the Indian Navy, as also the Divisional Head quarters of East Coast Railways and is also the seat of Andhra University. Further, the City is popularly known as Steel City or the City of Destiny. The total geographical area of the City is about 550 sq. km. According to 2001 census, the population of the City was around 15 lakhs and that of Visakhapatnam Urban Agglomeration (GVMC) is 20 lakh now.

Visakhapatnam is an amalgamation of the old and the new where ancient temples lie in the shadows of gigantic Hindustan Shipyard. The City is a visitors' delight, with its beautiful beach, stretching endlessly against a backdrop of low hills, dotted with secluded caves and creeks. The 3rd century B.C. to 2nd century A.D. Buddhist ruins of Totlakonda and Bhavikonda are just at the outskirts of the City. Several Dutch and English buildings dated back to 17th and 18th century A.D. are the highlights of the City. The City's biggest advantage is its closeness to the most of the countries buzzling with activities in South Asia like Hong Kong, Singapore, Japan, Malaysia, Korea etc.

A Historic Profile

This City was ruled by several dynasties including famous Kalingas during 7th century AD, Chalukyas during 8th century AD, Rajahmundry Reddy kings, Cholas, Golkonda Nawabs etc. The antiquity of the Region is evident in its mention in the *Ramayana* and the *Mahabharata*. The former tells of the forests through which Lord Sri Rama travelled in search of His abducted wife Sita Devi, and where He met his devotee, Shabari, who directed Him to the mountains where Hanuman lived. Sri Rama also met Jambhavan, a bear man, who helped him in His battle with Ravana. It was heard too, that Bheema defeated the demon Bakasura. The Pandava's huge stone club can be seen in the village of Uppalam, 40 kms away. This region, formerly part of the great Kalinga Empire that stretched up to the Godavari, has also been mentioned in Hindu and Buddhist texts from the 5th and 6th century B.C., as well as by Sanskrit grammarians, like Panini, Katyayana etc. in the 4th century B.C. After Independence this was the biggest District in the country, which was then divided into different districts viz. Srikakulam, Vijayanagaram and Visakhapatnam.

Physical Characteristics of The City

Based on topographical conditions, the City and its environs can be divided into four categories, namely, hilly regions, uplands tracts, rolling plains and plains. The major hill ranges of the City are Kailasa range and Yarada Range. The Kailasa range stretches from Simhachalam to Muvalavanipalem Colony, while on the other side, from Malkapuram to Gajuwaka on the south. A considerable number of hillocks and residual hills are found in various parts of the City. The rolling plains stretch from the foothills to the plains. The uplands tracts are found in the hillocks and residual hills. The altitude of Kailasa range is in between 0 to 507 meters above the mean sea level (MSL), while the altitude of Yarada ranges between 0 to 367 meters above MSL. The heights of residual hill& and hillocks are less than 30 metres. The topography of the rolling plains has gentle to smooth undulation with an altitude of 20 to 30 metres above the MSL. The coastal plains are irregular with headlands, beach sand and mud flats.

Climate

Visakhapatnam and its environs come under semi-arid category. The mean annual range of temperature is as low as I8.4^{0}C, which is a characteristic feature of coastal situation. May is the hottest month with the maximum temperature touching 34^{0}C and January the coldest month with the minimum temperature of 14^{0}c, the relative humidity is very high (80-84 per cent) from April to September on account of monsoonal rains. The maximum rainfall (427mm) occurs in the months of September-October during the retreating monsoon period. October is the wettest month, with maximum rainfall of 259 mm, while January is the driest month with a minimum rainfall of only 7.2 mm. The climate of Visakhapatnam City is not extreme due to maritime conditions. Hence, the climate is comfortable and pleasant.

Soils

The main categories of soils in this City are red sands, alluvial and sediments, saline coastal sandy soils, skeletal soils etc. Red sandy soils, which cover 50 percent of the tract, are associated with Khondalites and granite with high percentage of sand (80.00) and low clay content (less than 15) with pH 7.0 to 8.0. The soil is usually associated with rolling plains, which are medium to fine in texture with pH 7.0 to 9.0. The coastal sandy soils are coarse to fine textured, rich in heavy minerals like monazite, yemenite and zircon with pH ranging from 6.5 to 8.0. Skeletal soils (colluviums and lateritic gravel) occur on eroded foot slopes of the hills. They are infertile, highly permeable with pH ranging from 4.0 to 6.0.

Vegetation

The vegetation in the tract is of tropical moist deciduous type. The soils support rich vegetation spots of thick foliage, both natural and orchard (mango, jack-fruit, cashew etc) are grown on the lower debris slope (5.15), where water trickles down in the form of springs. The dry deciduous and thorny forest is found at lower elevation hill slopes. Both dry and wet crops are cultivated in the plains. Most parts of the tract are strewn with small shrubs, and palymyrah trees. Maritime bushy grasses cover the coastal sand dunes. 'Avitinnia Alba' grows in the saline marshes. Coconut, cashew and casuarinas are grown on the beach and on the dune sands as commercial plantations.

Rainfall

The District receives an annual normal rainfall of 1202 mm of which SouthWest Monsoon accounted for 70.9 percent of the normal, while the Northeast Monsoon contributed 8.6 percent of the normal rainfall during 2000-2001. The rest is shared by summer showers and winter rains. Agency and inland Mandals receive larger rainfall from the Southwest Monsoon, while coastal Mandals get similarly larger rainfall from Northeast Monsoon. But both the monsoons play truant, variations of Southwest Monsoon accounting for 13 percent of normal and Northwest Monsoon to 26 percent of normal. Since the variation for most periods is on the negative side of log 'V and since even the years of normal rainfall are characterised by long dry spells during one or more parts of the crop seasons. The District experiences drought conditions too often, as no major irrigation system exists to cushion the vagaries of the monsoon.

Drainage

Visakhapatnam and its environs have a fairly good surface drainage system. A number of non-perennial mountain streams and perennial spring waters contribute to the total drainage system of the area. All the streams follow gravity, the general slope directions of the tract before joining the Bay of Bengal. Mostly, the drainage pattern in he tract is dendrite and sub-pattern, which occur in the valleys of strike ridges and dissected pediments.

Land-use Pattern

The City has witnessed accelerated growth since mid 1990s. The proposals for further expansion of the steel plant, establishment of SEZ and the initiatives taken by the Central and State government, as a result of economic reforms, to establish/expand medium to heavy industries in the spheres of chemicals (Petroleum), IT based industries, Pharmaceuticals, etc. might be the cause of this growth. Thus, land-use pattern data has been analysed. The comparative land use statistics at the point of time is presented in Table 3.2. Out of the total geographical areas of Hal, 1.72 lakhs the built up land has been increased from 15302 Ha in 1997 to 16601Ha in 2002 or from 8.89 percent to 9.58 percent of the geographical area, followed by recreational/open space was 2759 Ha (1.60 percent) which has been marginally decreased to 2533 Ha constituting 1.46 percent. Transportation and communication was with Ha 731 (0.42 percent) in 1997 which has been slightly increased to Ha 793 constituting 0.47 percent in 2002. While, according to the satellite based imagery, agricultural land was 90630 Ha (52.66 percent) in 1997 which has been decreased to 89712 Ha (51.98 percent) during 2002.

According to 1997 forestland/hills were 18962 Ha constituting 11.02 percent which has increased to 21100 Ha with (12.26 percent). Waste land according to 1997 was 34971 Ha (20.22 percent) which was decreased to 32203 Ha constituting 18.77 percent. Area of water bodies was 5194 Ha (3.20 percent) which has been decreased to 5397 Ha (3.13 percent). Area of river / streams were 1829 Ha (0.87 percent) in 1997 which has been increased to 1804 Ha (1.05 percent). While, others in 1997 was 1902 Ha (1.11) percent and increased to 1957 Ha (1.13) percent in 2002.

Table - 3.1
Comparative Land use statistics from 1997 and 2002

(Area in ha)

Sl No	*Name*	*Area2002 based on Satellite Imagery*	*Percentage to total*	*Area 1997*	*Percentage to total*
1.	Built up land	16601	9.58	15302	8.89
2.	Recreational/open Space	2533	1.46	2759	1.60
3.	Transportation/ Communication	793	0.47	731	0.42
4.	Agricultural land	89712	51.98	90630	52.66
5	Forest land / hills	21100	12.26	18962	11.02
6.	Waste land	32203	18.77	34791	20..22
7.	Water Bodies	5397	3.13	5194	3.20
8.	River/streams	1804	1.05	1829	0.87
9.	Others	1957	1.13	1902	1.11
	Total	1,72,100	100.00	1,72,100	100.00

Source: Master Plan/or VMR-2021.

Population

Table 3.2 presents the trends in population growth in the Visakhapatnam City. The population of the City in the beginning of the last century (1901) was only 40 thousand. The City population remained more or less stable up to 1921, but recorded a moderate growth during 1931-41, and an exploding growth after 1951, the highest decadal growth was reported, during 1951-1961(95.47 percent).

The Urban Agglomeration data are available from 1961 onwards. The period 1961-91, was experienced as the population explosion period, in which population has increased at a rate of growth of 7 percent per annum, one of the highest in the Asian cities during the period. This is primarily because of the growth in the industrial activity. The growth rate was the lowest during 1991-2001 (25.76 percent).

Table -3.2

Population Growth in Visakhapatnam City

Year	*Population*	*Decadal Variation*	*Percentage of Growth*
1901	40,892	—	—
1911	43,413	+2,521	6.17
1921	44,711	+ 1,298	2.99
1931	57,303	+12,592	28.16
1941	70,243	+12,940	22.16
1951	1,08,042	+37,799	53.81
1961	2,11,190	+1,03,148	95.47
1971	3,55,045	+1,43,855	68.12
1981	6,75,163	+3,20,118	62.00
1991	10,57,118	+4,81,955	76.43
2001	13,29,472	+2,72,354	25.76

Source: Census of India, 1971, 1981, *1991and 2001.*

According to the 2001 provisional census figures, the urban population is 39.85 percent of the total population of the District[2]. They reside in the 10 hierarchic urban settlements. The share of female population is 49.74 percent. Total workers in the urban area are 2,05,200 forming 27.35 percent. Women workers in Visakhapatnam City alone are 38,888 in member accounting for a mere 7.54 percent of total female population of the City. The share of female workers is 12.47 percent.

Sex Ratio

Table 3.3 shows the sex ratio of Visakhapatnam City during the period 1951 - 2001. It is obvious from the Table that the sex ratio of Visakhapatnam City has declined from 978 in 1951 to 920 in 1961 and then increased to 971 by 2001. It can also be observed from the Table that the ratio of females to males is very low in 1961 i.e., 920 females per 1000 males and very high in 1951 i.e. 978 females per 1000 males. Sex ratio of females to males is very low because of the proportion people living below poverty line is high and high infant mortality rate, extremely unhygienic conditions of living and absence of pre-natal and post- natal care. Besides this, high mortality rate among women in reproductive age is also responsible for a declining female sex ratio.

Table - 3.3

Sex Ratio in Visakhapatnam

Year	*Sex Ratio (Females per, 1,000 Males)*
1951	978
1961	920
1971	921
1981	925
1991	939
2001	971

Source: District Census Report of Andhra Pradesh, Government of India

Levels of Literacy

Table -3.4 presents the levels of literacy in Visakhapatnam City as a whole. The literacy rate is about 77.10 percent in 2001 which shows an increasing trend compared to 1961 (48 percent). The female literacy rate is lower than that of males. The male literacy rate which was 31 percent in 1961 shooted to 83.75 percent by 2001. Similarly for females it was 17 percent in 1961 and it tremendously increased to 70 percent in 2001.

Table -3.4
Levels of literacy in Visakhapatnam City: 1961-2001

Year	*1961*	*1971*	*1981*	*1991*	*2001*
Total population	1,8,803	3,55,045	6,75,163	10,57,118	13,29,472
Total male Population	94,803	1,84,820	2,98,757	3,87,784	6,74,080
Total female Population	87,201	1,70,225	2,76,406	3,64,253	6,55,392
Total male literates	55,542	1,14,073	1,97,893	3,12,370	5,64,676
Total female literates	31,090	68,244	1,30,513	2,31,119	4,60,347
Total Literates	96,632	1,82,317	3,28,406	5,43,489	10,25,023
Non-literate Males	39,261	70,747	1,00,864	75,414	1,09,404
Non-literate Females	56,261	1,01,981	1,45,893	1,33,134	1,95,045
% of literate males in total Population	30.52	32.13	34.41	41.51	83.75
% of literate females in total Population	17.09	19.23	22.70	30.71	70.24
% of total literate in total Population	47.61	51.36	57.11	72.22	77.10

Workforce

According to 2001 census, the workforce in Visakhapatnam City was 2, 18,695, (Table -3.5) and significant proportion are in trade and commerce (17.51 %), transport (16.75 %) and industry (14.54 %), while the lowest is found in cultivators group (0.15 %) in 2001.

The percentage share of workforce is showing an increase during 1971- 2001 in the workers' categories of livestock, (2.47 t0 2.56), construction (7.53 t0 7.60), trade and commerce (13.56 to 17.51) and other allied services (30.84 to 39.45). On the other hand, some other categories like house ho1d industry (1.30 to 0.56) and cultivators (0.52 to 0.15) other than household industry (16.00 to 14.54), showed a decreasing trend in their shares during 1971-2001.

Table – 3.5

Occupational Structure: 1971 – 2001

Sl.No	*Occupation*	*2001* No of workers	*2001* % to the total workers	*% of workers in 1971*
1.	Cultivation	318	0.15	0.52
2	Agricultural	1,460	0.67	0.83
3	Livestock	5,605	2.56	2.47
4	Mining & Quarrying	458	0.21	0.43
5	Household Industry	1,232	0.56	1.30
6	Industrial workers	31,809	14.54	16.00
7	Construction	16,614	7.60	7.53
8	Trade &Commerce	38,309	17.51	13.56
9	Transport	36,611	16.75	26.52
10	Other	86,279	39 45	30.84
11	Total	2,18,695	100.00	100.00

Source: *Hand Book of Statistics-2001*, Visakhapatnam District

Infrastructure Development of the Visakhapatnam City

Industries

As already mentioned, Visakhapatnam is one of the fastest growing cities in India, located on the northeastern coast of the state of Andhra Pradesh. The District of Visakhapatnam itself is rapidly industrializing having 33 major and medium industries and over 4,120 small-scale industrial units.

The City had 345 factories in 1986 besides heavy industries such as Visakhapatnam Steel Plant, Bharat Heavy Plates and Vessels (B.H.P.V.), Hindustan Petroleum and Chemicals Limited etc. By virtue of having a big natural port, this city has a "Free Trade Zone" established by the Central Government in order to boost exports.

Industrial development is conspicuous in Visakhapatnam urban agglomeration with the large scale industries like Hindustan Shipyard, Hindustan Petroleum Corporation Ltd, Coromandal Fertilizers Ltd, Bharath Heavy Plates and Vessels Ltd, L.G. Polymers Ltd; Hindustan Zinc Plant Ltd, and recent giant Visakhapatnam Steel Plant and a host of other ancillary industries. The Visakhapatnam Steel Plant is the biggest with an authorised share capital of Rs.7466 crores with a licensed capacity of 2.8 million tonnes of salable steel, 3.0 millions tonnes of Pig Iron and 832 lakhs tonnes of byproduct. About 25,000 persons are expected to be employed. The Project has provided employment to 16300 persons. On the countryside the agro-based industries like sugar factories, jute mills and rice mills are established besides brick and tile units. The District has 1063 registered factories under the Factories Act functioning with a workforce of 77203 persons during 2002-2003.

Education and Medical facilities

There are 3550 Primary Schools with 2.80 lakh children on enrolment, 489 Upper Primary Schools with an enrolment of 1.28 lakh, 447 High Schools with 2.04 lakh pupils on roll, 196 Junior, Degree and Professional Institutions with 0.83 lakh students during 2002-2003. Regarding medical facilities, there are 159 Government Hospitals and dispensaries both Allopathic and Indian Medicine with 2819 bed strength and 596 doctors.

Power

Power consumption by industries in the city is 42.45 million KWH while it is 70.17 MKWH for Agricultural purposes in the District. All the 3,335 habitations in the District have been electrified including solar power system during 2002-2003.

Banking

In the District there are 215 public sector bank branches, 29 private sector bank branches, 52 RRB branches, and 32 District Central Cooperative Bank branches, all put together 318 Bank branches exist to cater to the credit needs and banking activities of the people.

Communication

The District has a road length of 7336 kms of which the National Highway-5 runs to a length of 134.28 Kms, State Highways at a length of 277 Kms and remaining are the roads maintained by Roads and Buildings, Zilla Praja Parishad and Mandal Praja Parishads. The number of vehicles registered during 2002-2003 were 390,322 of which 326,295 are Motor Cycles. There are 660 Post Offices, 7 Telegraph Offices and 96 Telephone Exchanges with 156,993 Telephone connections in the District.

City shifts from South to North

The City was once a small fishermen village, the old town area, until the British arrived here. They developed Bhimunipatnam as the port and Waltair uplands as their residential colony. The City extended up to Poorna Market, the only commercial center for the entire City even up to 1970. After construction of Jagadamba Theatre, the City moved towards north and the commercial activity spread up to the so- called Jagadamba center in 1970's. Thereafter the City expanded further northwards after the construction of the RTC Complex and the City's tallest building by the LIC in 1980's. The entire Dabagardens area had become a hub of electronic goods trade. In 1990's the prestigious NH -5 Project brought the City shift towards further to the north. With the proposed construction of LT towers in the old T.B. Hospital area, the City is destined to create a hub for IT activity. The old town area is specialised in fishing.

Slums and Informal Sector

Along with the increase in urban population, the number of slums also increased. In 1971 the city had 40 urban slums and 36 village slums. By 1985 the number of slums increased to 170 and by the 2000 the number increased to more than 200. With this increase in the number of slums, the slum population also increased rapidly. In 1971 the slum population was 51,337 and in 1981 it increased threefold to 1,52,115 which accounts for approximately a quarter of the city's total population.[3] Though the data on slum population are scanty at present it is estimated that it accounts for 40 percent of the total city population. These slum dwellers mostly belong to the backward and scheduled castes and tribes individually earning less than or equal to Rs.400 per month. They are mostly illiterate or less educated.

Table – 3.6
Distribution of Slums in Visakhapatnam City

S.No.	*Area*	*No. of Slums*
1.	Corporation Land	190
2.	Temple Land	10
3.	Govt. and Private Land	51
	Total	251

Source: Housing Section, Visakhapatnam Municipal Corporation, Visakhapatnam

The Distribution of slums in Visakhapatnam City according to the land type is given in Table 3.6. It may be seen from the Table that there are 190 slums in the corporation land, 51 slums in Government and private land and 10 slums in Temple land. In total there are 251 slums consisting of 51855 for easy access to price of employment dwelling units most of families with 2,37,437 population. i.e. these slums are developing around the commercial centres of the city along side the Railway track and on the hill slopes, along side the large city drains (Geddas), along side of beach, old core of the city and marginal lands. These slums on private land are also in the old city, which provide easy access to place of employment.

Along with the industrial growth, the urban informal sector (IFS) is also growing by creating employment opportunities for the urban people. A number of small industrial units, trade and business establishments have come up, and smaller units of less than 10 workers form over 90 percent of all establishments employing a large number of workers in the IFS. Trade and Business establishments account for more than 50 percent in these informal sector establishments.[4]

In the year 1988 National Institute of Urban Affairs conducted a study on women workers in the informal sector (IFS).

Visakhapatnam City is one of the selected cities. According to the study about 70 percent of the total informal sector activities of women belongs to trade and service categories in Visakhapatnam. Self-employment occupies highest place (46.24%), followed by regular wage employment (22.78%) in providing employment for women in IFS. Details of the women workers in IFS of the City by industrial employment category are given in Table 3.7 and Table 3.8 respectively.

Table 3.7

Women Population in the IFS by Industrial Employment Category in Visakhapatnam city: 1988

Activity	*Percentage*
Primary	7.92
Construction	17.95
Manufacturing & Processing	3.47
Trade	34.75
Service	34.75
Miscellaneous	1.16

Source: NIUA, First Survey, 1988

Table 3.8

Women (15 Years +) in the IFS by Employment Status in Visakhapatnam city: 1988

Employment status	*Percentage*
Self employed	46.24
Employer	
Worker in family enterprise	11.68
Regular wage	22.78
Casual wage	18.63
Piece rate	0.67

Source: As shown ante

According to an evaluation study conducted by the Institute for Development and Planning Studies, Visakhapatnam, Table - 3.9 presents the number of slums, households and population in Visakhapatnam Metropolitan Region. In the City itself there are 268 slums habitants 60,231 households with a population of 2,51,530. After the successful implementation of the slum improvement project in Hyderabad, the ODA (UK) sanctioned a similar project to Visakhapatnam in 1988-89. The major objective of the Visakhapatnam Slum Improvement Project (VSIP) was to meet the basic needs of the urban poor through physical improvement of slums and to improve the quality of life for nearly two lakh people with an initial grant of Rs. 20.70 crores, out of which Rs. 15.67 crores (75.70%) was allotted to the improvement of physical infrastructure. The VSIP evaluation study observed that the physical infrastructure of slums has been totally changed. All the slums are provided with C. C. roads, streetlights, dustbins and protected water through pipelines. The quality of housing has improved with 55 percent of households constructing pucca houses, and another 16 percent have semi -pucca houses. The respondents reported that the house rents have recorded an increase from Rs.75/- to Rs.116/- in 1991. With the increased access to the slums, frequent visits of the officials to the slums and skill improvement progammes, there was an increase in work participation rates and gainful employment. In 1991, nearly 50 percent of the work force was engaged in unskilled labour and 25 percent were in skilled jobs. However, women workers in skilled labour category were only about 4 percent. Per household monthly income in real terms increased from Rs.956 in 1988 to Rs.1108 in 1991. Even though one cannot attribute this entirely to the VSIP. It is a remarkable improvement in the economic status of slum households. Development through community participation is the basic approach of the VSIP. It is reported that about three- fourths of the respondents are aware of the development programme, but only one-fifths have actually participated in them. Only about 60 percent of the respondents reported the visit of Sanitary / Health officials of the Municipal Corporation. With the establishments of Primary Health Care Centers (PHCCs), people reported that death rate is decreasing day by day. Institutional deliveries have increased from 42 percent in 1988 to 72 percent in 1991. As much as 83 percent of children were immunized fully. Family Planning acceptance rate has increased from 64 percent in 1988 to 67 percent in1991. The summative evaluation of the VSIP brings out clearly the substantial and significant improvement in physical and social infrastructure and in the levels of living of the slum dwellers particularly in the matters of housing, consumption expenditure, health, immunization of women and children, family planning and literacy. However the Study brings out certain features. The lowest income groups in the slum communities have not apparently shared adequately in the overall changes in the level of living. The relative disadvantage situation of the womenfolk in the slums in respect of occupation, wage earnings and vocational literacy has not improved. The Study also brought out that the community participation in the management of the newly created infrastructure has not shown any great improvement or strength. These findings should be matters of serious concern and the VMC should pay more attention in the future to rectify these inequalities and deficiencies.

Table – 3.9
Trends in Socioeconomic Indicators in Vizag Slums

SI No	*Socio-economic indicators*	*1998*		*1991*		*1996*	
		No.	*%*	*No*	*%*	*No*	*%*
1	Demographic change						
	No. of sample households		612		612		300
	Total sample population		2806		2889		1288
	Average Household Size		4.58		4.72		4.30
2	Literacy						
	Literacy rate (overall)						
	Males	923	64.73	1093	74.00	494	75.54
	Females	585	42.39	725	51.34	380	59.94
	Total	1508	53.74	1818	62.93	874	67.86
	Literacy rate (15 yrs & above						
	Males	524	61.00	632	67.38	366	87.14
	Females	245	28.13	316	34.96	240	58.82
	Total	769	44.45	948	51.47	606	73.19

Table – 3.9 (Contd.)

Sl No	*Socio-economic indicators*	*1998* *No.*	*%*	*1991* *No*	*%*	*1996* *No*	*%*
	Literacy rate of S.C. population (total)	289	50.44	388	63.82	441	50.46
3	Housing and Environment						
	Residence owning the house	533	87.09	542	88.56	267	89.00
	Households with Pucca houses	182	29.74	339	55.39	205	68.33
	S.C. household with Pucca houses	26	19.85	78	59.54	97	69.78
	S.C Household with separate latrine	72	11.76	133	21.73	70	23.33
	Households using tap water for drinking	325	53..10	345	56.37	166	55.33
	Household using dustbins	108	17.65	282	46.08	180	60.00
4	Labour Force						
	Gainfully employed (15 yrs & above)						
	Males	715	83.24	743	79.21	373	88.81
	Females	182	20.89	224	24.78	175	42.79
	Total	897	51.85	967	52.49	548	66.10
3	Incomes(Rs)	1988	1991	1996			
	Per household real income	956		1108		1295	
	Per capita income	208		235		302	
	Per workers real income earned-						
	Males	702		761		847	
	Females	313		312		415	
	Total	622		654		709	
	S.C. per worker real income (earned)						

Table – 3.9 (Contd.)

Sl No	*Socio-economic indicators*	*1998* No.	*1998* %	*1991* No	*1991* %	*1996* No	*1996* %
	Males	677		623		842	
	Females	251		324		377	
	Total	576		542		701	
6	Income distribution (Gini Co-efficient)	0.265		0.308		19.113	
	Health, status, immunization and family planning						
	Fully immunized children (1-3 yrs age)	56	24.67	92	82.88	32	96.97
	Partially immunized children (1-3yrs age)	152	66.96	18	16.22	1	3.03
	Not immunized children(1-3yrs)	19	8.37	1	0.90	0	0
	No. of vasectomies	106	35.22	106	27.18	50	28.09
	No. of Tubectomioes	193	64.12	262	67.18	124	69.66
	Births attended by trained person at the house or residence	16	45.71	7	53.85	3	60.66
	General sickness (in last 14days)	43	1.53.	130	4.50	66	5.12

Source: Institute for Development and Planning Studies, Visakhapatnam.

REFERENCES

1. http://timesofindia.indiatimes.com/articleshow/2481744.cms
2. *Handbook of Statistics, Visakhapatnam District 2000-2001*, Chief Planning Officer, Visakhapatnam
3. *Women in the Urban Informal Sector*, Research Study series, 1991, p. 32.
4. (a) NIUA (1991): *op cit.*

   (b) Dr. Ramana, K.V. and Dr. Krishna, K. S. "Structure and Working of Unorganised Sector in the Visakhapatnam City", Volume-I, *Department of Economics*, Andhra University, Visakhapatnam.

4

The Socioeconomic Background of Women Vendors

Introduction

In this Chapter an attempt is made to analyse the socio-economic characteristics of the sample women vendors. The Chapter is divided into two Sections. Section – I presents the household particulars of the sample women vendors while Section – II deals with characteristics of women vendors.

Household Particulars of the Sample Women Vendors

As mentioned earlier, the vegetable and fish vending is traditionally operated by Backward and Scheduled castes. It is also believed that caste in social structure inhibits other castes to enter into this trade. But changing social relations, level of unemployment, awareness of economic opportunities etc. motivate other castes to enter this trade. To examine this, the social background of the sample vendors has been analyzed. The social structure appears to exert a significant influence on economic activities. Religion and castes are considered to be the most important variable in the social structure. Every woman being a member of this system is influenced by this structure.

Religion

Distribution of the households of the sample women vendor according to the religion is presented in Table 4.1. It could be observed from the table that majority of the vendors are Hindus

(73.73%), followed by Christians (23.61%), Muslims (2.22%) and the others constitute 0.85 percent.

Table – 4.1

Distribution of the Sample Women Vendor Households by Religion

Type and level of trade		*Hindus*	*Christians*	*Muslims*	*Others*	*Total*
Fish vendors	Street Vendors	37 (61.67)	23 (38.33)	—	—	60 (100)
	Small Petty Vendors	43 (71.67)	17 (28.33)	—	—	60 (100)
	Petty Vendors	51 (85.00)	9 (15.00)	—	—	60 (100)
	Total	131 (72.78)	49 (27.22)	—	—	180 (100)
Vegetable Vendors	Street Vendors	40 (66.67)	20 (33.33)	—	—	60 (100)
	Small Petty Vendors	49 (81.67)	6 (10.00)	3 (5.00)	2 (3.33)	60 (100)
	Petty Vendors	44 (73.33)	10 (16.67)	5 (8.33)	1 (1.67)	60 (100)
	Total	133 (73.89)	36 (20.00)	8 (4.44)	3 (1.68)	180 (100)
Total Vendors	Street Vendors	77 (64.16)	43 (35.83)	—	—	120 (100)
	Small Petty Vendors	92 (76.67)	23 (19.17)	3 (2.50)	2 (1.66)	120 (100)
	Petty Vendors	95 (79.17)	19 (15.83)	5 (4.16)	1 (0.83)	120 (100)
	Total	264 (73.34)	85 (23.61)	8 (2.22)	3 (0.83)	360 (100)

Source: Computed from the primary data. Figures in parentheses indicate percentages to row total.

Among the fish vendors 72.78% are Hindus, 27.22% are Christians. Among vegetable vendors 73.89% are Hindus, 20.00% are Christians and 4.44% are Muslims and 1.68% are others.

Table – 4.2
Distribution of Sample Women Vendors Household by Caste

Types and level of Trade		OC				BC				SC				Total
		Panta Reddy	*Ksha-tritya*	*Others*	*Total*	*VodaBalji*	*Jalari*	*Othrs*	*Total*	*Relliy*	*Mala Madiga*	*Others*	*Total*	
Fish Vendors	Street Vendors	4 (6.67)	3 (5.00)	5 (8.33)	12 (20.00)	14 (23.33)	6 (10.00)	8 (13.33)	28 (46.67)	9 (15.00)	5 (8.33)	6 (10.00)	20 (33.33)	60 (100.00)
	Small Petty Vendors	7 (11.67)	4 (6.67)	4 (6.67)	15 (25.00)	18 (30.00)	8 (13.33)	6 (10.00)	32 (53.33)	6 (10.00)	3 (5.00)	4 (6.67)	13 (21.67)	60 (100.00)
	Petty Vendors	10 (16.67)	3 (5.00)	4 (6.67)	17 (28.33)	19 (31.67)	10 (16.67)	5 (8.33)	34 (56.67)	5 (8.33)	1 (1.67)	3 (5.00)	9 (15.00)	60 (100.00)
	Total	21 (11.67)	10 (5.56)	13 (7.22)	44 (24.44)	51 (28.33)	24 (13.33)	19 (10.56)	94 (52.22)	20 (11.11)	9 (5.00)	13 (7.22)	42 (23.33)	180 (100.00)
Vegetable Vendors	Street Vendors	9 (15.00)	8 (13.33)	4 (6.67)	21 (35.00)	6 (10.00)	4 (6.67)	16 (26.67)	26 (43.33)	5 (8.33)	3 (5.00)	5 (8.33)	13 (21.67)	60 (100.00)
	Small Petty Vendors	12 (20.00)	9 (15.00)	5 (8.33)	26 (43.33)	5 (8.33)	3 (5.00)	14 (23.33)	22 (36.67)	3 (5.00)	2 (3.33)	7 (11.67)	12 (20.00)	60 (100.00)
	Petty Vendors	11 (18.33)	10 (16.67)	9 (15.00)	30 (50.00)	7 (11.67)	5 (8.33)	15 (25.00)	27 (45.00)	2 (3.33)	1 (1.67)	0 (0.00)	3 (5.00)	60 (100.00)
	Total	32 (17.78)	27 (15.00)	18 (10.00)	77 (42.78)	18 (10.00)	12 (6.67)	45 (25.00)	75 (41.67)	10 (5.56)	6 (3.33)	12 (6.67)	28 (15.56)	180 (100.00)

Total Vendors	Street Vendors	13 (10.83)	11 (9.17)	9 (7.50)	33 (27.50)	20 (16.67)	10 (8.33)	24 (20.00)	54 (45.00)	14 (11.67)	8 (6.67)	11 (9.17)	33 (27.50)	120 (100.00)
	Small Petty Vendors	19 (15.83)	13 (10.83)	9 (7.50)	41 (34.17)	23 (19.17)	11 (9.17)	20 (16.67)	54 (45.00)	9 (7.50)	5 (4.17)	11 (9.17)	25 (20.83)	120 (100.00)
	Petty Vendors	21 (17.50)	13 (10.83)	13 (10.83)	47 (39.17)	26 (21.67)	15 (12.50)	20 (16.67)	61 (50.83)	7 (5.83)	2 (1.67)	3 (2.50)	12 (10.00)	120 (100.00)
	Total	53 (14.72)	37 (10.28)	31 (8.61)	121 (33.61)	69 (19.17)	36 (10.00)	64 (17.78)	169 (46.94)	30 (8.33)	15 (4.17)	25 (6.94)	70 (19.44)	360 (100.00)

Source: Computed from the primary data. Figures in parentheses indicate percentages to the row total

Caste

The sample women vendors are classified into three social groups, namely Open Category (OC), Backward Category (BC), and Scheduled Caste (SC) considering their caste as the parameter. The distribution of women vendors based on the caste classification is presented in Table 4.2.

It could be observed from the table that majority of the women vendors are from Backward Classes (46.94%), then by the OC category (33.61%), and Scheduled Castes (19.44%). Among all the castes of 3 social groups, it is the Vadabalija, Jalari, Relli castes which are traditionally involved in the vegetable and fish vending activity.

Among the fish vendors, about 24.44% are OCs, 52.22% are BCs, and 23.33 % are SCs. In vegetable vendors, 42.78 percent are OCs, 41.07% are BCs and 15.56% are SCs.

Family Size

Family size affects the activities of each member of the family and the combination of different members within the family group. The family is the Social unit within which all women live, work and have their identity. Family network and its size are important as supporting system for women to work and earn money.

The distribution of the sample women vendors by the size of the family is presented in Table 4.3. The households are classified into three groups; 1-3 members; 4-5 members; above 5 members.

It could be observed from the Table 4.3 that 39.17% of the households have more than 5 members. Percentage of households having family size of 4-5 is 34.44%. Only 26.30% have less than 4 members. Among fish vendors 20.56% have the family size 1-3; 32.78% have 4-5 family members; and the remaining 46.67 percent have more than 6 members. Among the vegetable vendors, 32.22% have 1-3 family size; 36.11 have 4-5 family size; 31.67% have 6 and above family size.

Dependency Ratio

Work force participation rate and dependency ratio are to important aspects which indicate the economic situation of the

Table – 4.3
Distribution of the Selected Women Vendor Households by Size of family

Types and level of Trade		*Range* 1 – 3	4 – 5	*Total* 6 and a bove	
Fish Vendors	Street Vendors	9 (15.00)	16 (26.67)	35 (58.33)	60 (100)
	Small Petty Vendors	11 (18.33)	20 (33.33)	29 (48.34)	60 (100)
	Petty Vendors	17 (28.34)	23 (38.33)	20 (33.33)	60 (100)
	Total	37 (20.56)	59 (32.78)	84 (46.67)	180 (100)
Vegetable Vendors	Street Vendors	15 (25.00)	21 (35.00)	24 (40.00)	60 (100)
	Small Petty Vendors	20 (33.33)	25 (41.67)	15 (25.00)	60 (100)
	Petty Vendors	23 (38.33)	19 (31.67)	18 (30.00)	60 (100)
	Total	58 (32.22)	65 (36.11)	57 (31.67)	180 (100)
Total Vendors	Street Vendors	24 (20.00)	37 (30.83)	59 (49.17)	120 (100)
	Small Petty Vendors	31 (25.83)	45 (37.50)	44 (36.67)	120 (100
	Petty Vendors	40 (33.33)	42 (35.00)	38 (31.67)	120 (100
	Total	95 (26.38)	124 (34.44)	141 (39.17)	360 (100)

Source: Computed from the primary data. Figures in parentheses indicate percentages to the row total.

household. Data regarding the earners, non-earners and dependency ratio are presented in Table 4.4.

Table – 4.4

Earners, Non-earners and Dependency Ratio among the Sample Women Vendor Households

Types and level of Trade		*Number of members*	*Item Average Family Size*	*Earners*	*Dependents*	*Earners Dependents Ratio*
Fish Vendors	Street Vendors	303 (60)	5.05	112	191	1.70
	Small Petty Vendors	298 (60)	4.96	109	189	1.73
	Petty Vendors	270 (60)	4.50	112	158	1.41
	Total	871 (180)	4.83	333	538	1.61
Vegetable Vendors	Street Vendors	289 (60)	4.81	124	165	1.33
	Small Petty Vendors	289 (60)	4.81	124	138	1.11
	Petty Vendors	253 (60)	4.21	102	151	1.48
	Total	804 (180)	4.46	350	454	1.29
Total Vendors	Street Vendors	563 (120)	4.69	236	356	1.50
	Small Petty Vendors	560 (120)	4.66	233	327	1.40
	Petty Vendors	523 (120)	4.35	214	309	1.44
	Total	1675 (360)	4.65	683	992	1.45

Source: Computed from the primary data. Figures in parentheses indicate percentages to the row total

From Table-4.4 it could be observed that in the sample of women vendor households, the percentage of earners is 41 and the dependency ratio is 1.45. Among the sample fish vending households, the percentage of earners is 38 and the dependency ratio is 1.61, while the percentage of earners in the vegetable vendor's households is 43 and the dependency ratio is 1.29.

Table – 4.5
Distribution of the Sample Women Vendor by Average Households Monthly Income

Types and level of Trade		*Monthly family income (in Rs.)* Below 2500	2600-3500	3600-4500	Above 4600	*Total*
Fish Vendors	Street Vendors	1970(10)	2696(8)	4174(16)	5075(26)	4000(60)
	Small Petty Vendors	1993 (10)	2734 (17)	4164 (12)	5166 (21)	3748 (60)
	Petty Vendors	——	——	3846 (16)	6122 (44)	5515 (60)
	Total	1981 (20)	2722 (25)	4052 (44)	5602 (91)	4421 (180)
Vegetable Vendors	Street Vendors	2060 (4)	2402 (5)	4020 (19)	5239 (32)	4404 (60)
	Small Petty Vendors	——	3003 (5)	3980 (7)	5681 (32)	5259 (60)
	Petty Vendors	——	——	3921 (18)	5731 (48)	5188 (60)
	Total	2060 (4)	2702 (10)	3973 (44)	5582 (122)	4951 (180)
Total Vendors	Street Vendors	1996 (14)	2583 (13)	4090 (35)	5165 (58)	4202 (120)
	Small Petty Vendors	1993 (10)	2795 (22)	4096 (19)	5224 (69)	4503 (120)
	Petty Vendors	——	——	3886 (34)	5931 (86)	5352 (120)
	Total	1994 (24)	2716 (35)	4012 (88)	5591 (213)	4686 (360)

Source: Computed from the primary data. Figures in parentheses indicate percentages to the row total.

Average Households Monthly Income of the Women Vendor

The information about the average monthly income of the sample households is presented in Table 4.5. It could be observed from the table that the average monthly income of the sample women vendor households is Rs. 4686; sample fish vendor households is Rs. 4421 and sample vegetable vendor households is Rs. 4951.

Based on the household income all the households are classified into four categories; below Rs. 2500; Rs. 2600- Rs. 3500; Rs. 3600 – Rs. 4500: and Rs. 4600 and above.

The average incomes of the total women vendor households under these four categories are Rs. 1994, Rs. 2716, Rs. 4012, Rs. 5591 respectively. In case of fish vendor households the average incomes are Rs. 1981, Rs. 2722, Rs. 4052, Rs. 5582. In case of vegetable vending households the respective averages are Rs. 2060, Rs. 2702, Rs. 3973, Rs. 5502.

Per Capita Income

The per capita income of the women vendor households is presented in Table 4.6. The data shows that the per capita income of the vegetable vendor households (Rs. 1108) is higher than the fish vendor households (Rs. 913). For the total vendors the per capita income is Rs. 1007.

Housing Status of the Women Vendors

The distribution of the women vendor households based on the own and rented housing status is presented in Table 4.7 It could be seen from the table that out of the total women vendor households 65% have their own house. In case of fish vendor households it is 60 % and n case of vegetable vendor households it is 70%.

Electrification status of the women vendor households

The living standards of the women vendor households could be assessed by various parameters. Electrification of the houses is one such good indicator. The electrification status if the women vendor household is presented in Table 4.8. According the information 51% of the total sample women vendors have

Table – 4.6
Distribution of the Sample Women Vendor Households by Monthly Per Capital Income

Types and level of Trade		*Per-capita income* < 500	500-1000	1000-1500	1500 and above	*Total*
Fish Vendors	Street Vendors	399 (11)	752 (32)	1235 (14)	1693 (3)	792 (60)
	Small Petty Vendors	420 (14)	817 (39)	1184 (6)	1916 (1)	754 (60)
	Petty Vendors	—	818 (16)	1196 (25)	1869 (19)	1225 (60)
	Total	410 (25)	793 (87)	1206 (45)	1850 (23)	913 (180)
Vegetable Vendors	Street Vendors	426 (6)	793 (30)	1113 (14)	1642 (10)	970 (60)
	Small Petty Vendors	—	822 (19)	1185 (19)	1768 (22)	1204 (60)
	Petty Vendors	—	811 (15)	1209 (26)	1905 (19)	1230 (60)
	Total	426(6)	806 (64)	1177 (59)	1793 (51)	1108 (180)
Total Vendors	Street Vendors	407 (17)	772 (62)	1169 (28)	1653 (13)	851 (120)
	Small Petty Vendors	420 (14)	819 (58)	1185 (25)	1773 (23)	965 (120)
	Petty Vendors	—	814 (31)	1202 (51)	1886 (38)	1228 (120)
	Total	413 (31)	789 (151)	1189 (104)	1811 (74)	1007 (360)

Source: Computed from the primary data. Figures in parentheses indicate percentages to the row total

Table – 4.7
Housing Status of the Sample Women Vendors

Types and level of Trade		*Own House*				*Rent House*				*Total*
		Pucca	*Semi Pucca*	*Kutcha*	*Total*	*Pucca*	*Semi Pucca*	*Kutcha*	*Total*	
Fish Vendors	Street Vendors	8 (13.33)	10 (16.67)	12 (20.00)	30 (50.00)	8 (13.33)	9 (15.00)	13 (21.67)	30 (50.00)	60 (100)
	Small Petty Vendors	12 (20.00)	13 (21.66)	12 (20.00)	37 (61.66)	6 (10.00)	7 (11.66)	10 (16.66)	23 (38.33)	60 (100)
	Petty Vendors	14 (23.34)	19 (31.67)	9 (15.00)	42 (70.00)	5 (8.33)	8 (13.33)	5 (8.33)	18 (30.00)	60 (100)
	Total	34 (18.89)	42 (23.35)	33 (18.33)	109 (60.56)	19 (10.55)	24 (13.33)	28 (15.55)	71 (39.44)	180 (100)
Vegetable Vendors	Street Vendors	15 (25.02)	10 (16.66)	13 (21.67)	38 (63.33)	4 (6.66)	8 (13.33)	10 (16.66)	22 (36.67)	60 (100)
	Small Petty Vendors	15 (25.02)	22 (36.66)	4 (6.66)	41 (68.34)	6 (10.00)	7 (11.66)	6 (10.66)	19 (31.66)	60 (100)
	Petty Vendors	19 (31.67)	24 (40.02)	4 (6.66)	47 (78.34)	5 (8.33)	7 (11.66)	1 (1.66)	13 (21.66)	60 (100)
	Total	49 (27.22)	56 (31.13)	21 (11.66)	126 (70.00)	15 (8.33)	22 (12.22)	17 (9.44)	54 (30.00)	*180 (100)*

Total Vendors	Street Vendors	23 (19.16)	20 (16.66)	25 (20.86)	68 (56.67)	12 (10.00)	17 (14.16)	23 (19.16)	52 (43.33)	120 (100)
	Small Petty Vendors	27 (22.50)	35 (29.18)	16 (13.33)	78 (65.00)	12 (10.00)	14 (11.66)	16 (13.33)	42 (35.00)	120 (100)
	Petty Vendors	33 (27.50)	43 (35.84)	13 (10.83)	89 (74.16)	10 (8.33)	15 (12.50)	6 (5.00)	31 (25.83)	120 (100)
	Total	83 (23.05)	98 (27.24)	54 (15.00)	235 (65.28)	34 (9.44)	46 (12.77)	45 (12.50)	125 (34.72)	360 (100)

Source: Computed from the primary data. Figures in parentheses indicate percentages to the row total

Table – 4.8

Distribution of Households according to Facility of Electrification

Types and level of Trade		Description		Total
		Yes	No	
Fish Vendors	Street Vendors	23(38.33)	37(61.67)	60(100)
	Small Petty Vendors	27(45.00)	33(55.00)	60(100)
	Petty Vendors	36(60.00)	24(40.00)	60(100)
	Total	86(47.78)	94(52.22)	180(100)
Vegetable Vendors	Street Vendors	28(46.67)	32(53.33)	60(100)
	Small Petty Vendors	32(53.33)	28(46.67)	60(100)
	Petty Vendors	39(65.00)	21(35.00)	60(100)
	Total	99(55.00)	81(45.00)	180(100)
Total Vendors	Street Vendors	51(42.50)	69(57.50)	120(100)
	Small Petty Vendors	59(49.17)	61(50.83)	120(100)
	Petty Vendors	75(62.50)	45(37.50)	120(100)
	Total	185(51.39)	175(48.61)	360(100)

Source: Computed from the primary data. Figures in parentheses indicate percentages to the row total.

electrification for their houses. Among the fish vendors 47.78% and among the vegetable vendors 55% have electrification to their houses.

Sources of water supply

The distribution of the households based on the sources of water supply is presented in Table 4.9. According to the table 22.5% of the total women vendors have own source of water supply. In case of fish vendors the percentage is 17.78 and in case of vegetable vendors the percentage is 27.22.

Sanitary facilities

The sanitary facilities available at the sample women vendor households are presented in Table 4.10. Out of the total women vending households only 15% have their own sanitary facilities.

In case of fish vendors the percentage still low (17.78%) and in case of vegetable vendor households the percentage is 27.22.

Cooking fuel

The type of cooking fuel used by the sample women vendor households is given in the Table 4.11. The major sources are firewood, kerosene and LPG. Majority of the households are still dependent on the Firewood. Out of the total households 40.55% use firewood for cooking purpose, whereas in case of fish vendors it is 41.67% and in case of vegetable vendors it is 39%. The percentage of vendor households who use LPG is 20.95 % in total households, 23.33% in fish vendors and 30 % in vegetable vendors.

Table – 4.9

Distribution of Households by the Source of Protected Water Supply

Types and level of Trade		*Description*		*Total*
		Own	*Public*	
Fish Vendors	Street Vendors	7(11.67)	53(88.33)	60(100)
	Small Petty Vendors	11(18.33)	49(81.67)	60(100)
	Petty Vendors	14(23.33)	46(76.67)	60(100)
	Total	32(17.78)	148(82.22)	180(100)
Vegetable Vendors	Street Vendors	12(20.00)	48(80.00)	60(100)
	Small Petty Vendors	16(26.67)	44(73.33)	60(100)
	Petty Vendors	21(35.00)	39(65.00)	60(100)
	Total	49(27.22)	131(72.78)	180(100)
Total Vendors	Street Vendors	19(15.83)	101(84.17)	120(100)
	Small Petty Vendors	27(22.50)	93(77.50)	120(100)
	Petty Vendors	35(29.17)	85(70.83)	120(100)
	Total	81(22.50)	279(77.50)	360(100)

Source: Computed from the primary data. Figures in parentheses indicate percentages to the row total.

Table – 4.10

Status of Sanitary Facility by Women Vendors

Types and level of Trade		*Description*		*Total*
		Own	*Public*	
Fish Vendors	Street Vendors	3(5.00)	57(95.00)	60(100)
	Small Petty Vendors	8(13.33)	52(86.67)	60(100)
	Petty Vendors	11(18.33)	49(81.67)	60(100)
	Total	22(12.22)	158(87.78)	180(100)
Vegetable Vendors	Street Vendors	4(6.67)	56(93.33)	60(100)
	Small Petty Vendors	12(20.00)	48(80.00)	60(100)
	Petty Vendors	16(26.67)	44(73.33)	60(100)
	Total	32(17.78)	148(82.22)	180(100)
Total Vendors	Street Vendors	7(17.78)	113(82.22)	120(100)
	Small Petty Vendors	20(16.67)	100(83.33)	120(100)
	Petty Vendors	27(22.50)	93(77.50)	120(100)
	Total	54(15.00)	306(85.00)	360(100)

Source: Computed from the primary data. Figures in parentheses indicate percentages to the row total

Table – 4.11

Type of Cooking Fuel

Types and level of Trade		*Description*			*Total*
		Fire Wood	*Kerosene*	*LPG*	
Fish Vendors	Street Vendors	34 (56.67)	20 (33.33)	6 (10.00)	60 (100)
	Small Petty Vendors	21 (35.00)	25 (41.67)	14 (23.33)	60 (100)
	Petty Vendors	20 (33.33)	18 (30.00)	22 (36.67)	60 (100)
	Total	75 (41.67)	63 (35.00)	42 (23.33)	180 (100)

Vegetable Vendors	Street Vendors	28 (46.67)	22 (36.67)	10 (16.66)	60 (100)
	Small Petty Vendors	25 (41.67)	18 (30.00)	17 (28.33)	60 (100)
	Petty Vendors	18 (30.00)	14 (23.33)	28 (46.67)	60 (100)
	Total	71 (39.41)	54 (30.00)	55 (30.56)	180 (100)
Total Vendors	Street Vendors	62 (51.66)	42 (35.00)	16 (13.33)	120 (100)
	Small Petty Vendors	46 (38.33)	43 (35.83)	31 (25.83)	120 (100
	Petty Vendors	38 (31.67)	32 (26.66)	50 (41.67)	120 (100
	Total	146(40.55)	117(32.50)	97(26.95)	360(100)

Source: Computed from the primary data. Figures in parentheses indicate percentages to the row total

Characteristics of Women Vendors

The characteristics of women vendors like age, marital status, literacy, language spoken experience, origin of business, no. of working hours, are present in the following sub-section.

Age-wise distribution of the sample women vendors

The distribution of the sample women vendors according to the age group is presented in Table 4.12. They were grouped into 18-25 years, 26-30 years, 31-45 years, 46-55 years, 56 and above years. Majority of the vendors fall in the category of 31-45 years age group followed by 56 and above and then by 26-30 age group. In case of fish vendors majority fall under the category of 26-30 followed by 56 and above category. In case of vegetable vendors majority are in the age group of 31-45 and almost equal percentage are there in the three age group (26-30, 46-55, 56 and above).

Table – 4.12

Age-wise Distribution of the Sample Women Vendors

Types and level of Trade		*Age Wise - Levels*					*Total*
		18-25 Years	*26-30 Years*	*31-45 Years*	*46-55 Years*	*56 and above years*	
Fish Vendors	Street Vendors	12(20.00)	8(13.00)	18(30.00)	6(10.00)	16(26.66)	60(100)
	Small Petty Vendors	5(8.33)	16(26.67)	9(15.00)	11(18.33)	19(31.67)	60(100)
	Petty Vendors	3(5.00)	17(28.34)	10(16.66)	12(20.00)	18(30.00)	60(100)
	Total	20(11.11)	41(27.77)	37(20.55)	29(16.11)	53(29.44)	180(100)
Vegetable Vendors	Street Vendors	9(15.00)	7(11.66)	19(31.68)	13(21.66)	12(20.00)	60(100)
	Small Petty Vendors	6(10.00)	13(21.67)	18(30.00)	12(20.00)	11(18.33)	60(100)
	Petty Vendors	4(6.66)	17(28.34)	14(23.34)	12(20.00)	13(21.66)	60(100)
	Total	19(10.55)	37(20.55)	51(28.33)	37(20.55)	36(20.00)	180(100)
Total Vendors	Street Vendors	21(17.50)	15(12.50)	37(30.84)	19(15.83)	28(23.33)	120(100)
	Small Petty Vendors	11(9.16)	29(24.16)	27(22.50)	23(19.16)	30(25.00)	120(100)
	Petty Vendors	7(5.83)	34(28.34)	24(20.00)	24(20.00)	31(25.83)	120(100)
	Total	39(10.83)	78(21.66)	88(24.44)	66(18.33)	89(24.72)	360(100)

Source: Computed from the primary data. Figures in parentheses indicate percentages to the row total

Table – 4.13
Marital Status of the Sample Women Vendors

Types and level of Trade		*Married*					*Total*
		Unmarried	*United*	*Widowed*	*Second Wife*	*Total*	
Fish Vendors	Street Vendors	14(23.33)	26(43.33)	13(21.67)	7(11.67)	46(76.66)	60(100)
	Small Petty Vendors	16(26.67)	30(50.00)	9(15.00)	11(18.33)	44(73.33)	60(100)
	Petty Vendors	16(26.67)	36(60.00)	6(10.00)	14(23.33)	44(73.33)	180(100)
	Total	46(25.56)	92(51.11)	28(15.56)	32(53.33)	134(74.44)	180(100.00)
Vegetable Vendors	Street Vendors	12(20.00)	33(55.00)	9(15.00)	6(10.00)	48(80.00)	60(100)
	Small Petty Vendors	15(25.00)	34(56.67)	6(10.00)	10(16.67)	45(75.00)	60(100)
	Petty Vendors	16(26.67)	37(61.67)	4(6.67)	13(21.67)	44(73.33)	60(100)
	Total	43(23.89)	104(57.78)	19(10.56)	29(48.33)	137(76.11)	180(100)
Total Vendors	Street Vendors	26(21.67)	59(49.17)	22(18.33)	13(21.67)	94(78.33)	120(100)
	Small Petty Vendors	31(25.83)	64(53.33)	15(12.50)	21(35.00)	89(74.16)	120(100)
	Petty Vendors	32(26.67)	73(60.83)	10(8.33)	27(45.00)	88(73.33)	120(100)
	Total	8924.72	196(54.44)	47(13.06)	61(16.94)	271(75.27)	360(100)

Source: Computed from the primary data. Figures in parentheses indicate percentages to the row total

Table – 4.14
Distribution of the Sample Women Vendors by Literacy Levels

Types and level of Trade		*Literacy Levels*						*Total*
		Illiteracy	*1 – 5 Class*	*6 – 7 Class*	*8 – 10 Class*	*Inter-mediate*	*Total*	
Fish Vendors	Street Vendors	48(80.00)	9(15.00)	2(3.33)	1(1.67)	—	12(20.00)	60(100)
	Small Petty Vendors	47(78.33)	8(13.33)	3(5.00)	2(3.33)	—	13(21.66)	60(100)
	Petty Vendors	43(71.67)	11(18.33)	4(6.67)	1(1.67)	1(1.67)	17(28.33)	60(100)
	Total	138(76.67)	28(15.56)	9(5.00)	4(2.22)	1(0.36)	42(23.33)	180(100)
Vegetable Vendors	Street Vendors	46(76.67)	11(18.33)	2(3.33)	1(1.67)	—	14(23.33)	60(100)
	Small Petty Vendors	44(73.33)	8(13.33)	4(6.67)	3(5.00)	1(1.67)	16(26.66)	60(100)
	Petty Vendors	45(75.00)	6(10.00)	4(6.67)	3(5.00)	2(3.33)	15(25.00)	60(100)
	Total	135(75.00)	25(13.89)	10(5.56)	7(3.89)	3(1.67)	45(25.00)	180(100)
Total Vendors	Street Vendors	94(78.33)	20(16.67)	4(3.33)	2(1.67)	—	26(21.66)	120(100)
	Small Petty Vendors	91(75.83)	16(13.33)	7(5.83)	5(4.17)	1(0.83)	29(24.16)	120(100)
	Petty Vendors	88(73.33)	17(14.17)	8(6.67)	4(3.33)	3(2.5)	32(26.66)	120(100)
	Total	273(75.83)	53(14.72)	19(5.28)	11(3.06)	4(1.11)	87(24.16)	360(100)

Source: Computed from the primary data. Figures in parentheses indicate percentages to the row total

Marital status

The marital status of the women vendors is presented in the Table 4.13. They are categorized into four namely, unmarried, married, widowed, second wife. It could be observed from the table that nearly 25 percent of the women vendors, both fish and vegetable categories are unmarried.

Literacy levels of the women vendors

The literacy levels of the women vendors are presented in Table 4.14. It could be observed from the table that about 75% of the women vendors are illiterates.

Spoken Language of women vendors

The information on the language spoken by the women vendors generally in the marketyard is provided in the Table 4.15. Generally five languages are spoken by them. They are Telugu, Hindi, English, Oriya, Relli.

Experience

The distribution of the women vendors based on the years of experience is presented in Table 4.16. The percentage of vendors below 5 years of experience accounts for 12.5 % in total vendors, 8.33 in fish vendors and 16.66 in vegetable vendors. It could said that vegetable vending is the trade where the new entrants were seen than in the fish vending. In fish vending activity they traditionally involve in that and gain more than 10 years of experience.

Origin of business

The information about the origin of the business is presented in Table 4.17. Majority of the vendors involved in the activity because of the caste based nature of the activity. Next people are involved in the vending activity because they inherited that. The next reason for that no technical skill is required to start the vending activity. Based on this classification the vendors are distributed for origin of business.

Table-4.15
Distribution of the Sample Women Vendors by Language

Types and level of Trade		Language						Total
		Telugu	Telugu Hindi	Telugu English	Oriya Telugu	Telugu, Hindi English	Relli Telugu	
Fish Vendors	Street Vendors	27(45.00)	6(10.00)	3(5.00)	8(13.33)	—	16(26.66)	60(100)
	Small Petty Vendors	26(43.33)	13(21.66)	4(6.66)	5(8.33)	2(3.33)	10(16.66)	60(100)
	Petty Vendors	18(30.01)	12(20.00)	9(15.00)	10(16.66)	6(10.00)	5(8.33)	60(100)
	Total	71(39.45)	31(17.23)	16(8.88)	23(12.77)	8(4.44)	31(17.23)	180(100)
Vegetable Vendors	Street Vendors	42(70.00)	5(8.33)	2(3.33)	3(5.00)	—	8(13.34)	60(100)
	Small Petty Vendors	13(21.66)	15(25.00)	7(11.66)	13(21.66)	5(8.33)	7(11.66)	60(100)
	Petty Vendors	12(20.00)	14(23.34)	9(15.00)	15(25.00)	9(15.00)	1(1.66)	60(100)
	Total	67(37.24)	34(18.89)	18(10.00)	31(17.22)	14(7.00)	16(8.88)	180(100)
Total Vendors	Street Vendors	69(57.50)	11(9.16)	5(4.16)	11(9.16)	—	24(20.00)	120(100)
	Small Petty Vendors	39(32.50)	28(23.33)	11(9.16)	18(15.00)	7(5.83)	17(14.16)	120(100)
	Petty Vendors	30(25.00)	26(21.66)	18(15.00)	25(20.83)	15(12.50)	6(5.00)	120(100)
	Total	138(38.33)	65(18.05)	34(9.44)	54(15.00)	22(6.11)	47(13.05)	360(100)

Source: Computed from the primary data. Figures in parentheses indicate percentages to the row total/

Table – 4.16

Experience of the Sample Women Vendors

Types and level of Trade		*Experience*					*Total*
		Below-5	*6-10*	*11-15*	*16-25*	*25 and above*	
Fish Vendors	Street Vendors	5(8.33)	32(53.33)	6(10.00)	8(13.33)	9(15.00)	60(100)
	Small Petty Vendors	2(3.33)	25(41.66)	11(18.33)	9(15.00)	13(21.66)	60(100)
	Petty Vendors	8(13.33)	36(60.00)	5(8.33)	5(8.33)	6(10.00)	60(100)
	Total	15(8.33)	93(51.66)	22(12.22)	22(12.22)	28(15.55)	180(100)
Vegetable Vendors	Street Vendors	23(38.33)	30(50.00)	2(3.33)	2(3.33)	3(5.00)	60(100)
	Small Petty Vendors	5(8.33)	32(53.33)	9(15.00)	6(10.00)	8(13.33)	60(100)
	Petty Vendors	2(3.33)	41(68.33)	6(10.00)	4(6.66)	7(11.66)	60(100)
	Total	30(16.66)	103(57.22)	17(9.44)	12(6.66)	18(10.00)	180(100)
Total Vendors	Street Vendors	28(23.33)	62(51.66)	8(6.66)	10(8.33)	12(10.00)	120(100)
	Small Petty Vendors	7(5.83)	57(47.51)	20(16.66)	15(12.50)	21(17.50)	120(100)
	Petty Vendors	10(8.33)	77(64.16)	11(9.16)	9(7.50)	13(10.83)	120(100)
	Total	45(12.50)	196(54.44)	39(10.83)	34(9.44)	46(12.77)	360(100)

Source: Computed from the primary data. Figures in parentheses indicate percentages to the row total.

It could be observed from the table that 45% of the total vendors, 43.34% of fish vendors, and 41.12% of vegetable vendors are originated because of the caste based nature. The next majority is inheritance. 43% of total vendors, 42, 24% of fish vendors, 45% of vegetable vendors engaged in that because of inheritance. The rest are new entrants.

Table – 4.17
Distribution of the Selected Women Vendors by Origin of Business

Types and level of Trade		*Description*			*Total*
		Caste Base	*Inherited*	*Un skilled*	
Fish Vendors	Street Vendors	21 (35.00)	34 (56.67)	5 (8.33)	60 (100)
	Small Petty Vendors	30 (50.00)	23 (38.37)	7 (11.66)	60 (100)
	Petty Vendors	39 (65.00)	19 (31.66)	2 (3.33)	60 (100)
	Total	90 (43.34)	76 (42.23)	14 (7.77)	180 (100)
Vegetable Vendors	Street Vendors	26 (31.66)	22 (36.66)	12 (20.00)	60 (100)
	Small Petty Vendors	19 (48.34)	36 (60.00)	5 (8.33)	60 (100)
	Petty Vendors	29 (48.34)	23 (38.33)	8 (13.33)	60 (100)
	Total	74 (41.12)	81 (45.00)	25 (13.88)	180 (100)
Total Vendors	Street Vendors	47 (39.16)	56 (46.66)	17 (14.16)	120 (100)
	Small Petty Vendors	49 (40.83)	59 (49.17)	12 (10.00)	120 (100)
	Petty Vendors	68 (56.66)	42 (35.00)	10 (8.33)	120 (100)
	Total	164 (45.55)	157 (43.61)	39 (10.83)	360 (100)

Source: Computed from the primary data. Figures in parentheses indicate percentages to the row total

Table – 4.18
Working Hours of the Selected Women Vendors

Types and level of Trade		*Working hours*				*Total*
		Below 4 hours	*5 -7 Hours*	*8 -10 hours*	*11 and above hours*	
Fish Vendors	Street Vendors	29(48.33)	28(46.66)	3(5.00)	—	60(100)
	Small Petty Vendors	8(13.33)	37(61.66)	15(25.00)	—	60(100)
	Petty Vendors	—	20(33.34)	24(40.00)	16(26.66)	60(100)
	Total	37(20.55)	85(47.22)	42(23.33)	16(8.88)	180(100)
Vegetable Vendors	Street Vendors	36(60.00)	24(40.00)	—	—	60(100)
	Small Petty Vendors	5(8.34)	31(51.66)	24(40.00)	—	60(100)
	Petty Vendors	3(5.00)	10(16.66)	28(46.66)	19(31.66)	60(100)
	Total	44(24.44)	65(36.11)	52(28.88)	19(10.55)	180(100)
Total Vendors	Street Vendors	65(54.17)	52(43.33)	3(2.30)	—	120(100)
	Small Petty Vendors	13(10.83)	68(56.66)	39(32.50)	—	120(100)
	Petty Vendors	3(2.50)	30(25.00)	52(43.33)	35(29.16)	120(100)
	Total	81(22.50)	150(41.66)	94(26.11)	35(9.72)	360(100)

Source: Computed from the primary data. Figures in parentheses indicate percentages to the row total.

Working hours of the women vendors

Generally these activities require some specific timing which is presented in Table 4.18. There exists peak vending hours etc. Therefore, total time spent on the activity is divided into 4 categories namely below 4 hours, 5-7 hours, 8-10 hours and 11 and above hours. It could be observed from the Table that majority of the vendors (26.11%) are spending 8-10 hours. In case of fish vendors 47.22% are spending 5-7 hours while in case of vegetable vending 36.11% are spending 5-7 hours.

5

Migration of Women Vendors

Introduction

Migration has become an essential characteristic feature of modern society. It is increasing rapidly along with and because of industrialization and urbanization. Though the moment of population is an ongoing phenomenon since time immemorial, the advances made in the field of science and technologies have given it a grater flip. Given that there are various typologies of migration all equal active, yet rural to urban migration is becoming more and more significant. Everyday, thousands of people, especially in underdeveloped and developing countries leave their villages to find a new way of life and living in one of the cities. Internal migration i.e., population mobility within a country, may have important socioeconomic consequences for the country as a whole, for the area of origin and destination and for the migrants themselves.

Migration by people from one place to another is caused by many factors like economic, social, political and environmental. But in many studies, it is observed that main motivation behind migration is economic in nature. Upreti[1] says that migration is a search of economic emancipation. It is both a cause and a consequence of social and economic change. It is a general tendency to presume that the migrants tend to end up in the informal sector because of a lack of adequate and required knowledge about alternative opportunities. In fact, informal sector has long been viewed as a transitory sector serving as an entry point for new migrants.[2] Therefore, there has been always a tendency to identify informal sector with migrant population in the cities since there is a correlation between migrants on the one hand, and urban poverty in slum areas in the other.[3] However, ILO's world employment programme suggested that informal sector is not a transitory concept but a permanent feature of third world urban economies. Mazumdar[4] observes that there is no evidence to suggest that informal sector plays a predominant role as a point of entry into the labour market for fresh migrants to the urban areas.

The Concept of Migration

The word migration has been derived from the Latin 'Migrate' which means to change one's residence. Literally it means the settlements or shifting of an individual or a group of individuals from one cultural area or place of habitation to another, more or less permanently. In the *International Encyclopedia of Social Sciences* migration has been defined "as the relatively permanent movement of persons over a significant distance.[5]

In *Encyclopedia Americana* it has been stated that "migration is a coordinated voluntary movement of a considerable number of people from an accustomed habitat to a new one."[6] The out come of migration depends upon the possibility of gaining a foothold in the region entered. Neither the wandering of nomads or venture constitutes migration, nor does the term apply to rhythmic changes of base by pastoral people who move their herds seasonally within a familiar region.

According to Helen I. Safa, "migration is normally viewed as an economic phenomenon. Though non-economic factors obviously have some bearing. Most studies concur that migrants leave their area of origin primarily because of lack of employment opportunities and in the hope of finding better opportunities elsewhere.[7] It has also been pointed out that most of the migrants move from rural areas to urban centers to find out better economic opportunities. A few well educated, socially and economically better-off people are attracted by the vast opportunities of fulfilling their aspirations and acquiring better status and changes of further achievement in society.

Fucks and Demko have stated that, "migration, is a highly selective process. It removes the younger, stronger, best educated, most skilled people from rural areas, and efforts to revitalize or modernize the rural economy are hindered by this drain."[8]

"Migration is a form of geographical mobility or spatial mobility or spatial between one geographical unit and another, generally involving a change in residence from the place of origin or place of departure to the place of destination or place of arrival, such migration is called permanent migration and should be distinguished from other forms of movement which do not involve a permanent change of residence'.[9]

In the words of Lee, "migration is defined broadly as permanent or semi-permanent change of residence. No restriction is placed upon the distance of the move or upon the voluntary or involuntary nature of the act, and no distinction is made between external or internal migration.[10]

Jansen on the other hand, regards migration as a "demographic problem which influences the size of population at both the places – the place of origin as well as place of migration.[11]

The term mobility is perhaps the most general concept in migration studies. It includes all kinds of territorial movements both temporary and permanent. Over various distances migration is much restricted and relates to a permanent change of residence. In contemporary India with the growth of industries, commerce and trade, gaps between the rural and the urban sectors, with respect to wages and employment opportunities have considerably widened. Due to these factors urban areas are expanding and people are migrating to cities, especially to metropolitan centers.

Causes of Migration

Economic and non-economic factors are identified as causes of migration. Increasing pauperization in rural areas has led to streams of migration and polarization between rural and urban areas with considerable concentration of wealth and social services in the urban economy. This is because agricultural sector happens to be the backward sector in most of the developing countries. Insufficiency of cultivable land, lack of irrigation facilities and low rate of working capital in agriculture have contributed to lower stagnant growth of income. Fragmentation and subdivision of land ownership due to increasing pressure of population resulting in high indebtedness, inequality in the distribution of land and other productive assets further worsened the levels of living in the rural sector. These causes constitute the push factors.[12]

The following studies may be cited as important in this regard.

Industrialization and thereby creation of better employment opportunities, comforts available in urban life, lack of jobs in rural areas in commensurate with literacy qualification act as urban pull factors. Thus the rural-urban migration can be explained primarily by the influence of economic factors. These include the standard "push" from subsistence rural sector and "pull" of relatively high urban wages.

Family disputes, attractiveness of city life, commercial fairs, wars and famines, family size and its structure, social factors outside their village such as literacy prospects for children, entertainment opportunities strongly contribute to migration. Presence of friends and relatives in towns who help in getting jobs and political factors may hasten migration. Emphases have variously been placed for example in, social factors including the desire of migrants to break away from traditional constraints of social organizations. Physical factors including elements and disasters like floods and droughts. Demographic factors include the reduction in mortality rates and the concomitant high rates of rural population growth. Cultural factors include the security of urban "extended family" relationships and the allurement of "bright city lights." Communication factors including improved transportation, urban–oriented literacyal systems, and the 'modernizing' impact of the introduction of radio, television, and the cinema.

However there now seems to be widespread agreement among economists and non- economists alike that rural-urban migration can be explained primarily by the influence of economic factors. Thus migration implies mobility of generally able bodied people in the working age group in search of higher income opportunities[13].

Types of Migration

Migration between one geographical unit and another, generally involves a change in residence from the place of origin or place of departure to the place of destination is called permanent migration.[14] In the case of seasonal migration the migrants like agricultural labour and marginal farmers go to nearby towns for work during offseason and return to village in peak agricultural season. In this case village is their permanent residence.[15]

Half-seasonal migration represents migration of rural poor (landless agricultural workers, marginal farmers and others) at the time of flood, drought and other natural calamities to safer places. They return to their native places after the natural calamity is over.[16] Zachariah[17] has classified migration in the basis of the distance of movement such as 'short distance migration' and 'long distance migration'. Census of India[18] classified internal migration into four types namely Rural to urban, Rural to rural, Urban to urban and Urban to rural.

Thus, migration could be classified based in distance, period of stay, region, cultural differentials and purpose of movement. Among all types of migration, rural to urban is the most common phenomenon of the modern world, specifically in the developing world. In the India context, rural to urban migration is the most common feature.

Migration and Economic Development

The recent urbanization process involving a rapid expansion of urban areas and a remarkable rise in urban population particularly noticed in developing economies has been described as a process of massive exodus of rural population due to the 'rural push' and the 'urban pull' factors.[19]

A rigorous analysis of the process of rural labour absorption in the urban modern sectors has been attempted by economists like Todaro, Lewis, Fei and Rains. Though models developed by them will be useful while considering the question of how the rural migrants may be absorbed in the urban sector side of the employment problem, they do not throw much light on the determinants of rural-urban labour supply. As such these models can hardly be a guide to estimate the magnitude of urban unemployment implication of alternative policies.[20] But relatively migration ought to be viewed as a two stage phenomenon. An understanding of migration process is of critical importance in formulating employment policies. The sensitivity of migration to changes in the demand for labour depends partly on the motivation that underline migration decisions and partly on various characteristics of the mechanism of recruitment and information dissemination. The history of economic development of any country was closely associated with migration and in fact it is often defined in terms of the movement of labour from rural to urban areas. The overall economic development was characterized by the gradual reallocation of labour out of agriculture and into industry through rural-urban migration.

The Lewis-Fei-Ranis Model of Development (L.F.R. Model)

The first comprehensive model of development to give consideration at least implicitly, to the process of rural-urban labour transfer was the one developed by Lewis (1954)[21] and later extended by Ranis - Fei (1961).[22] This model considers migration as an equilibrating mechanism which through transfer of labour from the labour-surplus sector to the labour-deficit sector, brings about equality between the two sectors. The model is based on the concept of dual economy comprising a traditional agricultural subsistence sector characterized by unemployment and under-employment and modern industrial sector characterized by full employment, where it is assumed that "Capitalists" always reinvest all of their profits. In the subsistence sector, the marginal productivity of labour is either zero or very low and workers are paid wage which equal their cost of subsistence. Thus in this sector wages exceed marginal productivity. In the modern sector, wages are maintained at levels much higher than the average agricultural wage. However, at this stage of constant urban wage, the supply of rural labour is considered to be perfectly elastic. The following provides a simple illustration of L.F.R.Model.

On the vertical exist the real wage and on horizontal axis the quantity of labour are represented. OA represents the average level of real subsistence in the traditional rural (agricultural) sector. OW is the real wage in the urban industrial sector. At this wage, the supply of rural labour is assumed to be 'unlimited'. So WS is the horizontal labour supply curve. Given a fixed supply of capital,

Diagram:

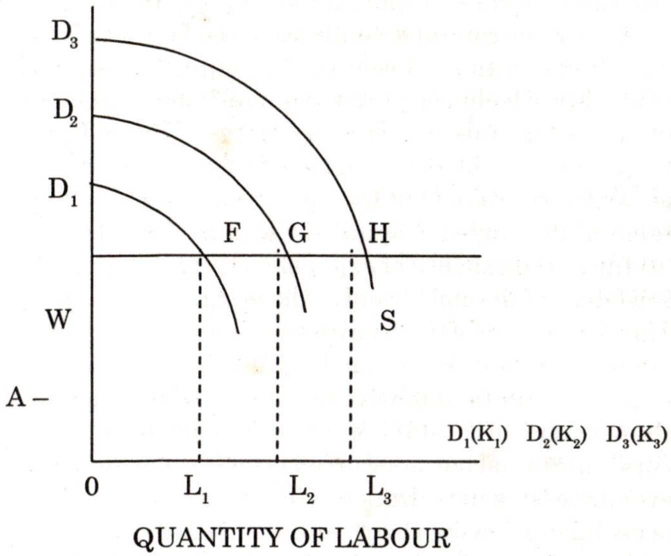

K_1, in the initial stage of modern sector growth, the demand curve for labour is determined by labour's declining marginal product as shown by curve D_1 (K_1). 'F' is the point of intersection between the labour demand and supply curves. Total modern sector employment would be equal to OL_1. So the surplus output would become profits to the capitalists i.e., $OD_1 FL_1$ - OW FL_1 = W D_1 F.

Since it is assumed that all the profits are reinvested, the total capital in the modern sector will rise from K_1 to K_2. This larger capital stock causes the total product curve to rise which in turn induces the demand curve to shift upwards. The outward shift in the labour demand curve is D_2 (K_2). A new equilibrium employment level will be established at point G with OL_2 workers now employed. Total output rises to OD_2 GL_2, while total wages and profits increase to $OWGL_2$ and WD_2 G respectively.

Once again the increase profits (WD G) are reinvested increasing the total capital stock to D_3 which again shifts the labour demand curve to D_3 (K_3) raising the level of modern sector employment to OL_3. Thus capital accumulation becomes a crucial determinant of the rate of growth of modern sector and thereby absorption of rural surplus labour. This indicates that the faster the rate of the capital accumulation the faster will be the rate of labour absorption. However the implicit assumption of the neutrality of technical progress is questioned although Lewis has recognized the role of technical progress. If the additions to capital stock embody labour saving technical progress, the total output grows substantially but the total wages and employment might remain unchanged. Capitalists gain in the form of increasing profits at the expense of expansion of employment. Further the existence of full employment in the urban sector is also questioned. This is so in most of the countries like India which followed inward-oriented strategy of development relying to a larger extent on the imports of capital intensive techniques of production. Moreover the existence of constant real wages in the urban sector until the rural surplus labour is absorbed is highly questionable due to the ever increasing unionization of urban labour. However, the model is useful in knowing about capitalist sector is usually associated with urban industrial sector; the subsistence sector is associated to rural agricultural sector.

Thus migration from the subsistence sector to the industrial sector increases production as well as the capitalist profits. The process of modern sector growth and employment expansion is assumed to continue until the entire surplus rural labour is absorbed.

Todaro Model of Rural-Urban Migration

Todaro believes that the decision to migrate includes perception by the potential migrant of an expected stream of income which is a function of both the prevailing urban wage structure and the subjective possibility of obtaining employment in the urban modern sector.[23] Expected income is measured by (1) the difference in rural incomes between rural and urban work and (2) the probability of a new migrant obtaining and urban job.

In essence, the theory assume that members of the labour force, both actual and potential, compare their expected incomes for a given time horizon in the urban sector with prevailing average rural incomes and migrate likely in the face of wide urban-rural expected income differential. Higher rate of urban unemployment is, therefore, inevitable outcome of the serious imbalance in economic opportunities between the urban and rural areas of less developed countries.

Migration and Informal Sector

Migration is one of the characteristics of the informal sector. They are persons who migrated to the city at different point of time on account of droughts, famines, displacement of supplementary occupation, high burden of indebtedness leading finally to transfer of property to creditors. The Urban Informal Sector gave ready-made employment market to the rural migrants. Usually the origin of informal sector is attributed to the massive outflow of surplus labour from the agricultural sector in the rural areas; these rural migrants form a substantial part of the urban poor in the informal sector.

Migration of Women

Migration of poor families from countryside to urban sites in search of livelihood and employment is a regular phenomenon in the economic life of India. The backwardness in agriculture, lack of irrigation facilities and famines have made a hazardous effect on the income and lives of poor peasants, and landless agricultural labourers.

The result is unending migration to the towns in search of better life. Women are also part of those poor families who experienced the sorts of hardships along with men and in few cases women exclusively are found migrating to other areas leaving their parents, husbands and children at native villages. There has been a significant empirical evidence on women's work and their migration. In the traditional rural sector, women significantly work as 'free wage labourers' or permanently bondage labour though the income derived thereby is insignificant. Further, seasonal fluctuations in employment are high for women. Various socioeconomic, cultural and psychological factors hinder the development of women. In such a situation, women migrate in search of better income-earning opportunities and thereby better levels of living.

Table – 5.1
Distribution of Sample Women Vendors by Migrants, Floating and Non-migrants

Types and level of Trade		*Description*			*Total*
		Migrants	*Floating*	*Non-Migrants*	
Fish Vendors	Street Vendor	23 (38.33)	20 (33.33)	17 (28.33)	60 (100.00)
	Small Petty Vendor	29 (48.33)	8 (13.33)	23 (38.33)	60 (100.00)
	Petty Vendor	44 (73.33)	6 (10.00)	10 (16.67)	60 (100.00)
	Total	96 (53.33)	34 (18.89)	50 (27.78)	180 (100.00)
Vegetable Vendors	Street Vendor	14 (23.33)	18 (30.00)	28 (46.67)	60 (100.00)
	Small Petty Vendor	32 (53.33)	12 (20.00)	16 (26.67)	16 (100.00)
	Petty Vendor	36 (60.00)	7 (11.67)	17 (28.33)	60 (100.00)
	Total	82 (45.56)	37 (20.56)	61 (33.89)	180 (100.00)
Total Vendors	Street Vendor	37 (30.83)	38 (31.67)	45 (37.50)	120 (100.00)
	Small Petty Vendor	61 (50.83)	2 (16.67)	39 (32.50)	120 (100.00)
	Petty Vendor	80 (66.67)	13 (10.83)	27 (22.50)	120 (100.00)
	Total	178 (49.44)	71 (19.72)	111 (30.83)	360 (100.00)

Source: Completed from the primary data. Figures in parentheses indicate percentages to the grand total.

Results of the Study

Table 5.1 shows that in the total women vendors, 49.44 percent constitute migrants. About 20 percent were floating vendors. It means that on the whole 70 percent are either permanently moved from the rural areas in search of employment or regarding coming to urban area(city) for the better earnings or profits for their production. Both the phenomenon are common due to lack of proper employment opportunities in rural areas as well as attractive profits that could be earned in the urban market.

In the case of fish vendors 53.33 percent were migrants, and 18.89 percent were floating vendors. The percentage of migrants in fish petty vendors is highest amount to 73.33 percent. In case of vegetable petty vendors also they account for 60 percent. Floating vendors are generally more in street vendors whereas the migrants are more in petty vendors.

Migrant Women Vendors

Tables 5.2.1 to 5.2.5 present several aspects of migrant women vendors with respect to their occupation before migration place and distance from where they migrated, years of migration and the reasons for their migration.

Occupation of the Migrants before Migration

It could be observed from Table 5.2 that nearly 57 percent of the migrants are engaged in the same occupation before migrating to the city, followed by the artisan occupation (26 percent). This clearly indicates that over a period of time, the demand for the traditional rural crafts is declining gradually, which forces them to migrant to urban areas. In the case of fish vendors, the migration with respect to the same occupation is more. Across all the categories of fish vendors, non-agricultural labour and artisans are next major group of vendors. In the case of vegetable vendors, majority of the migrants are basically vegetable vendors, followed by non-agricultural labour. Agricultural labour and artisan consist equal proportion in migrants. It could also be observed from the table that across the various categories of vegetable vendors, 21.42 percent are agricultural labour and only 7.14 percent are non-agricultural labour.

Table – 5.2

Distribution of Sample Women Vendors by Migrant's Occupation Before Migration

Types andlevel of Trade		*Description*				*Total*
		Agricultural Labour	*Non-agricultural Labour*	*Same occupation*	*Artisan*	
Fish Vendors	Street Vendor	2 (8.69)	4 (17.39)	14 (60.86)	3 (13.04)	23 (100.00)
	Small Petty Vendor	3 (10.34)	3 (10.34)	19 (65.51)	4 (13.79)	29 (100.00)
	Petty Vendor	4 (9.09)	6 (13.63)	28 (63.63)	6 (13.63)	44 (100.00)
	Total	9 (9.37)	13 (13.54)	61 (63.54)	13 (13.54)	96 (100.00)
Vegetable Vendors	Street Vendor	3 (21.42)	1 (7.14)	6 (42.85)	4 (28.57)	14 (100.00)
	Small Petty Vendor	4 (12.50)	8 (25.00)	17 (53.13)	3 (9.37)	32 (100.00)
	Petty Vendor	6 (16.66)	8 (22.22)	16 (44.44)	6 (16.66)	36 (100.00)
	Total	13 (15.85)	17 (20.73)	39 (47.56)	13 (15.85)	82 (100.00)
Total Vendors	Street Vendor	5 (16.67)	5 (18.33)	20 (25.83)	7 (8.33)	37 (100.00)
	Small Petty Vendor	7 (18.33)	11 (18.33)	36 (25.83)	7 (5.00)	61 (100.00)
	Petty Vendor	10 (12.50)	14 (17.50)	44 (55.00)	12 (15.00)	80 (100.00)
	Total	22 (12.35)	30 (16.85)	100 (56.17)	26 (14.60)	178 (100.00)

Source: Computed from the primary data. Figures in parentheses indicate percentages to the totals.

Reasons for Migration

Table 5.2.1 shows reasons for migration of migrants. It could be observed that of the total women vendors 47.45 percent of the women vendors moved to the city based on the suggestions of the relatives. The next important reason is children education. In case of fish vendors more than nearly 40 percent migrated on the suggestions of the relatives, and about one fourth due to children's education. In case of vegetable vendors, above 55 percent were due to suggestion made by relatives and 20 percent are because of the children education. Among all the categories generally street vendors are migrating for the sake of their children education.

Place from which Vendors Migrated

The place from which migration took place is presented in Table 5.2.2. It could be observed from the table that out of the total vendors 64.04 percent were migrated from rural areas to the urban areas. In case of fish vendors as well as vegetable vendors, highest percentage (81.82 & 61.12 respectively) could be observed among petty vendors. On the whole, whatever may be the category of vendor, migration from the rural areas is more in fish vendors.

Distance from where Vendors Migrated

Generally when people are migrating from one area to another area in search of employment or livelihood, the distance they need to crop up also matters a lot. But, as majority of the women vendors are illiterates, they can't tell the distance exactly. Hence, from where they cropped into the city is presented under four categories, namely 'within the District', 'Surrounding the Districts', 'Distance Districts in A.P.' and 'other States'.

It could be observed from the Table 5.2.3 that majority of the vendors are migrating from 'surrounding the districts' and 'within the district' (37.66 percent and 30.89 percent respectively). A significant percent i.e., 14.60 percent is migrated from other states. In case of vegetable vendors the migration from other states is higher than the corresponding fish vendors. In case of vegetable vendors, migration 'within the District' is higher among street vendors, whereas in case of fish vendors migration from 'Surrounding the District' is the highest.

Table – 5.2.1
Distribution of Sample Women Vendors by Reasons for Migrations

		Description				
	Types and level of Trade	*Children Literacy*	*To clear Debts*	*Relatives Suggestion*	*To earn more money*	*Total*
Fish Vendors	Street Vendor	7(30.43)	4(17.39)	9(39.13)	3(13.04)	23(100.00)
	Small Petty Vendor	8(27.58)	4(13.79)	12(14.37)	5(17.24)	29(100.00)
	Petty Vendor	11(25.00)	7(15.90)	18(40.90)	8(18.18)	44(100.00)
	TOTAL	26(27.08)	15(15.67)	39(40.62)	16(16.66)	96(100.00)
Vegetable Vendors	Street Vendor	2(21.87)	2(14.28)	7(50.00)	3(21.42)	14(100.00)
	Small Petty Vendor	4(50.00)	7(21.87)	18(56.25)	3(9.37)	32(100.00)
	Petty Vendor	5(16.67)	6(16.67)	21(58.33)	4(11.11)	36(100.00)
	TOTAL	11(18.29)	15(18.29)	46(56.09)	10(12.19)	82(100.00)
Total Vendors	Street Vendor	9(24.32)	6(16.21)	16(43.24)	6(16.21)	37(100.00)
	Small Petty Vendor	12(19.67)	11(18.03)	30(49.18)	8(13.11)	61(100.00)
	Petty Vendor	16(20.00)	13(16.25)	39(48.75)	12(15.00)	80(100.00)
	TOTAL	37(20.78)	30(16.85)	85(47.75)	26(14.60)	178(100.00)

Source: Computed from the primary data. Figures in parentheses indicate percentages to the totals.

Table – 5.2.2

Distribution of Sample Women Petty Vendors by Rural and Urban Migration

Types andlevel of Trade		*Description*		
		Rural	*Urban*	*Total*
Fish	Street Vendor	14 (60.87)	9 (39.13)	23 (100.00)
Vendors	Small Petty Vendor	17 (58.63)	12 (41.37)	29 (100.00)
	Petty Vendor	36 (81.82)	8 (18.18)	44 (100.00)
	TOTAL	67 (69.79)	29 (30.20)	96 (100.00)
Vegetable	Street Vendor	8 (57.15)	6 (42.85)	14 (100.00)
Vendors	Small Petty Vendor	17 (53.13)	15 (46.87)	32 (100.00)
	Petty Vendor	22 (61.12)	14 (38.88)	36 (100.00)
	TOTAL	47 (57.32)	35 (42.68)	82 (100.00)
Total	Street Vendor	22 (61.12)	15 (40.54)	37(100.00)
Vendors	Small Petty Vendor	34 (55.74)	27(44.26)	61(100.00)
	Petty Vendor	58 (72.50)	22 (27.50)	80 (100.00)
	TOTAL	114 (64.04)	64(35.95)	178 (100.00)

Source: Computed from the primary data. Figures in parentheses indicate percentages to the totals.

Years of Migration

Table 5.2.4 presents the duration of migration. Among the total vendors about 52 percent were migrated just before 5 years followed by 6-10 years (20.22 percent). It could be observed from the table that there exists a spread based on the years of migration among fish street vendors. On the other hand, among the fish petty vendors, no vendor is having more than 15 years of migration. In case of vegetable vendors, the spread is very less compared to the fish vendors. Recent migration is high in the vegetable vendors. The maximum 'years of migration' is 25 years among vegetable petty vendors.

Table – 5.2.3

Distribution of Sample Women Petty Vendors by Place from where the Sample Households Migrated

Types andLevel of Trade		*Description*				
		With in the district	*Surrounding The districts*	*Other districts of A. P.*	*Other States*	*Total*
Fish Vendors	Street Vendor	7(30.43)	9(39.13)	4(17.39)	3(13.04)	23(100.00)
	Small Petty Vendor	9(31.03)	11(37.93)	5(17.25)	4(13.79)	29(100.00)
	Petty Vendor	15(34.09)	18(40.92)	5(11.36)	6(13.63)	44(100.00)
	TOTAL	31(32.29)	38(39.58)	14(14.58)	13(13.54)	96(100.00)
Vegetable Vendors	Street Vendor	6(42.87)	5(35.71)	1(7.14)	2(14.28)	14(100.00)
	Small Petty Vendor	8(25.01)	11(34.37)	7(21.87)	6(18.75)	32(100.00)
	Petty Vendor	10(27.77)	13(36.11)	8(22.22)	5(13.88)	36(100.00)
	TOTAL	24(29.26)	29(35.38)	16(19.51)	13(15.85)	82(100.00)
Total Vendors	Street Vendor	13(35.13)	14(37.85)	5(13.51)	5(13.51)	37(100.00)
	Small Petty Vendor	17(27.86)	22(36.08)	12(19.67)	10(16.39)	61(100.00)
	Petty Vendor	25(31.25)	31(38.75)	13(16.25)	11(13.75)	80(100.00)
	TOTAL	55(30.89)	67(37.66)	30(16.85)	26(14.60)	178(100.00)

Source: Computed from the primary data. Figures in parentheses indicate percentages to the totals.

Table – 5.2.4
Distribution of Sample WomenPetty Vendors by Years of Migration

Types andlevel of Trade		*Range*						
		0-5	*6-10*	*11-15*	*16-20*	*21-25*	*26-30*	*Total*
Fish Vendors	Street Vendor	6(26.09)	4(17.39)	5(21.74)	4(17.39)	3(13.04)	1(4.34)	23(100.00)
	Small Petty Vendor	13(44.85)	7(24.13)	4(13.79)	2(6.89)	3(10.34)	——	29(100.00)
	Petty Vendor	35(79.55)	5(11.36)	4(9.09)	——	——	——	44(100.00)
	TOTAL	54(56.25)	16(16.66)	13(13.54)	6(6.25)	6(6.25)	1(1.04)	96(100.00)
Vegetable Vendors	Street Vendor	7(50.00)	3(21.42)	1(7.14)	1(7.14)	——	2(14.28)	14(100.00)
	Small Petty Vendor	19(59.37)	8(25.00)	2(6.25)	1(3.12)	——	2(6.25)	32(100.00)
	Petty Vendor	12(33.35)	9(25.00)	6(16.66)	4(11.11)	5(13.88)	——	36(100.00)
	TOTAL	38(46.34)	20(24.39)	9(10.97)	6(7.31)	5(6.09)	4(4.85)	82(100.00)
Total Vendors	Street Vendor	13(35.13)	7(18.91)	6(16.21)	5(13.51)	3(8.10)	3(8.10)	37(100.00)
	Small Petty Vendor	32(52.45)	15(24.59)	6(9.83)	3(4.91)	3(4.91)	2(3.27)	61(100.00)
	Petty Vendor	47(58.75)	14(17.50)	10(12.50)	4(5.00)	5(6.25)	——	80(100.00)
	TOTAL	92(51.68)	36(20.22)	22(12.35)	12(6.74)	11(6.17)	5(2.80)	178(100.00)

Source: Computed from the primary data. Figures in parentheses indicate percentages to the totals.

Floating Women Vendors

Tables 5.3 to 5.3.4 present several of aspects of floating women vendors with respect to reasons for floating, distance of floating, place of floating, years of floatring, and mode of travelling.

Reasons for Floating

Table 5.3 shows the reasons for floating of the women vendors. Among the total vendors 60.58 percent of the vendors are floating to the city to increase their business volume or sales volume. About 28.16 percent are floating to earn more profits to their working capital. In case of fish petty vendors they are distributed equally, whereas majority of the fish street vendor (65 percent) are floating to increase their business volume. In case of small petty fish vendors 25 percent are floating as usual habit or in order to avoid. It is surprising to observe that only 5 percent of street fish vendors comes under this category. In case of vegetable vendors almost 16 percent constitute who usually float to the city both in street vendors and small petty vendors.

Distance of Floating

Table 5.3.1 presents the distance of floating of the women vendors. Only street vendors, both fish and vegetable, float from a distance of above 55 kilometers. In case of fish petty vendors 66 percent of vendors are floating from 35-45 kilometers. But, in case of vegetable petty vendors 42.85 percent were floating from a distance between 25-35 kilometers. Another interesting observation could be made from the table that majority of percentage of vegetable vendors are floating from 25-35 km. In case of fish vendors, majority are floating from a distance of 35-45 km.

Place from where Floating

It could be observed from the Table 5.3.2 that of the total vendors, 52 percent are floating from 'within the district' and 48 percent are floating from 'surrounding the district'. In case of fish vendors majority were floating from 'within the district', where as among vegetable vendors majority were floating from 'surrounding the district'.

Table – 5.3
Reasons for Floating

Types and level of Trade		*Description*			
		Business/ Sales	*Profits*	*No loss/ As usual*	*Total*
Fish Vendors	Street Vendor	13 (65.00)	6 (30.00)	1 (5.00)	20 (100.00)
	Small Petty Vendor	4 (50.00)	2 (25.00)	2 (25.00)	8 (100.00)
	Petty Vendor	3 (50.00)	3 (50.00)	—	6 (100.00)
	TOTAL	20 (58.82)	11 (32.35)	3 (8.82)	34 (100.00)
Vegetable Vendors	Street Vendor	11 (61.12)	4 (22.22)	3 (16.66)	18 (100.00)
	Small Petty Vendor	7 (58.34)	3 (25.00)	2 (16.66)	12 (100.00)
	Petty Vendor	5 (71.43)	2 (28.57)	—	7 (100.00)
	TOTAL	23 (62.16)	9 (34.32)	5 (13.51)	37 (100.00)
Total Vendors	Street Vendor	24 (63.17)	10 (26.31)	4 (10.52)	38 (100.00)
	Small Petty Vendor	11 (55.00)	5 (25.00)	4 (20.00)	20 (100.00)
	Petty Vendor	8 (61.54)	5 (38.46)	—	13 (100.00)
	TOTAL	43 (60.58)	20 (28.16)	8 (11.26)	71 (100.00)

Source: Computed from the primary data. Figures in parentheses indicate percentages to the totals.

Table – 5.3.1
Distance of Floating

Types and level of Trade		*Description*				
		25 – 35	*35 – 45*	*45– 55*	*55 and above*	*Total*
Fish Vendors	Street Vendor	4 (20.00)	5 (25.00)	8 (40.00)	3 (15.00)	20 (100.00)
	Small Petty Vendor	3 (37.50)	4 (50.00)	1 (12.50)	—	8 (100.00)
	Petty Vendor	2 (33.34)	4 (66.66)	—	—	6 (100.00)
	TOTAL	9 (26.47)	13 (38.23)	9 (26.47)	3 (8.82)	34 (100.00)
Vegetable Vendors	Street Vendor	7 (38.89)	4 (22.22)	5 (27.78)	2 (11.11)	18 (100.00)
	Small Petty Vendor	5 (41.66)	3 (25.00)	4 (33.33)	—	12 (100.00)
	Petty Vendor	3 (42.85)	2 (28.57)	2 (28.57)	—	7 (100.00)
	TOTAL	15 (40.54)	9 (24.32)	11 (29.72)	2 (5.40)	37 (100.00)
Total Vendors	Street Vendor	11 (28.95)	9 (23.68)	13 (34.22)	5 (13.15)	38 (100.00)
	Small Petty Vendor	8 (40.00)	7 (35.00)	5 (25.00)	—	20 (100.00)
	Petty Vendor	5 (38.46)	6 (46.16)	2 (15.38)	—	13 (100.00)
	TOTAL	24 (33.81)	22 (30.99)	20 (28.16)	5(7.04)	71 (100.00)

Source: Computed from the primary data. Figures inparentheses indicate percentages to the totals.

Table – 5.3.2
Place of Floating

Types and level of Trade		*Description*		
		With in the district	*Surround the districts*	*Total*
Fish Vendors	Street Vendor	12 (60.00)	8 (40.00)	20 (100.00)
	Small Petty Vendor	5 (62.50)	3 (37.50)	8 (100.00)
	Petty Vendor	4 (66.67)	2 (33.33)	6 (100.00)
	TOTAL	21 (61.76)	13 (55.56)	34 (100.00)
Vegetable Vendors	Street Vendor	8 (44.44)	10 (58.34)	18 (100.00)
	Small Petty Vendor	5 (41.66)	7 (58.34)	12 (100.00)
	Petty Vendor	3 (42.85)	4 (47.14)	7 (100.00)
	TOTAL	16 (43.24)	21 (56.75)	37 (100.00)
Total Vendors	Street Vendor	20 (52.64)	18 (47.36)	38 (100.00)
	Small Petty Vendor	10 (50.00)	10 (50.00)	20 (100.00)
	Petty Vendor	7 (53.85)	6 (46.15)	13 (100.00)
	TOTAL	37 (52.12)	34 (47.88)	71 (100.00)

Source: Computed from the primary data. Figures in parentheses indicate percentages to the totals.

Years of Floating

Table 5.3.3 presents the information about the years of floating. Among the women vendors, about 15% of the vendors have been floating to the city for more than 11 years. In case of fish vendors, majority of the vendors have been floating (47.05 percent) to the city for less than 5 years followed by 38.23 percent of the vendors, floating for 6-10 years. The same phenomenon could be observed with fish street vendors and fish petty vendors. Among the fish small petty vendors, majority have been floating for 6-10 years.

Table – 5.3.3
Years of Floating

Types and level of Trade		*Years*			*Total*
		Below – 5	*6 – 10*	*11 and above*	
Fish Vendors	Street Vendor	9 (45.00)	7 (35.00)	4 (20.00)	20 (100.00)
	Small Petty Vendor	3 (37.50)	4 (50.00)	1 (12.50)	8 (100.00)
	Petty Vendor	4 (66.66)	2 (33.33)	—-	6 (100.00)
	TOTAL	16 (47.05)	13 (38.23)	5 (14.70)	34 (100.00)
Vegetable Vendors	Street Vendor	7 (38.88)	8 (44.46)	3 (16.66)	18 (100.00)
	Small Petty Vendor	6 (50.00)	4 (66.66)	2 (16.66)	12 (100.00)
	Petty Vendor	4 (57.14)	3 (42.85)	—-	7 (100.00)
	TOTAL	17 (45.94)	15 (40.54)	5 (13.51)	37 (100.00)
Total Vendors	Street Vendor	16 (42.11)	15 (39.47)	7 (18.42)	38 (100.00)
	Small Petty Vendor	9 (45.00)	8 (40.00)	3 (15.00)	20 (100.00)
	Petty Vendor	8 (61.53)	5 (38.46)	—-	13 (100.00)
	Total	33 (46.47)	28 (39.43)	10 (14.08)	71 (100.00)

Source: Computed from the primary data. Figures in parentheses indicate percentages to the totals

In case of vegetable vendors, majority of the vendors (47.95 percent) have been floating to the city for less than 5 years followed by 40.54 percent of vendors, floating for 6-10 years. The same phenomenon could be observed with small petty vendors and petty vendors. Among the vegetable street vendors, 44.46 percent have been floating for 6-10 years.

Mode of Traveling

Table 5.3.4 presents the mode of traveling of the floating women vendors. Among the total vendors, 63.39 percent travel by train and 28.16 percent travel by bus. In case of fish vendors, 52.82 percent travel by train and 32.35 percent travel by bus, whereas in case of vegetable vendors, 67.57 percent travel by train and 24.32 percent travel by bus.

Table – 5.3.4
Mode of Traveling

Types and level of Trade		*Description*			
		Train	*Bus*	*Others*	*Total*
Fish Vendors	Street Vendor	11 (55.00)	7 (35.00)	2 (10.00)	20 (100.00)
	Small Petty Vendor	5 (62.50)	2 (25.00)	1 (12.00)	8 (100.00)
	Petty Vendor	4 (66.67)	2 (33.33)	—-	6 (100.00)
	TOTAL	20 (58.82)	11 (32.35)	3 (8.82)	34 (100.00)
Vegetable	Street Vendor	13 (72.23)	4 (22.22)	1 (5.55)	18 (100.00)
Vendors	Small Petty Vendor	7 (58.34)	3 (25.00)	2 (16.66)	12 (100.00)
	Petty Vendor	5 (71.43)	2 (28.57)	—-	7 (100.00)
	TOTAL	25 (67.57)	9 (24.32)	3 (8.11)	37 (100.00)

(contd...)

Total Vendors	Street Vendor	24 (63.15)	11 (28.94)	3 (7.89)	38 (100.00)
	Small Petty Vendor	12 (60.00)	5 (25.00)	3 (15.00)	20 (100.00)
	Petty Vendor	9 (69.23)	4 (30.76)	—	13 (100.00)
	TOTAL	45 (63.39)	20 (28.16)	6 (8.45)	71 (100.00)

Source: Computed from the primary data. Figures in parentheses indicate percentages to the totals.

Among the various categories of women vendors, similar observation could be made with both fish and vegetable vendors. The main reason supporting this observation could be the cheaper travel by train when compared to that by bus.

Average Profits of Women Vendors

Table 5.4 presents the average amount of profits of the women vendors according to migration status. Among all categories of women vendors, the profits earned by non-migrants are more compared to migrant and floating vendors.

Table - 5.4

Average Values of Profit of Women Vendors by Migrant, Floating and Non-migrant Status

Types and level of Trade		*Description*			
		Migrants	*Floating*	*Non-Migrants*	*Total*
Fish Vendors	Street Vendor	63.17 (23)	74.65 (20)	85.24 (17)	73.25 (60)
	Small Petty Vendor	66.03 (29)	66.13 (8)	83.35 (23)	72.68 (60)
	Petty Vendor	127.14 (44)	122.17 (6)	165.00 (10)	132.95 (60)
	Total	93.35 (96)	81.03 (34)	100.32 (50)	92.96 (180)

Vegetable Vendors	StreetVendor	71.43 (14)	78.67 (18)	87.11 (28)	80.92 (60)
	Small Petty Vendor	91.09 (32)	95.33 (12)	113 (16)	97.97 (60)
	Petty Vendor	131.94 (36)	127.00 (7)	137.76 (17)	133.02 (60)
	TOTAL	105.67 (82)	93.22 (37)	108.20 (61)	103.97 (180)
Total Vendors	StreetVendor	66.30 (37)	76.55 (38)	86.40 (45)	77.08 (120)
	Small Petty Vendor	79.18 (61)	83.65 (20)	95.79 (39)	85.33 (120)
	Petty Vendor	129.30 (80)	124.77 (13)	147.85 (27)	132.98 (120)
	TOTAL	99.02 (178)	87.38 (71)	104.64 (111)	98.46 (360)

Source: Computed from the primary data. Parentheses indicate percentages to the totals.

It is obvious from the table that among the fish street vendors, floating vendors earn more profits than migrant vendors (Rs.74.64 and Rs.63.17 respectively). The profits are equal for small petty fish vendors of these two types. In case of fish petty vendors, migrants are earning more profits than floating vendors (Rs.127.14 and Rs.122.17 respectively).

REFERENCES

1. Upreti, D.H.C. (1981): *Social Organization of Migration Group*, Himalaya Publishing House, Bombay.
2. International Council on Social Welfare(): *The Urban Dead End?*, Somaiya Publications, Pvt. Ltd. p. 99.
3. Sethuraman S.V. (1976): "The Urban Informal Sector: Concept Measurement and Policy," *International Labour Review*, July - Dec, p. 69-76.
4. Mazumdar, Dipak (1975): The Urban Informal Sector, *World Bank Staff Working Paper No. 211*, July, p. 59.
5. *International Encyclopedia of the Social Sciences*, Macmillan and Free, Press. Vol. 10, 1968,p. 286.

6. *Encyclopedia Americana*, America Corporation, New York, Vol. 19, 1968, p. 48.
7. Safa I Helen and Vrian M Dutoit (1975): *Migration and Development*, Mouton Publishers, The Haque, p. 1.
8. George J Demko and Ronald JJueks (1980):"Population Redistribution: Problems and Policies", *Populi*, Vol. 7, No. 4, p.30.
9. United Nations Organisation (1956): *Multilingual Demographic Dictionary*, ST/SOA/SER, *Population Studies*, No. 29, New York, p. 46.
10. Lee, ES. (1975):"A Theory of Migration"in CW Kamme, Kenneth (eds), *Population Studies*, Ronald MC Nally College Pub, Co., Chicago, p.191.
11. Jansen, C J.: "Some Sociological Aspects of Migration", in JA Jackson. (ed.). a). Murali Monohar, K.(1983):*Social Economic Status of Indian Women*, p. 10.

    b). Aziz Abdul (1983): Urban Poor and Urban Informal Sector, p. 22.

    c). Muzumdar, D.N. (1960): *Social Contours of an Industrial City*, Asia Publishing House, Bombay, p. 73.

    d). Mishra Srudar (1952): "Urban Employment and Migration of Agricultural Labour in U.P.", Rural India, Vol.3, March.

    e). Standing, G. and Skdeo, F.(): Labour Migration and Development in Gayana," *International Labour Review*, Nov-Dec., Vol. 116, No.3. pp.303-313.

    f). Frifin K. (1974): *Land Concentration and Rural Poverty*, London, Mcmillan.

    g). Kingsley Danis (1950): *The Population of India and Pakistan*, p.108.

13. The important studies are: a). Kingsley Danis (1950): *The Population of India and Pakistan*, Princeton, New Jersey.

    b). Gupta, O.P (1972): "Volume, Factors and Characteristics of Migration to Urban Delhi", *Indian Census Centenary Seminar*, Vol.1, Office of the Registraar General of India, Ministry of Home Affairs, New Delhi, p. 69.

    c). Ganguli, B.N.(1973): *Population and Development*, S. Chand and Co.Pvt. Ltd., New Delhi, p. 54.

d). John Connal and Biplab Das Gupta (1976): *Migration from Rural Areas,* Oxford University Press, Delhi, pp. 38-53.

14. United Nations Organisation : *Multi-lingual demographic Dictionary, op cit,* p. 46.

15. Everetts Lee (1975): *Theory of Migration,* Keneth , U.K. Kamneyer (ed.) 1975, *op cit,* p.191.

16. *Ibid.*

17. Zachariah, K.C (1961), *A Historical Study of Internal Migration in the Indian Subcontinent 1901-31.* Asia Publishing House, pp.250-51. 19

18. *Census of India.* Migration Tables, 1981.

19. Azizi Abdul, *op cit.,* p. 23.

20. *Ibid.,* p. 25.

21. Heather and Joshi (1976): *Surplus Labour and the City – A Study of Bombay,* p. 1.

22 Lewis, W.A. (1954): "Economic Development with unlimited supply of Labour", *Manchester School of Economics and Social Studies,* May, Vol. 22, pp.139-191.

23. Todaro, M.P. (1976): International Migration in Developing Countries, *International Labour Organisation,* Geneva

6

Seasonal Variations in the Profits of Women Vendors

Introduction

In this chapter an attempt is made to examine the seasonal variations in the profits earned by women vendors. Generally any type of trade experiences fluctuations in its path because of some reasons like seasons, festivals, customs etc., which is broadly named as 'seasonal variation'. Particularly, in case of the selected two trades, seasonal variations are much visible. Fish vending depends on the fish catchments of the fishermen, which inturn depends on the climate and weather conditions. In the case of vegetable vending also seasons like summer is well known for the scarcity of vegetables. Therefore, examination of the seasonal variations needs attention for the better understanding of these trades conducted by women.

In the first instance, the average per day profit of the women vendors for the three seasons and the financial year is analyzed. Whether there exist any significance differences in the profits of the women vendors across seasons is analyzed with the help of regression analysis. The analysis was carried out for total vendors, fish vendors, vegetable vendors separately both at aggregate and disaggregate levels.

The Functional Form Used

a) $P = a + b_1 S_1 D + b_2 S_2 D + \epsilon$ ——————————— (1)

where

P = Per Day Profit of the Woman Vendor

S_1D = Season dummy represented by 1 if the season is 1st August to 30th November, and '0' otherwise

S_2D = Season dummy represented by 1 if the season is 1st December to 31st March, and otherwise '0'

a, b_1, b_2 are estimated parameters and € is error term.

This chapter is divided into three Sections. Section – I presents the analysis of average per day profits of the Total Women Vendors during the three seasons as well as for the financial year. Section - II presents the analysis of average per day profits of the Women Fish Vendors during the three seasons as well as for the financial year. Section - III presents the analysis of average per day profits of the women vegetable vendors during the three seasons as well as for the financial year.

I

Total Women Vendors and Average Profits Per Day

Table 6.1 presents the average per day profits of the total women vendors as well as the three categories of vendors for the three seasons and for the financial year. It could be observed from the table that women vendors are getting higher profits in the 1st season followed by the 2nd and 3rd seasons. The average per day profit of the total women vendors is Rs 106.86 during the 1st season and around Rs. 94 for the other two seasons. The Intra-category analysis reveals that in case of Small Petty Vendors and Petty Vendors similar trend could be observed where as in case of Street Vendors the profits are low during the 2nd season (Rs. 71.20). Inter-category analysis revels that Petty Vendors are earning more profits than other two categories in almost all seasons. Thus, the analysis reveals considerable inter-category and intra category differences with respect to the three seasons.

The observation that could be made from Table 6.1.1 is the estimated coefficients are statistically significant. This states that the significant difference exists between average per day profits of women vendors during the three seasons. The sign of the estimated coefficients are negative implies that during the first season the

Table 6.1

Average per Day profit of the Women Vendors

(Value in Rs.)

Season	*Women Vendors*			
	Street Vendors	*Small Petty Vendors*	*Petty Vendors*	*Total*
1st April-31st July	83.8	94.32	142.46	106.86
1st Aug-30th Nov	71.2	81.80	129.76	94.25
1st Dec-31st March	76.27	79.86	126.75	94.29
Total Period	77.09	85.33	132.99	98.47

profits are higher than the other two seasons. The same could be observed for the three categories of vendors namely Street Vendors, Small Petty Vendors, and Petty Vendors.

In case of all the vendors taken together, the difference in average per day profits is Rs. 12.60 per day in the 1st season compared to the other two seasons. In case of Street Vendors the difference in average per day profits is Rs. 12.60 in the 1st season compared to 2nd season and is Rs. 7.52 compared to the 3rd season. In case of Small Petty Vendors the difference in average per day profits is Rs. 12.50 in the 1st season compared to 2nd season and is Rs. 14.45 compared to the 3rd season. In case of Petty Vendors the difference in average per day profits is Rs. 12.70 in the 1st season compared to 2nd season and higher by Rs. 15.71 compared to the 3rd season.

It could be inferred from the above analysis that the variation in the average per day profits during 1st and 2nd seasons is same for all the categories of vendors, where as the variation increase with the level of vending (starting from Street Vendors the ladder goes up towards Petty Vendors). Petty Vendors can reap more profits during the favourable season than street vendors.

Table 6.1.1

Seasonal Variations in profits- Estimated Parameters –Total Women Vendors

Category of Vendors	*Constant*	*S_1D*	*S_2D*	*Adjusted R^2*	*F-ratio*
Total Women Vendors	106.86* (62.78)	-12.606* (-5.23)	-12.567* (-5.22)	0.3313	18.22*
Street Vendors	83.80* (64.766)	-12.60* (-6.886)	-7.525* (-4.112)	0.114	24.006*
Small Petty Vendors	94.325* (52.635)	-12.517* (-4.939)	-14.458* (-5.705)	0.092	19.175*
Petty Vendors	142.467* (58.392)	-12.70* (-3.681)	-15.717* (-4.55)	0.056	11.686*

II

Women Fish Vendors and Average Profits Per Day

Table 6.2 presents the average per day profits of the women fish vendors as well as the three categories of fish vendors for the three seasons and for the financial year. It could be observed from the table that women fish vendors are getting higher profits in the 1st season followed by the 3rd season and 2nd season. The Intra-category analysis reveals that in case of Fish Street Vendors and Fish Small Petty Vendors similar trend could be observed where as in case of Fish Petty Vendors the average per day profit of women fish vendors is Rs 140.13 during the 1st season and Rs. 133.25 in the 2nd season and Rs. 125.52 in the 3rd season. Inter-category analysis reveals that fish petty vendors are earning more profits than other two categories in almost all seasons. Thus, the analysis reveals considerable inter-category and intra-category differences with respect to the three seasons.

Table 6.2
Average Per Day Profit of the Women Fish Vendors

(Value in Rs.)

Season	*Fish Vending*			
	Street Vendors	*Small Petty Vendors*	*Petty Vendors*	*Total*
1st April-31st July	74.93	76.50	140.13	97.18
1st Aug-30th Nov	70.66	66.43	133.25	90.11
1st Dec-31st March	74.00	75.10	125.50	91.58
Total Period	73.25	72.68	132.95	92.96

The following observations could be made form Table 6.2.1. The sign of the estimated coefficients are negative implies that during the first season the profits are higher than the other two seasons. The same could be observed for the three categories of vendors namely fish street vendors, fish small petty vendors, and fish petty vendors. Further, it could be observed that only in few cases the estimated coefficients are statistically significant. This means that there does not exists significant difference in the average per day profits of women fish vendors during the three seasons for all categories of fish vendors.

Table 6.2.1

Seasonal Variations in Profits- Estimated Parameters- Fish Vendors

Type of Vendor	*Constant*	*S_1D*	*S_2D*	*Adjusted R^2*	*F-ratio*
Total Fish Vendors	97.18* (36.25)	- 7.072 (-1.86)	- 5.606 (-1.47)	0.1031	1.93
Fish Street Vendors	74.93* (38.44)	-4.267 (-1.54)	-0.817 (-0.29)	0.0041	1.350
Fish Small Petty Vendors	76.50* (49.03)	- 10.067* (-4.56)	-1.383 (-0.62)	0. 1125	12.23*
Fish Petty Vendors	140.13* (33.05)	- 6.883 (-1.14)	- 14.617* (-2.43)	0.0223	2.976*

In case of all the Fish Vendors taken together, the difference in average per day profits is Rs. 7.07 per day in the 1st season compared to the 2nd season and Rs. 5.60 compared to the 3rd season. However, these two coefficients are not statistically significant. In case of fish street vendors the difference in average per day profits is Rs. 4.26 in the 1st season compared to 2nd season and is Rs. 0.81 compared to the 3rd season. These differences are statistically not significant. In case of fish small petty vendors the difference in average per day profits is Rs. 10.06 in the 1st season compared to 2nd season and is Rs. 1.383 compared to the 3rd season. These two coefficients are statistically significant indicated that there exists significant seasonal variations in the average per day profits earned by fish small petty vendors. In case of fish petty vendors the difference in average per day profits is Rs. 6.88 in the 1st season compared to 2nd season and higher by Rs. 14.617 compared to the 3rd season. However, the regression coefficient of S_1D not significant implies that the no considerable difference exists in the average per day profits of the fish petty vendors between 1st and 2nd season.

It could be inferred from the above analysis that there are no significant seasonal variations in the average per day profits of the Fish Vendors. But, the analysis at the disaggregate level Fish Small Petty Vendors have significant seasonal variations.

III

Women Vegetable Vendors and Average Profits Per Day

Table 6.3 presents the average per day profits of the women vegetable vendors as well as the three categories of vegetable vendors for the three seasons and for the financial year. It could be observed from the table that women vegetable vendors are getting higher profits in the 1st season followed by the 2nd and 3rd seasons. The Intra-category analysis reveals that in case of vegetable street vendors and vegetable petty vendors similar trend could be observed where as in case of fish small petty vendors the average per day profit of women vegetable vendors is Rs 112.15 during the 1st season and Rs. 97.18 in the 2nd season and Rs. 84.62

Table 6.3
Average per Day Profit of the Women Vegetable Vendors

(Value in Rs.)

Season	*Vegetable Vending*			
	Street Vendors	*Small Petty Vendors*	*Petty Vendors*	*Total*
1st April-31st July	92.66	112.15	144.8	116.53
1st Aug-30th Nov	71.73	97.18	126.28	98.40
1st Dec-31st March	78.43	84.61	127.98	97.01
Total Period	80.94	97.98	133.02	103.98

in the 3rd season. Inter-category analysis revels that vegetable petty vendors are earning more profits than other two categories in almost all seasons. Thus, the analysis reveals considerable inter-category and intra category differences with respect to the three seasons.

Table 6.3.1
Seasonal Variations in profits- Estimated Parameters- Vegetable Vendors

Type of Vendor	*Constant*	*S_1D*	*S_2D*	*Adjusted R^2*	*F-ratio*
Total Vegetable Vendors	116.539* (58.32)	- 18.139* (-6.41)	- 19.528* (-6.91)	0.9612	29.73
Vegetable Street Vendors	92.66* (65.35)	- 20.933* (-10.43)	- 14.233* (-7.09)	0.3840	56.83*
Vegetable Small Petty Vendors	112.15* (56.04)	- 14.967* (5.28)	- 27.533* (9.72)	0.3421	47.44*
Vegetable Petty Vendors	144.80* (59.98)	- 18.517* (-5.42)	- 16.817* (-4.92)	- 16.817*	

The following observations could be made form Table 6.3.1. The sign of the estimated coefficients are negative implies that during the first season the profits are higher than the other two seasons. The same could be observed for the three categories of vendors namely vegetable street vendors, vegetable small petty vendors, and vegetable petty vendors. Further, it could be observed that the estimated coefficients are statistically significant for all the categories of vegetable vendors. This means that there exists significant difference in the average per day profits of women vegetable vendors during the three seasons for all categories of vegetable vendors.

In case of all the vegetable vendors taken together, the difference in average per day profits is Rs. 18.13 per day in the 1st season compared to the 2nd season and Rs. 19.52 compared to the 3rd season. In case of vegetable street vendors the difference in average per day profits is Rs. 20.93 in the 1st season compared to 2nd season and is Rs. 14.23 compared to the 3rd season. In case of vegetable small petty vendors the difference in average per day profits is Rs. 14.96 in the 1st season compared to 2nd season and is Rs. 27.53 compared to the 3rd season. In case of vegetable petty vendors the difference in average per day profits is Rs. 18.51 in the 1st season compared to 2nd season and higher by Rs. 16.81 compared to the 3rd season.

These results indicated that there exist significant seasonal variations in the average per day profits earned by vegetable vendors. It could be inferred from the above analysis that the difference in the average per day profits during 1st and 2nd seasons and 1st and 3rd seasons is very close for vegetable petty vendors (Rs. 18 and Rs. 16) and for total vegetable vendors (Rs. 18 and Rs. 19), whereas, in case of street vegetable vendors the difference is wide (Rs. 20.93 and Rs. 14.23). In the similar manner the difference is also wide (Rs. 14.96 and Rs. 27.53) in the case of vegetable small petty vendors. Therefore, it is not evident for vegetable vendors that level of vending (starting from street vendors the ladder goes up towards petty vendors) can reap more profits during the favourable season.

Conclusion

It could also be concluded that there exists noticeable variation in the profits with respect to seasons. With respect to the seasonal variation in profits of fish vendors, street vendors are getting low profits during the 2nd season whereas petty vendors are getting low profits during 3rd seasons. In case of vegetable vendors, for all the categories of vendors profits are declining from 1st season to 3rd season. But these variations in the profits are pertinent in case of vegetable vendors than in case of fish vendors.

7

Influence of Working Capital on Profits of Women Vendors

Introduction

In this chapter an attempt is made to examine the influence of working capital on the profits earned by women vendors. In general, profit from any trade is the difference between the revenue and cost. In case of vending activity, it is the difference between the total expenses incurred by the vendors for purchasing the goods as well as bringing them to the market value, and the total amount they earned by selling the goods. Therefore, the purchasing expenses depend on the quantity they purchase, if higher the quantity, the bargaining power of the vendor increases, so that they purchase higher quantity at lower prices, which in turn influences the margin of profits. But the working capital requirement of these vendors is limited by the storage capability and the mode of operation of vending venture.

In case of street vendors, they have to carry the head-load; they prefer to purchase low quantities. Generally, they prefer either one or two varieties of items as they can't separately carry various items. This limits their profitability, in terms of attracting more number of customers, who need verities of items. In case of small petty vendors also, who operate the enterprise without any proper shelter or space may not be interested to purchase more quantity in order to get the benefits of economies of scale. Lack of proper storage space forces these two types of vendors to sell their quantity totally by the end of the day even for low prices, sometimes leads to incur losses.

On the other hand, the petty vendors, who have a small shelter in the marketyard, purchase more quantity, which can be stored even for the next day, in case if they couldn't sell the quantity for a reasonable price. Hence, they have double advantage of economies of scale as well as earning the targeted profits. Whatever may be the limitations, working capital definitely determines the extent of profits. But differences may exist in the degree of influence among these three categories of vendors.

This chapter analyses the average working capital of the women vendors during the three seasons as well as for the financial year by various categories of women vendors belonging to fish and vegetable vending. The influence of working capital on profits across various seasons is also analyzed with the help of simple regression.

Average Working Capital

The average amount of working capital invested by the total women vendors as well as the three categories of vendors for the three seasons and for the financial year is presented in Table 7.1.

Table -7.1
Average Working Capital of Women Vendors

(Value in Rs. Per day)

Seasons	*Total Women Vendors*			
	Street vendors	*Small petty vendors*	*Petty vendors*	*Total*
1st April-31st July	147.76	183.65	240.82	190.75
1st Aug-30th Nov	120.02	133.29	221.66	158.32
1st Dec-31st March	171.43	143.14	211.45	175.32
Total period	146.41	153.36	224.63	174.80

It could be observed from the table that the average working capital ranges from a maximum of Rs. 224.63 to Rs. 120.02. It could be observed that the working capital invested is highest during 1st season by petty vendors (Rs. 240.82) and lowest during 2nd season by street vendors. Intra-category analysis shows that working capital of petty vendors is the highest and working capital of the street vendors is the lowest. Inter-category analysis shows that generally during 2nd season working capital is low, except for petty vendors.

Table -7.1.1
Average Working Capital of Women Fish Vendors

(Value in Rs. Per day)

Seasons	*Fish Vending*			
	Street vendors	*Small petty vendors*	*Petty vendors*	*Total*
1st April-31st July	123.56	135.60	227.75	162.30
1st Aug-30th Nov	109.1	117.20	211.95	146.08
1st Dec-31st March	195.86	126.42	185.51	169.28
Total period	142.84	126.42	208.40	159.22

Table 7.1.1 presents the average working capital invested by women fish vendors as well as the three categories of Fish Vendors for the three seasons and for the financial year. It could be observed from the table that the average working capital ranges from a maximum of Rs. 227.75 to Rs. 109.10. It could be observed that the working capital invested is highest during 1st season by petty vendors (Rs. 227.75) and lowest during 2nd season by street vendors. Intra-category analysis shows that working capital of petty vendors is the highest and working capital of the street vendors is the lowest. Inter-category analysis shows that generally during 2nd season working capital is low, except for petty vendors.

Table -7.1.2
Average Working Capital of Women Vegetable Vendors

(Value in Rs. Per day)

Seasons	*Vegetable Vending*			
	Street vendors	*Small petty vendors*	*Petty vendors*	*Total*
1st April-31st July	171.98	231.7	253.90	219.19
1st Aug-30th Nov	130.95	149.38	231.38	170.57
1st Dec-31st March	147.00	160.00	237.28	181.36
Total period	149.98	180.30	240.85	190.38

Table 7.1.2 presents the average working capital invested by women fish vendors as well as the three categories of vegetable Vendors for the three seasons and for the financial year. It could be observed from the table that the average working capital ranges from a maximum of Rs. 253.90 to Rs. 130.95. It could be observed that the working capital invested is highest during 1st season by petty vendors (Rs. 253.90) and lowest during 2nd season by street vendors. Intra-category analysis shows that working capital of petty vendors is the highest and working capital of the street vendors is the lowest. Inter-category analysis shows that working capital is low during 2nd season.

The Basic Forms of Linear Regress function

The influence of working capital is assessed with help of simple regression technique for the three seasons and three categories of women vendors belonging to two trades separately.

1) $P = a + b_1 WC + €$ ———— (1)

where

WC = Working Capital per day

a, b_1 are estimated parameters and € is error term.

Results of the analysis

The impact of the amount of working capital on the profits is analyzed with the help the regression analysis.

Model Specification

The specific regression equation used is

$P_i = a + b\,WC_i + u_i$

where,

P_i = per day profit in rupees of i-th woman vendor,

WC_i = Amount of working capital in rupees by the i-th woman vendor

'a' is intercept and 'b' is regression parameters, and u_i the stochastic disturbance term, and

Total Women Vendors

Table 7.2

Results of the Estimated Regression Equations (Profits Vs Working Capital) – Women Vendors (i= 1 to 360 or n=360)

Season	*Dependent Variable*	*Constant*	*Working Capital*	R^2	*F*
1st April-31st July	Profit	9.33	0.51* (29.63)	0.710	878.271*
1st Aug-30th Nov	Profit	20.14	0.46* (32.59)	0.748	1062.104*
1st Dec-31st March	Profit	38.04	0.32* (16.05)	0.419	257.890*
Total	Profit	6.62	0.52* (42.23)	0.833	1783.826*

Note: Figures in parentheses indicate t values.
* Significant at 1 percent level

Table 7.2 presents the results of the regression analysis for the total women vendors. Except for the 3rd period, The R-bar square value is above 0.7. It indicates that working capital could able to explain more than 70 percent variations in the profits of the women vendors. The F- ratios is also significant and the variable also significant at 1 % level. An increase in the working capital by one rupee per day will yield a profit of 51 paise per day during 1st season, 46 paise per day during 2nd season, 32 paise per day during 3rd season, and 52 paise, on average during the financial year 2007-08. The 't' test reveals that all these estimated values are significant at 1% level.

Fish Vendors

Table 7.3 presents the results of the regression analysis for the Fish vendors. For the 3rd season, the R-bar square value is only 0.22. It indicates that working capital could able to explain only 22 percent variations in the profits of the women fish vendors during this season. The F- ratios is significant and the variable also significant at 1 % level in the functions.

Table 7.3

Results of the Estimated Regression Equations (Profits Vs Working Capital)- Fish Vendors

(i= 1 to 180 or n=180)

Season	*Dependent Variable*	*Constant*	*Working Capital*	*R^2*	*F*
1st April-31st July	Profit	0.99	0.59* (20.57)	0.704	423.425*
1st Aug-30th Nov	Profit	21.57	0.46* (26.81)	0.802	718.803*
1st Dec-31st March	Profit	54.37	0.22* (7.06)	0.219	49.899*
Total Period	Profit	7.83	0.53* (25.25)	0.782	637.860*

Note: Figures in parentheses indicate t values.

* Significant at 1 percent level.

Table 7.3.1

Results of the Estimated Regression Equations (Profits Vs Working Capital)- Fish Street Vendors

(i= 1 to 60 or n =60)

Season	*Dependent Variable*	*Constant*	*Capital Working*	*R^2*	*F*
1st April-31st July	Profit	20.75	0.43* (6.15)	0.395	37.933*
1st Aug-30th Nov	Profit	-9.19	0.73* (9.65)	0.617	93.297*
1st Dec-31st March	Profit	26.29	0.24* (10.44)	0.653	109.117*
Total Period	Profit	19.08	0.379* (11.12)	0.681	123.772*

Note: Figures in parentheses indicate t values.

* Significant at 1 percent level

From the above Table it could be inferred that an increase in the working capital by one rupee per day will yield a profit of 59 paise per day during 1st season, 46 paise per day during 2nd season, 22 paise per day during 3rd season, and 52 paise, on average during the financial year 2007-08. The 't' test reveals that all these estimated values are significant at 1% level.

Table 7.3.1 presents the results of the regression analysis for the fish street vendors. Except for the 1st period, the R-bar square value is about 0.6. It indicates that working capital could able to explain more than 60 percent variations in the profits of the women vendors. The F-ratios is also significant and the variable also significant at 1 % level. From the Table could be inferred that an increase in the working capital by one rupee per day will yield a profit of 43 paise per day during 1st season, 73 paise per day during 2nd season, 24 paise per day during 3rd season, and 38 paise, on average during the financial year 2007-08. The 't' test reveals that all these estimated values are significant at 1% level.

Table 7.3.2

Results of the Estimated Regression Equations (Profits Vs Working Capital)- Fish Small Petty Vendors

(i= 1 to 60 or n =60)

Season	*Dependent Variable*	*Constant*	*Capital Working*	R^2	*F*
1st April-31st July	Profit	28.21	0.35* (13.10)	0.747	171.634*
1st Aug-30th Nov	Profit	42.39	0.20* (16.66)	0.827	277.658*
1st Dec-31st March	Profit	42.42	0.20* (16.66)	0.446	46.672*
Total Period	Profit	33.77	0.30* (18.02)	0.849	324.967*

Note: Figures in parentheses indicate t values.

* Significant at 1 percent level

The results of the regression analysis for the small petty fish vendors are presented in Table 7.3.2. Except for the 3rd period, The R-bar square value is about 0.8. It indicates that working capital could able to explain about 80 percent variations in the profits of the women vendors. The F- ratios is also significant and the variable also significant at 1 % level. From the Table, it could be inferred that an increase in the working capital by one rupee per day will yield a profit of 35 paise per day during 1st season, 20 paise per day during 2nd season, 20 paise per day during 3rd season, and 30 paise, on average during the financial year 2007-08. The 't' test reveals that all these estimated values are significant at 1% level.

The regression results of the fish petty vendors are presented in Table 7.3.3. Except for the 1st period, The R-bar square value is about 0.8. It indicates that working capital could able to explain about 80 percent variations in the profits of the women vendors. The F- ratios is also significant and the variable also significant at 1 % level.

Table -7.3.3

Results of the Estimated Regression Equations (Profits Vs Working Capital)- Fish Petty Vendors

(i= 1 to 60 or n =60)

Season	*Dependent Variable*	*Constant*	*Working Capital*	R^2	*F*
1st April-31st July	Profit	0.75	0.61* (7.32)	0.480	53.613*
1st Aug-30th Nov	Profit	74.91	0.27* (13.61)	0.762	185.300*
1st Dec-31st March	Profit	101.10	0.13* (19.92)	0.873	397.057*
Total Period	Profit	55.63	0.37* (12.78)	0.738	163.441*

Note: Figures in parentheses indicate t values.
* Significant at 1 percent level.

From the above Table, it could be inferred that an increase in the working capital by one rupee per day will yield a profit of 61 paise per day during 1st season, 27 paise per day during 2nd season, 13 paise per day during 3rd season, and 37 paise, on average during the financial year 2007-08. The 't' test reveals that all these estimated values are significant at 1% level.

Vegetable Vendors

The regression results relating to vegetable vendors are presented in Table 7.4. R-bar square value is 0.753, 0.662, and 0.777 for the three seasons respectively. In case of total period it is 0.934 which indicates that 93 percent of variation in the profits of vegetable vendors could be explained by the working capital. The F-ratios are also significant. From the Table, it could be inferred that an increase in the working capital by one rupee per day will yield a profit of 49 paise per day during 1st season, 48 paise per day during 2nd season, 47 paise per day during 3rd season, and 55 paise, on average during the financial year 2007-08. The 't' test reveals that all these estimated values are significant at 1% level.

Table 7.4

Results of the Estimated Regression Equations (Profits Vs Working Capital)– Vegetable Vendors

(i= 1 to 180 or n =180)

Season	*Dependent Variable*	*Constant*	*Working Capital*	R^2	*F*
1st April-31st July	Profit	8.86	0.49* (23.30)	0.753	543.04*
1st Aug-30th Nov	Profit	15.75	0.48* (18.68)	0.662	349.05*
1st Dec-31st March	Profit	11.48	0.47* (24.91)	0.777	620.80*
Financial Year	Profit	-1.62	0.55* (50.32)	0.934	2532.90*

Note: Figures in parentheses indicate t values.

* Significant at 1 percent level.

The regression results relating to vegetable street vendors are presented in Table 7.4.1. R-bar square values are around 0.7 for all the seasons. In case of total period it is 0.934 which indicates that 93 percent of variation in the profits of vegetable vendors could be explained by the working capital. The F-ratios are also significant.

Table 7.4.1

Results of the Estimated Regression Equations (Profits Vs Working Capital) – Vegetable Street Vendors

(i= 1 to 60 or n =60)

Season	*Dependent Variable*	*Constant*	*Capital Working*	R^2	*F*
1st April-31st July	Profit	66.09	0.15* (11.42)	0.692	130.420*
1st Aug-30th Nov	Profit	-20.19	0.70* (11.25)	0.686	126.706*
1st Dec-31st March	Profit	5.42	0.49* (18.39)	0.854	338.400*
Financial Year	Profit	17.68	0.42* (30.70)	0.942	942.864*

Note: Figures in parentheses indicate t values.
* Significant at 1 percent level.

Table 7.4.2

Results of the Estimated Regression Equations (Profits Vs Working Capital)– Vegetable Small Petty Vendors

(i= 1 to 60 or n =60)

Season	*Dependent Variable*	*Constant*	*Working Capital*	R^2	*F*
1st April-31st July	Profit	9.51 (18.21)	0.44*	0.851	331.615*
1st Aug-30th Nov	Profit	70.85	0.17* (16.32)	0.821	266.346*
1st Dec-31st March	Profit	73.79	0.06 (1.06)	0.019	1.125
Financial Year	Profit	16.86	0.45* (16.39)	0.823	268.842*

Note: Figures in parentheses indicate t values.
* Significant at 1 percent level

From Table 7.4.1, it could be inferred that an increase in the working capital by one rupee per day will yield a profit of 15 paise per day during 1st season, 70 paise per day during 2nd season, 49 paise per day during 3rd season, and 42 paise, on average during the financial year 2007-08. The 't' test reveals that all these estimated values are significant at 1% level.

The regression results of the small petty vegetable vendors are presented in Table 7.4.2. Except for the 3rd period, the R-bar square value is about 0.8. It indicates that working capital could able to explain about 80 percent variations in the profits of the women vendors. The F- ratios is also significant and the variable also significant at 1 % level. From the Table 7.4.2, it could be inferred that an increase in the working capital by one rupee per day will yield a profit of 44 paise per day during 1st season, 17 paise per day during 2nd season, 6 paise per day during 3rd season, and 45 paise, on average during the financial year 2007-08. The 't' test reveals that all these estimated values are significant at 1% level.

Table 7.4.3

Results of the Estimated Regression Equations (Profits Vs Working Capital)– Vegetable Petty Vendors

(i= 1 to 60 or n =60)

Season	*Dependent Variable*	*Constant*	*Working Capital*	$\bar{R}^2$	*F*
1st April-31st July	Profit	-84.88* (-8.06)	0.90* (21.89)	0.892	479.256*
1st Aug-30th Nov	Profit	-79.24 (-1.09)	0.88* (2.84)	0.123	8.108*
1st Dec-31st March	Profit	-77.08* (-15.48)	0.21* (10.24)	0.644	104.968*
Financial Year	Profit	-56.06* (-3.45)	0.78* (11.66)	0.701	136.060*

Note: Figures in parentheses indicate t values.

* Significant at 1 percent level.

The regression results of the petty vegetable vendors are presented in Table 7.4.3. Except for the 2nd period, the R-bar square value is 0.892 for the 1st season, 0.644 for the 3rd season. For the total period, it is 0.7. The F- ratios is also significant and the variable also significant at 1 % level. From the Table, it could be inferred that an increase in the working capital by one rupee per day will yield a profit of 90 paise per day during 1st season, 88 paise per day during 2nd season, 21 paise per day during 3rd season, and 78 paise, on average during the financial year 2007-08. The 't' test reveals that all these estimated values are significant at 1% level.

Conclusion

The average working capital of the vegetable vendors is higher than the average working capital of the fish vendors. In all the categories of vendors the same thing could be observed. During the 2nd season the working capital is low. The working capital turned out to be a significant variable in the regression analysis, implies that the influence of the working capital is more in determining the profits. With respect to the fish vendors, working capital yields about 30 paise per day for one rupee increase in working capital. Inter category analysis reveals that maximum profits are for the fish petty vendors. With respect to the various categories of vegetable vendors, working capital yields highest profits for the vegetable petty vendors and lowest in the case of vegetable small petty vendors. With respect to the seasons the working capital yields maximum profits per day during the 1st season.

8

Factors Influencing the Profits of Women Vendors: Human Capital Approach

In the preceding Chapter the influence and importance of the working capital is examined. When the scope for increasing the working capital is limited by other factors, what are the other factors that cause variation in the profits of these various categories of vendors?

In this regard, the human capital approach may throw some insights into the divergence of the profits across these categories of vendors.[1] In this approach the characteristics of the vendors like age, education, and experience can be considered as important determinants of profits of vendors as these characteristics project the dynamism of the vendor.

Along with working capital, the experience, literacy level, and age of the vendors also influence the functioning of the activities. Particularly, in case of women the marital status also plays an important role. The analysis is carried out for the three categories of the women vendors' viz., street vendors, small petty vendors and petty vendors belonging to both the fish vending and vegetable vending for the three seasons separately. To examine the determinants of the profits, simple and multiple regression models were used in the study.

Vending and trading, with some notable exceptions, are seldom lucrative occupations for women. Irrespective of gender, available data suggest that even the more successful street vendors earn an income that is at, or close to, the poverty level. If one measures economic success in terms of expanding one's business, it is clear that both the vending environment (an oversupply of goods and vendors) and the small scale of the businesses limit women's potential for upward mobility. Increasingly, expenses and consumer resistance to price increases reduce profitability for hawkers and vendors. The high cost of credit is another constraint.

The re-investment behaviour of the vendor is influenced by various factors. Once they enter this marginal economic world, women experience limited opportunities for building up the assets they need to help their businesses grow. When there is growth of the business — as measured by hiring a part-time worker or acquiring assets, like fixed shelter — it is very slow and gradual in case of women. Some eventually leave the activity at times of stabilization due to reasons like getting married.

Another important aspect for their reluctance to reinvestment might be that operating in highly competitive markets and in environments where demand is constrained by limited purchasing power, women vendors often focus on reducing their vulnerability to crisis and economic shocks by limiting their investment only to a certain level to earn stable income.

Consequently, not all women reinvest their earnings in their businesses and instead apply them to other asset-creating endeavors. For example, many women use an intergenerational strategy by which they maintain the original vending enterprise to ensure stable income and then use the surplus to educate the next generation so that younger family members can have access to higher-earning occupations.

Therefore, the earnings as well as the working capital invested vary according to the age, literacy, marital status and experience.

This chapter is divided into Three sections. Section –I presents the average working capital with respect to literacy, marital status, age and experience of the women vendors. Section – II presents the average profits with respect to literacy, marital status, age and experience of the women vendors. Section –III presents the results of the multiple regression analysis on the profits of the women vendors.

I

Average Per Day Working Capital and Literacy

Tables 8.1.1, 8.1.2 and 8.1.3 present the average per day working capital of the women vendors during the three seasons according to the literacy level.

It could be observed from Table 8.1.1 that the average per day working capital of women vendors varies in between three seasons (Rs.190.75, Rs.158.33, and Rs.175.33). And also the average per day working capital of literate women vendors is higher than the illiterate women vendors in all the three categories of vendors. The difference between the working capital ranges between Rs. 50 to Rs. 70 per day.

It is evident from Table 8.1.2 that in case of fish vendors, the difference in working capital among three seasons is not wide (Rs.162.31, Rs.146.08, and Rs.169.28). But considerable difference exists in the average per day working capital of literate and illiterate women fish vendors of all the categories. Particularly, in the 2nd season, the difference in working capital between illiterate and literate small fish vendors is only Rs. 20 (Rs. 105.02 and Rs. 125.42 respectively) where as in the same season; the difference in working capital between illiterate and literate fish petty vendors is Rs. 100 (Rs. 183.90 and Rs. 284.94 respectively).

It could be seen from Table 8.1.3 that among vegetable vendors also, the difference in working capital among three seasons is not wide (Rs.219.19, Rs.170.57, and Rs.181.37). But considerable difference exists in the average per day working capital of literate and illiterate women fish vendors of all the categories. In case of women small petty vegetable vendors, the variations are more. During 1st period the difference is Rs. 75 and in 3rd period there is no difference.

Table 8.1.1: Average Working Capital of the Women Vendors - Literacy Level

(Value in Rs. Per day)

Season	Fish and Vegetable Vendors											
	Street Vendors			Smell Petty Vendors			Petty Vendors			Total		
	illiteracy	literacy	Total	Illiteracy	Literacy	Total	Illiteracy	literacy	Total	illiteracy	literacy	Total
1st April-31st July	135.36	192.65	147.78	162.04	248.47	183.65	220.57	279.85	240.83	170.09	246.77	190.75
1st Aug-30th Nov	115.27	137.23	120.03	122.41	165.93	133.29	203.05	257.54	221.67	144.08	196.96	158.33
1st Dec-31st March	156.72	224.62	171.43	137.57	159.87	143.14	188.66	255.22	211.40	159.76	217.53	175.33
Total period	135.81	184.81	146.43	140.66	191.47	153.36	204.11	264.15	224.63	157.98	220.40	174.80
n	94	26	120	91	29	120	88	32	120	273	87	360

Table -8.1.2

Average Working Capital of the Women Fish Vendors - Literacy Level

(Value in Rs. Per day)

Seasons	*Fish Vendors*											
	Street Vendors			*Small Petty Vendors*			*Petty Vendors*			*Total*		
	Illiteracy	*Literacy*	*Total*	*Illiteracy*	*Literacy*	*Total*	*Illiteracy*	*Literacy*	*Total*	*Illiteracy*	*Literacy*	*Total*
1st April -31st July	113.90	162.25	123.57	117.91	199.54	135.60	204.16	287.41	227.75	143.39	224.45	162.31
1st Aug -30th Nov	105.02	125.42	109.10	103.98	165.00	117.20	183.09	284.94	211.95	128.99	202.24	146.08
1st Dec -31st March	176.06	275.08	195.87	117.47	159.00	126.47	156.37	259.24	185.52	149.97	232.74	169.28
Total period	131.71	187.58	142.88	113.11	174.62	126.43	181.26	277.06	208.40	140.81	219.79	159.24
n	48	12	60	47	13	60	43	17	60	138	42	180

Table -8.1.3

Average Working Capital of the Women Vegetable Vendors - Literacy Level

(Value in Rs. Per day)

Seasons	Vegetable Vendors											
	Street Vendors			Small Petty Vendors			Petty Vendors			Total		
	Illiteracy	Literacy	Total	Illiteracy	Literacy	Total	Illiteracy	Literacy	Total	Illiteracy	Literacy	Total
1st April-31st July	157.76	218.71	171.98	210.28	285.88	231.70	240.17	274.50	253.90	199.56	263.82	219.19
1st Aug-30th Nov	125.96	147.36	130.95	142.56	166.65	149.38	226.89	238.13	231.38	160.74	192.93	170.57
1st Dec-31st March	136.54	181.36	147.00	159.53	160.53	159.82	227.22	252.38	237.28	170.57	205.91	181.37
Total period	140.09	182.43	149.97	170.77	204.35	180.28	231.42	255.00	240.85	176.94	220.87	190.37
n	46	14	60	43	17	60	36	24	60	125	55	180

Average Working Capital and Marital Status

Tables 8.2.1, 8.2.2 and 8.2.3 present the average per day working capital of women vendors during the three seasons according to the marital status.

It could be observed from the Table 8.2.1 that the average per day working capital of married women vendors is higher than the unmarried women vendors during all the seasons for all the categories of vendors. But the difference between average working capital of married petty vendors and unmarried petty vendors is lowest to Rs. 2 in case of petty vendors in the 1st season and highest to Rs. 46 in the 3rd season for the street vendors.

Table 8.2.2 presents the average per day working capital of the women fish vendors. It could be observed from the table that the trend is similar as above. The average per day working capital of married women fish vendors is higher than the unmarried fish vendors for all the seasons for all the categories of fish vendors. The lowest difference is Rs. 10 in case of street fish vendors in the 2nd season and highest difference is Rs. 55 in case of petty fish vendors. But the difference is large in case of fish petty vendors in all the seasons.

In case of vegetable vendors (Table-8.2.3), the average per day working capital of the unmarried vendors is lower than the married vendors in case of small petty vegetable vendors and vegetable street vendors. In case of vegetable petty vendors unmarried vegetable vendors are putting more working capital than unmarried vendors. All most there is no difference in the working capital of the small petty vegetable vendors during the 3rd season (Rs. 159.64 and Rs. 160) .

Table -8.2.1

Average Working Capital of the Women Vendors – Marital Status

(Value in Rs. Per day)

Seasons	*Fish and Vegetable Vendors*											
	Street Vendors			*Small Petty Vendors*			*Petty Vendors*			*Total*		
	Married	*Unmarried*	*Total*	*Married*	*Unmarried*	*Total*	*Married*	*Unmarried*	*Total*	*Married*	*Unmarried*	*Total*
1st April-31st July	155.81	118.69	147.7	194.44	152.64	183.65	241.37	239.31	240.82	196.28	173.88	190.75
1st Aug-30th Nov	122.69	110.38	120.0	139.65	115.03	133.29	227.61	205.31	221.66	162.331	146.13	158.32
1st Dec-31st March	181.41	135.34	171.43	146.14	134.51	143.14	214.53	202.78	211.4	180.58	159.30	175.32
Total period	153.33	121.47	146.41	160.08	134.06	153.36	227.84	215.80	224.63	179.73	159.77	174.80
n	94	26	120	89	31	120	88	32	120	271	89	360

Table -8.2.2

Average Working Capital of the Women Fish Vendors – Marital Status

(Value in Rs. Per day)

Seasons	*Fish Vendors*											
	Street Vendors			*Small Petty Vendors*			*Petty Vendors*			*Total*		
	Married	*Unmarried*	*Total*	*Married*	*Unmarried*	*Total*	*Married*	*Unmarried*	*Total*	*Married*	*Unmarried*	*Total*
1st April-31st July	129.78	103.14	123.56	144.88	110.06	135.6	239.56	195.25	227.75	170.79	137.58	162.30
1st Aug-30th Nov	111.47	101.28	109.1	124.90	96	117.2	226.59	171.68	211.95	153.68	123.93	146.08
1st Dec-31st March	211.17	145.57	195.86	132.34	110.31	126.46	199.40	147.31	185.51	181.42	133.91	169.28
Total period	150.81	116.67	142.84	134.04	105.46	126.42	221.85	171.42	208.40	168.63	131.81	159.22
n	46	14	60	44	16	60	44	16	60	14	46	180

Table -8.2.3

Average Working Capital of the Women Vegetable Vendors – Marital Status

(Value in Rs. Per day)

Seasons	*Season Vegetables Vendors*											
	Street Vendors			*Small Petty Vendors*			*Petty Vendors*			*Total*		
	Married	*Unmarried*	*Total*	*Married*	*Unmarried*	*Total*	*Married*	*Unmarried*	*Total*	*Married*	*Unmarried*	*Total*
1st April-31st July	180.77	136.83	171.98	242.91	198.06	231.70	243.18	283.37	253.90	221.22	212.72	219.194
1st Aug-30th Nov	133.43	121	130.95	154.06	135.33	149.38	228.63	238.93	231.38	170.78	169.88	170.5
1st Dec-31st March	152.89	123.41	147	159.64	160.33	159.81	229.65	258.25	237.28	179.76	186.46	181.36
TotalPeriod	155.70	127.08	149.98	185.54	164.58	180.30	233.82	260.19	240.85	190.59	189.69	190.38
n	48	12	60	45	15	60	44	16	60	137	43	180

Average Per Day Working Capital and Age Groups

The Tables 8.3.1, 8.3.2 and 8.3.3 present the average per day working capital of the women vendors during the three seasons according to the age groups.

From Table 8.3.1 it could be inferred that, irrespective of the seasons and categories of vendors, the average per day working capital of the women vendors is increasing along with the age group. For the street vendors and small petty vendors the working capital is low during 2nd season (Rs. 120.03, and Rs. 133.29) where as in case of petty vendors a gradual decline of the average per day working capital could be observed from 1st season to 3rd season. The similar observation could be made with respect to the three age groups of the all the categories of vendors.

Table 8.3.2 presents the average per day working capital of the total fish vendor and all the categories of fish vendors with respect to age groups for the three seasons. The average per day working capital is the highest (Rs. 270.23) for the fish petty vendors of the age group ≥ 50 years and the lowest is Rs. 179.27 by the Street Vendors of age group ≤ 30 years during the 3rd season.

Table 8.3.3 presents the average per day working capital of the vegetable vendors. Similar results as for the total vendors could be observed in this type of vendors trades also.

It could be inferred that on the average and in comparison with the three categories of vendors, the average per day working capital is higher for fish vendors than vegetable vendors.

Average Per Day Working Capital and Experience

The Tables 8.4.1, 8.4.2 and 8.4.3 present the average per day working capital of the women vendors during the three seasons according to the years of experience.

From Table 8.4.1 it could be inferred that, irrespective of the years of experience, during 2nd season the average per day working capital of the women vendors is low compared to the other two seasons. In case of petty vendors the average per day working capital is low during 3rd season. The average per day working

Table -8.3.1

Average Working Capital of the Women Vendors – Age-wise

(Value in Rs. Per day)

Seasons	Fish and Vegetable Vendors															
	Street Vendors				Small Petty Vendors				Petty Vendors				Total			
	≤ 30	31-50	≥51	Total	≤ 30	31-50	≥51	Total	≤ 30	31-50	≥51	Total	≤ 30	31-50	≥51	Total
1st April-31st July	116.08	158.87	168.36	147.78	150.03	196.84	208.92	183.65	203.27	254.24	270.23	240.83	158.24	199.59	221.38	190.75
1st Aug-30th Nov	109.89	121.79	131.64	120.03	111.63	140.05	153.63	133.29	187.20	236.49	244.57	221.67	137.57	161.57	183.16	158.33
1st Dec-31st March	130.56	179.82	214.68	171.43	129.90	143.45	164.50	143.14	179.27	224.57	233.80	211.40	147.40	180.75	206.38	175.33
Total period	118.83	153.53	171.55	146.43	130.55	160.05	175.75	153.36	189.98	238.41	249.47	224.63	147.77	180.62	203.63	174.80
n	36	62	22	120	40	56	24	120	41	49	30	120	117	167	76	360

Table -8.3.2

Average Working Capital of the Women Fish Vendors – Age-wise

(Value in Rs. Per day)

Seasons	*Fish Vendors*															
	Street Vendors				*Small Petty Vendors*				*Petty Vendors*				*Total*			
	≤ 30	*31-50*	*≥51*	*Total*	*≤ 30*	*31-50*	*≥51*	*Total*	*≤ 30*	*31-50*	*≥51*	*Total*	*≤ 30*	*31-50*	*≥51*	*Total*
1st April-31st July	101.95	127.46	150.50	123.57	110.29	140.96	164.00	135.60	170.95	251.22	262.82	227.75	127.44	169.36	199.30	162.31
1st Aug-30th Nov	100.90	109.36	122.17	109.10	94.52	117.52	150.64	117.20	151.15	236.83	249.82	211.95	115.18	150.62	181.91	146.08
1st Dec-31st March	137.20	212.79	254.17	195.87	110.24	129.72	145.00	126.47	136.55	203.13	219.29	185.52	127.70	182.54	204.84	169.28
Total period	113.35	149.96	175.58	142.88	105.05	129.36	153.29	126.43	153.00	230.35	243.88	208.40	123.49	167.51	195.33	159.24
n	20	28	12	60	21	25	14	60	20	23	17	60	61	76	43	180

Table -8.3.3

Average Working Capital of the Women Vegetable Vendors – Age-wise

(Value in Rs. Per day)

Seasons	Vegetable Vendors															
	Street Vendors				Small Petty Vendors				Petty Vendors				Total			
	≤ 30	31-50	≥51	Total	≤ 30	31-50	≥51	Total	≤ 30	31-50	≥51	Total	≤ 30	31-50	≥51	Total
1st April-31st July	133.75	184.74	189.80	171.98	193.95	241.90	271.80	231.70	234.05	256.92	279.92	253.90	191.79	224.84	250.15	219.19
1st Aug-30th Nov	121.13	132.03	143.00	130.95	130.53	158.23	157.80	149.38	221.52	236.19	237.69	231.38	161.96	170.71	184.79	170.57
1st Dec-31st March	122.25	152.68	167.30	147.00	151.63	154.52	191.80	159.82	219.95	243.54	252.77	237.28	168.86	179.26	208.39	181.37
Total period	125.69	156.47	166.70	149.97	158.74	184.81	207.20	180.28	225.19	245.54	256.77	240.85	174.21	191.57	214.45	190.37
n	16	34	10	60	19	31	10	60	21	26	13	60	56	91	33	180

capital increases with the years of experience in all the categories of vendors.

Table 8.4.2 presents the average per day working capital of the fish vendors according to the years of experience. The average per day working capital of the street fish vendors, small petty fish vendors is low during 2nd season for all the groups of experience. In case of petty fish vendors it is low during 3rd season for all the years of experience. Whatever may be the category, the women fish vendors who have more than 10 years of experience putting higher working capital compared to the other two levels. The similar trend could be observed with respect to vegetable vendors (Table 8.4.3). The average per day working capital is least in case of Vegetable Street Vendors during 2nd season (Rs. 121. 09) by the < 5 years of experience, where as in case of Fish Small Petty vendors Rs. 58 during 2nd season by the group <5 years experience is the least.

II

Average Per Day Profit and Literacy Level

It is well known that most of the women vendors in the informal sector are illiterate. The advent of literacy programmes by the Government of India, in order to achieve 100% literacy, added incentives for education of girl child, adult education programmes, the general literacy level has increased and even the younger generations are at least able to read and write. This may have the positive impact on the earnings of the women vendors. Based on the literacy level all the women vendors are categorized as illiterate vendors and literate vendors.

Average Profits and Literacy – Total Women Vendors

The Tables 8.5.1 presents the average per day profit of the women vendors during the three seasons and for the financial year according to the literacy level.

It could be observed from the Table that the average per day profit of the literate women vendors is higher than the illiterate women vendors for all the three seasons as well for the whole year.

Table 8.4.1

Average Working Capital of the Women Vendors – Experience

(Value in Rs. Per day)

Seasons	Total															
	Street Vendors				Small Petty Vendors				Petty Vendors				Total			
	< 5	6-10	> 11	Total	< 5	6-10	> 11	Total	< 5	6-10	> 11	Total	< 5	6-10	> 11	Total
1st April-31st July	131.07	145.50	168.07	147.78	135.29	168.18	205.45	183.65	148.20	233.68	285.58	240.83	135.53	186.73	218.24	190.75
1st Aug-30th Nov	117.43	117.18	128.33	120.03	101.14	123.58	147.20	133.29	146.20	214.04	262.33	221.67	121.29	157.09	174.37	158.33
1st Dec-31st March	123.43	157.05	245.97	171.43	132.43	143.07	144.55	143.14	138.00	200.25	259.67	211.40	128.07	169.95	202.04	175.33
Total period	123.96	139.95	180.77	146.43	123.14	144.89	165.75	153.36	144.30	215.99	269.12	224.63	128.36	171.26	198.20	174.80
n	28	62	30	120	7	57	56	120	10	77	33	120	45	196	119	360

Table -8.4.2

Average Working Capital of the Women Fish Vendors – Experience

(Value in Rs. Per day)

Seasons	Fish Vendors															
	Street Vendors				*Small Petty Vendors*				*Petty Vendors*				*Total*			
	< 5	6-10	> 11	Total	< 5	6-10	> 11	Total	< 5	6-10	> 11	Total	< 5	6-10	> 11	Total
1st April-31st July	104.80	106.59	151.26	123.57	101.00	111.20	156.18	135.60	132.50	221.50	289.44	227.75	119.07	152.31	184.22	162.31
1st Aug-30th Nov	100.60	103.16	119.22	109.10	58.00	98.64	134.85	117.20	130.00	196.67	287.31	211.95	110.60	138.14	163.74	146.08
1st Dec-31st March	121.60	160.59	261.09	195.87	101.00	111.16	139.61	126.47	120.00	166.00	262.19	185.52	118.00	149.40	205.65	169.28
Total period	109.00	123.50	177.22	142.88	87.00	106.96	143.58	126.43	127.63	194.75	279.50	208.40	116.00	146.63	184.53	159.24
n	5	32	23	60	2	25	33	60	8	36	16	60	15	93	72	180

Table -8.4.3

Average Working Capital of the Women Vegetable Vendors – Experience

(Value in Rs. Per day)

Seasons	*Vegetable* Vendors															
	Street Vendors				*Small Petty Vendors*				*Petty Vendors*				*Total*			
	< 5	6-10	> 11	Total	< 5	6-10	> 11	Total	< 5	6-10	> 11	Total	< 5	6-10	> 11	Total
1st April-31st July	136.78	187.00	223.29	171.98	149.00	212.69	276.13	231.70	211.00	244.37	281.94	253.90	143.77	217.82	270.36	219.19
1st Aug-30th Nov	121.09	132.13	158.29	130.95	118.40	143.06	164.91	149.38	211.00	229.29	238.82	231.38	126.63	174.20	190.66	170.57
1st Dec-31st March	123.83	153.27	196.29	147.00	145.00	168.00	151.65	159.82	210.00	230.32	257.29	237.28	133.10	188.51	196.51	181.37
Total period	127.22	157.50	192.43	149.97	137.60	174.53	197.57	180.28	211.00	234.63	259.35	240.85	134.53	193.50	219.15	190.37
n	23	30	7	60	5	32	23	60	2	41	17	60	30	103	47	180

The results of the regression analysis presented in Table 8.5.1(a) reveal significant differences in profits derived by literate and illiterate women vendors. The coefficient of dummy variable indicates the difference between the profits of the literate and illiterate vendors are statistically significant at 1% level in all seasons and for the total period.

Table -8.5.1

Average Profits of the Women Vendors - Literacy Level

(Value in Rs. Per day)

Seasons	*Total*		
	Illiteracy	*Literacy*	*Total*
1st April-31st July	97.71	135.59	106.86
1st Aug-30th Nov	88.43	112.55	94.26
1st Dec-31st March	89.54	109.23	94.30
Total period	91.87	119.16	98.46
n	273	87	360

Table -8.5.1(a)

Results of the Estimated Regression Equations

(Profits Vs Literacy) – Women Traders

(i= 1 to 360 or n=360)

Season	*Dependent Variable*	*Constant*	D_1	R^2	*F*
1st April-31st July	Profit	97.71* (46.05)	37.87* (8.77)	0.177	77.031*
1st Aug-30th Nov	Profit	88.42* (50.07)	24.12* (6.71)	0.112	45.097*
1st Dec-31st March	Profit	89.53* (59.68)	19.69* (6.45)	0.104	41.643*
Total Period	Profit	91.86* (54.82)	27.29* (8.00)	0.152	64.103*

Note: Figures in the parentheses indicate Students' t - ratio.

* Indicates significance at 1 per cent level.

The difference in average per day profits is maximum (Rs. 37.87) in 1st season and minimum (Rs. 19.69) in 3rd season with respect to the literacy level. It could be inferred that literate women vendors able to reap higher profits during 1st season.

Average Profits and Literacy – Total Women Fish Vendors

The Table 8.5.2 presents the average per day profit of the Women Fish Vendors during the three seasons and for the financial year according to the literacy level. It could be observed from the Table that the average per day profit of the literate women fish vendors is higher than the illiterate women fish vendors for all the three seasons as well for the whole year for all the categories of vendors namely fish street vendors, fish small petty vendors, and fish petty vendors

The results of the regression analysis presented in Tables from 8.5.2(a) to 8.5.2(d) reveal significant differences in profits derived by literate and illiterate women fish Vendors. The coefficient of dummy variable indicates the difference between the profits of the literate and illiterate women fish vendors are statistically significant at 1% level in all seasons and for the total period for all the categories of vendors.

Among the Total Fish Vendors the difference in average per day profits is maximum (Rs. 43.35) in 1st season and minimum (Rs. 22.18) in 3rd season. Among the fish street vendors the difference in average per day profits is maximum (Rs. 27.66) in 3rd season and minimum (Rs. 14.27) in 2nd season. Among the fish small petty vendors the difference in average per day profits is maximum (Rs. 25.97) in 1st season and minimum (Rs. 14.28) in 3rd season. Among the fish petty vendors the difference in average per day profits is maximum (Rs. 59.65) in 1st season and minimum (Rs. 12.33) in 3rd season.

It could be inferred that literacy level influences the average per day profits of the fish vendors in general and highly influences the average per day profits of the fish petty vendors in particular.

Table -8.5.2

Average Profits of the Women Fish Vendors - Literacy Level

(Value in Rs. Per day)

Seasons	*Fish Vendors*											
	Street Vendors			*Small PettyVendors*			*Petty Vendors*			*Total*		
	Illiteracy	*Literacy*	*Total*	*Illiteracy*	*Literacy*	*Total*	*Illiteracy*	*Literacy*	*Total*	*Illiteracy*	*Literacy*	*Total*
1st April-31st July	70.54	92.50	74.93	70.87	96.85	76.50	123.23	182.88	140.13	87.07	130.43	97.19
1st Aug-30th Nov	67.81	82.08	70.67	63.09	78.54	66.43	121.65	162.59	133.25	82.98	113.57	90.12
1st Dec-31st March	68.58	96.25	74.12	72.02	86.31	75.12	122.02	134.35	125.52	86.41	108.60	91.58
Total period	68.98	90.33	73.25	68.66	87.23	72.68	122.28	159.94	132.95	85.48	117.55	92.96
n	48	12	60	47	13	60	43	17	60	138	42	180

Table -8.5.2(a)

Results of the Estimated Regression Equations (Profits Vs Literacy)

Fish Trade (i= 1 to 180 or n=180)

Season	*Dependent Variable*	*Constant*	*D_1*	*R^2*	*F*
1st April-31st July	Profit	87.07* (24.94)	43.35* (6.00)	0.168	35.999*
1st Aug-30th Nov	Profit	82.97* (31.24)	30.59* (5.56)	0.148	30.973*
1st Dec-31st March	Profit	86.40* (39.81)	22.18* (4.93)	0.121	24.388*
Total Period	Profit	85.47* (32.70)	32.06* (5.92)	0.165	35.124*

Table 8.5.2(b)

Results of the Estimated Regression Equations (Profits Vs Literacy)- Fish Street Vendors

(i= 1 to 60 or n =60)

Season	*Dependent Variable*	*Constant*	*D_1*	*R^2*	*F*
1st April-31st July	Profit	70.54* * (33.27)	21.95* (4.63)	0.270	21.459*
1st Aug-30th Nov	Profit	67.81* (59.84)	14.27* (5.63)	0.354	31.726*
1st Dec-31st March	Profit	68.58* (35.62)	27.66* (6.42)	0.416	41.299*
Total Period	Profit	68.97* (43.82)	21.35* (6.06)	0.388	36.820*

Note: Figures in the parentheses indicate Students' t - ratio.

* Indicates significance at 1 per cent level.

Table 8.5.2 (c)

Results of the Estimated Regression Equations (Profits Vs Literacy)- Fish Small Petty Vendors

(i= 1 to 60 or n =60)

Season	*Dependent Variable*	*Constant*	D_1	R^2	*F*
1st April-31st July	Profit	70.87* (40.81)	25.97* (6.96)	0.455	48.470*
1st Aug-30th Nov	Profit	63.08* (75.66)	15.45* (8.62)	0.562	74.435*
1st Dec-31st March	Profit	72.02* (56.98)	14.28* (5.26)	0.323	27.689*
Total Period	Profit	68.66* (59.93)	18.57* (7.45)	0.495	56.950*

Table 8.5.2(d)

Results of the Estimated Regression Equations (Profits Vs Literacy)- Fish Petty Vendors

(i= 1 to 60 or n =60)

Season	*Dependent Variable*	*Constant*	D_1	R^2	*F*
1st April-31st July	Profit	123.23* (17.90)	59.65* (4.61)	0.268	21.275*
1st Aug-30th Nov	Profit	121.65* (85.22)	40.93* (15.26)	0.801	233.025*
1st Dec-31st March	Profit	122.02* (137.82)	12.33* (7.41)	0.487	54.952*
Total Period	Profit	122.27* (41.78)	37.66* (6.85)	0.447	46.921*

Average Profits and Literacy – Total Women Vegetable Vendors

The Tables 8.5.3 presents the average per day profit of the Women vegetable vendors during the three seasons and for the f~ancial year according to the literacy level. It could be observed from the Table that the average per day profit of the literate women

Table-8.5.3

Average Profits of the Women Vegetable Vendors - Literacy Level

(Value in Rs. Per day)

Seasons	Vegetable Vendors											
	Street Vendors			Small Petty Vendors			Petty Vendors			Total		
	Illiteracy	Literacy	Total	Illiteracy	Literacy	Total	Illiteracy	Literacy	Total	Illiteracy	Literacy	Total
1st April-31st July	91.09	97.86	92.67	101.00	142.81	112.15	133.89	177.53	144.80	108.59	140.40	116.54
1st Aug-30th Nov	66.72	88.21	71.73	95.86	100.81	97.18	120.07	144.93	126.28	94.00	111.60	98.40
1st Dec-31st March	72.63	97.50	78.43	79.70	98.13	84.62	126.04	133.80	127.98	92.74	109.82	97.01
Total period	76.76	94.57	80.92	92.16	113.94	97.97	126.62	152.20	133.02	98.40	120.67	103.97
n	46	14	60	44	16	60	45	15	60	135	45	180

vegetable vendors is higher than the illiterate women vegetable vendors for all the three seasons as well for the whole year for all the categories of vendors namely vegetable street vendors, vegetable small petty vendors, and vegetable petty vendors

The results of the regression analysis presented in Tables from 8.5.3(a) to 8.5.3(d) reveal significant differences in profits derived by literate and illiterate women vegetable vendors. The coefficient of dummy variable indicates the difference between the profits of the literate and illiterate women vegetable vendors are statistically significant at 1% level in all seasons and for the total period for all the categories of vendors.

Among the Total Vegetable Vendors the difference in average per day profits is maximum (Rs. 31.81) in 1st season and minimum (Rs. 17.08) in 3rd season. Among the vegetable street vendors the difference in average per day profits is maximum (Rs. 24.87) in 3rd season and minimum (Rs. 6.77) in 1st season. Among the fish small petty vendors the difference in average per day profits is maximum (Rs. 41.81) in 1st season and minimum (Rs. 4.94) in 2nd season. Among the vegetable petty vendors the difference in average per day profits is maximum (Rs. 43.64) in 1st season and minimum (Rs. 7.75) in 3rd season.

Table -8.5.3(a)

Results of the Estimated Regression Equations (Profits Vs Literacy)- Vegetable Vendors

(i= 1 to 180 or n =180)

Season	*Dependent Variable*	*Constant*	D_1	R^2	*F*
1st April-31st July	Profit	108.58 (51.49) *	31.81 (7.54) *	0.242	56.917*
1st Aug-30th Nov	Profit	94.00 (41.51) *	17.60 (3.88) *	0.078	15.104*
1st Dec-31st March	Profit	92.74 (45.13) *	17.08 (4.15)*	0.088	17.280*
Total Period	Profit	98.40 * (49.48)	22.26 (5.59)*	0.150	31.341*

Note: Figures in the parentheses indicate Students' t - ratio.

* Indicates significance at 1 per cent level.

It could be inferred that literacy level influences the average per day profits of the vegetable vendors in general and highly influences the average per day profits of the vegetable small petty vendors and vegetable petty vendors in particular during 1st season.

Table 8.5.3(b)

Results of the Estimated Regression Equations (Profits Vs Literacy)- Vegetable Street Vendors

(i= 1 to 60 or n =60)

Season	*Dependent Variable*	*Constant*	D_1	R^2	*F*
1st April-31st July	Profit	91.08 (110.18)*	6.77 (3.95)*	0.212	15.641*
1st Aug-30th Nov	Profit	66.71 (59.22)*	21.49 (9.21)*	0.594	84.970*
1st Dec-31st March	Profit	72.63 (58.90)*	24.87 (9.74)*	0.621	94.924*
Total Period	Profit	76.76 (76.56)*	17.81 (8.58)*	0.559	73.636*

Note: Figures in the parentheses indicate Students' t - ratio.
* Indicates significance at 1 per cent level.

Table 8.5.3(c)

Results of the Estimated Regression Equations (Profits Vs Literacy)- Vegetable Small Petty Vendors (i= 1 to 60 or n =60)

Season	*Dependent Variable*	*Constant*	D_1	R^2	*F*
1st April-31st July	Profit	101.00* (52.63)	41.81 (11.25)*	0.686	126.592*
1st Aug-30th Nov	Profit	95.86 (257.529)*	4.949 (6.86)*	0.448	47.133*
1st Dec-31st March	Profit	79.70 (45.03)*	18.42 (5.37)*	0.332	28.890*
Total Period	Profit	92.15 (79.48)*	21.77 (9.70)*	0.619	94.08*

Note: Figures in the parentheses indicate Students' t - ratio.
* Indicates significance at 1 per cent level.

Table 8.5.3(d)

Results of the Estimated Regression Equations (Profits Vs Literacy)- Vegetable Petty Vendors (i= 1 to 60 or n =60)

Season	*Dependent Variable*	*Constant*	D_1	R^2	*F*
1st April-31st July	Profit	133.88 (107.24) *	43.64 (17.47)	0.840	305.519*
1st Aug-30th Nov	Profit	120.06 (36.45)*	24.86 (3.77) *	0.197	14.253*
1st Dec-31st March	Profit	126.04 (301.44) *	7.75 (9.27)	0.597	86.009*
Total Period	Profit	126.62 (94.81)*	25.57 (9.57)*	0..613	91.704*

Note: Figures in the parentheses indicate Students' t - ratio.

* Indicates significance at 1 per cent level.

Average Per Day Profit and Marital Status

As discussed in the earlier section, the marital status of the women vendor influences the reinvestment or the level of investment in the vending activity. There is a scope for existence of the deference in the profits with respect to the marital status. Based on the marital status all the women vendors are categorized as married vendors and unmarried vendors.

Average Profits and Marital Status–Total Women Vendors

The Tables 8.6.1 presents the average per day profit of the women vendors during the three seasons and for the financial year according to the marital status.

It could be observed from the Table that the average per day profit of the unmarried women vendors is higher than the married women vendors for all the three seasons as well for the whole year.

The results of the regression analysis presented in Table 8.6.1(a) reveal significant differences in profits derived by married and unmarried women vendors. The coefficient of dummy variable indicates the difference between the profits of the married and unmarried vendors are statistically significant at 1% level in all seasons and for the total period.

Table -8.6.1

Average Profits of the Women Vendors - Marital Status

(Value in Rs. Per day)

Seasons	Total		
	Unmarried	Married	Total
1st April-31st July	103.75	107.89	106.86
1st Aug-30th Nov	92.40	94.87	94.26
1st Dec-31st March	88.39	96.24	94.30
Total period	94.89	99.64	98.46
n	89	271	360

Table -8.6.1(a)

Results of the Estimated Regression Equations (Profits Vs Marital status)– Women Traders

(i= 1 to 360 or n=360)

Season	Dependent Variable	Constant	D_1	R^2	F
1st April-31st July	Profit	103.75 (25.35) *	4.13 (0.87) *	0.002	0.768*
1st Aug-30th Nov	Profit	92.40 * (28.17)	2.46 (0.65)	0.001	0.424*
1st Dec-31st March	Profit	88.39 (32.11) *	7.84 (2.47) *	0.017	6.112*
Total Period	Profit	94.88 (29.84) *	4.75 (1.29) *	0.005	1.681*

Note: Figures in the parentheses indicate Students' t - ratio.

* Indicates significance at 1 per cent level.

The difference in average per day profits is maximum (Rs. 7.84) in 3rd season and minimum (Rs. 2.46) in 2nd season with

Table -8.6.2

Average Profits of the Women Fish Vendors – Marital Status

Season	*Fish Vendors*											
	Street Vendors			*Small Petty vendors*			*Petty Vendors*			*Total*		
	Unmarried	*Married*	*Total*	*Unmarried*	*Married*	*Total*	*Unmarried*	*Married*	*Total*	*Unmarried*	*Married*	*Total*
1st April-31st July	65.93	77.67	74.93	64.38	80.91	76.50	121.94	146.75	140.13	84.87	101.42	97.19
1st Aug-30th Nov	63.14	72.96	70.67	61.06	68.39	66.43	120.13	138.02	133.25	82.24	92.82	90.12
1st Dec-31st March	63.00	77.50	74.12	66.13	78.39	75.12	121.50	126.98	125.52	84.43	94.04	91.58
Total period	64.07	76.04	73.25	63.88	75.89	72.68	121.19	137.23	132.95	83.87	96.08	92.96
n	14	46	60	16	44	60	16	44	60	46	134	180

respect to the literacy level. It could be inferred that unmarried women vendors able to reap higher profits during 3rd season.

Average Profits and Marital Status – Total Women Fish Vendors

The Tables 8.6.2 presents the average per day profit of the women fish vendors during the three seasons and for the financial year according to the marital status. It could be observed from the Table that the average per day profit of the married women fish vendors is higher than the unmarried women fish vendors for all the three seasons as well for the whole year for all the categories of vendors namely Fish street vendors, Fish small petty vendors, and Fish petty vendors.

Table -8.6.2(a)

Results of the Estimated Regression Equations (Profits Vs Marital Status) Fish Trade

(i= 1 to 180 or n=180)

Season	*Dependent Variable*	*Constant*	D_1	R^2	*F*
1st April-31st July	Profit	84.87* (12.97)	16.54 (2.18)	0.026	4.763*
1st Aug-30th Nov	Profit	82.23* (16.66)	10.58 (1.85)	0.019	3.421*
1st Dec-31st March	Profit	84.43* (21.32)	9.60 (2.09)	0.024	4.377*
Total Period	Profit	83.87* (17.15)	12.21 (2.15)	0.025	4.642*

Note: Figures in the parentheses indicate Students' t - ratio.

* Indicates significance at 1 per cent level.

The results of the regression analysis presented in Tables from 8.6.2(a) to 8.6.2(d) reveal that only in some cases, significant differences exists in profits derived by married and unmarried women fish vendors. The coefficient of dummy variable indicates the difference between the profits of the married and unmarried women fish vendors. In case of fish street vendors and fish small petty vendors for all the seasons and for the financial year, the differences are statistically significant at 1% level, where as in case of fish petty vendors they are significant for 2nd, 3rd and total year.

Among the total fish vendors the difference in average per day profits is maximum (Rs. 16.54) in 1st season and minimum (Rs. 9.60) in 3rd season. Among the fish street vendors the difference in average per day profits is maximum (Rs. 14.50) in 3rd season and minimum (Rs. 9.81) in 2nd season. Among the fish small petty vendors the difference in average per day profits is maximum (Rs. 16.53) in 1st season and minimum (Rs. 9.32) in 2nd season. Among the fish petty vendors the difference in average per day profits is maximum (Rs. 24.81) in 1st season and minimum (Rs.5. 47) in 3rd season.

It could be inferred that difference in average per day profit based on the marital status of the fish vendors in general is not very significant, but in case of fish street vendors and fish small petty vendors the differences are significant.

Table 8.6.2(b)

Results of the Estimated Regression Equations (Profits Vs Marital Status)- Fish Street Vendors

(i= 1 to 60 or n =60)

Season	*Dependent Variable*	*Constant*	D_1	R^2	*F*
1st April-31st July	Profit	65.92* (15.01)	11.74* (2.34)	0.086	5.484*
1st Aug-30th Nov	Profit	63.14* (26.83)	9.81* (3.65)	0.187	13.336*
1st Dec-31st March	Profit	63.00* (14.46)	14.50* (2.91)	0.128	8.493*
Total Period	Profit	64.07* (18.50)	11.97* (3.02)	0.136	9.166*

Note: Figures in the parentheses indicate Students' t - ratio.
* Indicates significance at 1 per cent level.

Table 8.6.2(c)

Results of the Estimated Regression Equations (Profits Vs Marital Status)- Fish Small Petty Vendors

(i= 1 to 60 or n =60)

Season	*Dependent Variable*	*Constant*	D_1	R^2	*F*
1st April-31st July	Profit	64.37* (17.99)	16.53* (3.95)	0.213	15.656*
1st Aug-30th Nov	Profit	61.06* (30.59)	7.32* (3.14)	0.145	9.873*
1st Dec-31st March	Profit	66.12* (29.48)	12.26* (4.68)	0.274	21.917*
Total Period	Profit	63.87* (26.48)	12.01* (4.26)	0.239	18.195*

Note: Figures in the parentheses indicate Students' t - ratio.

* Indicates significance at 1 per cent level.

Table 8.6.2(d)

Results of the Estimated Regression Equations (Profits Vs Marital Status)- Fish Petty Vendors

(i= 1 to 60 or n =60)

Season	*Dependent Variable*	*Constant*	D_1	R^2	*F*
1st April-31st July	Profit	121.93* (9.45)	24.81 (1.64)	0.045	2.715*
1st Aug-30th Nov	Profit	120.12* (24.81)	17.89* (3.16)	0.147	10.027*
1st Dec-31st March	Profit	121.50* (62.96)	5.47* (2.43)	0.092	5.909*
Total Period	Profit	121.18* (19.56)	16.04* (2.21)	0.078	4.915*

Note: Figures in the parentheses indicate Students' t - ratio.

* Indicates significance at 1 per cent level.

Average Profits and Marital Status– Total Women Vegetable Vendors

The Tables 8.6.3 presents the average per day profit of the women vegetable vendors during the three seasons and for the financial year according to the marital status. It could be observed from the Table that the average per day profit of the married women vegetable vendors is lower than the unmarried women vegetable vendors for 1st and 3rd seasons as well for the whole year, but in the 2nd season married women are earning more profits.

The results of the regression analysis presented in Tables from 8.6.3(a) to 8.6.3(d) reveal significant differences in profits derived by married and unmarried women vegetable vendors. The coefficient of dummy variable indicates the difference between the profits of the unmarried and married women vegetable vendors are statistically significant at 1% level in all seasons and for the total period for all the categories of vendors. The + ve sign of the coefficient of dummy variable indicates that during that seasons married women vegetable vendors are earning more and the –ve sign of the coefficient of dummy variable indicate that during that season unmarried vegetable vendors are earning more profits.

Among the Total Vegetable Vendors the difference in average per day profits is maximum (Rs. 31.81) in 1st season and minimum (Rs. 17.08) in 3rd season. Among the vegetable street vendors the difference in average per day profits is maximum (Rs. 24.87) in 3rd season and minimum (Rs. 6.77) in 1st season. Among the fish small petty vendors the difference in average per day profits is maximum (Rs. 41.81) in 1st season and minimum (Rs. 4.94) in 2nd season. Among the vegetable petty vendors the difference in average per day profits is maximum (Rs. 43.64) in 1st season and minimum (Rs. 7.75) in 3rd season.

It could be inferred that the average per day profits of the unmarried vegetable petty vendors are more than the married vegetable petty vendor. Marital status highly influences the average per day profits of the vegetable small petty vendors and vegetable petty vendors in particular during 1st season.

Table -8.6.3

Average Profits of the Women Vegetable Vendors – Marital Status

(Value in Rs. Per day)

Seasons	*Vegetable Vendors*											
	Street Vendors			*Small Petty Vendors*			*Petty Vendors*			*Total*		
	Unmarried	*Married*	*Total*	*Unmarried*	*Married*	*Total*	*Unmarried*	*Married*	*Total*	*Unmarried*	*Married*	*Total*
1st April-31st July	86.83	94.13	92.67	97.07	117.18	112.15	177.00	133.09	144.80	123.95	114.21	116.54
1st Aug-30th Nov	59.83	74.71	71.73	94.93	97.93	97.18	143.69	119.95	126.28	103.28	96.87	98.40
1st Dec-31st March	64.75	81.85	78.43	71.13	89.11	84.62	133.69	125.91	127.98	92.63	98.39	97.01
Total period	70.42	83.54	80.92	87.80	101.36	97.97	151.56	126.27	133.02	106.67	103.12	103.97
n	12	48	60	15	45	60	16	44	60	43	137	180

Table -8.6.3(a)

Results of the Estimated Regression Equations (Profits Vs Marital Status)- Vegetable Vendors

(i= 1 to 180 or n =180)

Season	*Dependent Variable*	*Constant*	D_1	R^2	*F*
1st April-31st July	Profit	123.95* (29.20)	-9.74* (-2.00)	0.022	4.009*
1st Aug-30th Nov	Profit	103.27* (24.84)	-6.41 (-1.34)	0.010	1.809*
1st Dec-31st March	Profit	92.62* (24.41)	5.75 (1.32)	0.010	1.753*
Total Period	Profit	106.67* (27.96)	-3.55 (0.84)	0.004	0.662*

Note: Figures in the parentheses indicate Students' t - ratio.
* Indicates significance at 1 per cent level.

Table 8.6.3(b)

Results of the Estimated Regression Equations (Profits Vs Marital Status)- Vegetable Street Vendors

(i= 1 to 60 or n =60)

Season	*Dependent Variable*	*Constant*	D_1	R^2	*F*
1st April-31st July	Profit	86.83* (53.92)	7.29* (4.05)	0.220	16.402*
1st Aug-30th Nov	Profit	59.83* (20.01)	14.87* (4.45)	0.255	19.802*
1st Dec-31st March	Profit	64.57* (19.23)	17.10* (4.54)	0.265	20.655*
Total Period	Profit	70.41* (27.91)	13.12* (4.65)	0.272	21.638*

Note: Figures in the parentheses indicate Students' t - ratio.
* Indicates significance at 1 per cent level.

Table 8.6.3(c)
Results of the Estimated Regression Equations (Profits Vs Marital Status)- Vegetable Small Petty Vendors

(i= 1 to 60 or n =60)

Season	*Dependent Variable*	*Constant*	D_1	R^2	*F*
1st April-31st July	Profit	97.06* (17.97)	20.1* (3.22)	0.152	10.406*
1st Aug-30th Nov	Profit	94.93* (120.52)	3.00* (3.29)	0.158	10.880*
1st Dec-31st March	Profit	71.13* (22.97)	17.97* (5.02)	0.304	25.292*
Total Period	Profit	87.80* (31.11)	13.55* (4.16)	0.230	17.305*

Note: Figures in the parentheses indicate Students' t - ratio.
* Indicates significance at 1 per cent level.

Table 8.6.3(d)
Results of the Estimated Regression Equations (Profits Vs Marital Status)- Vegetable Petty Vendors

(i= 1 to 60 or n =60)

Season	*Dependent Variable*	*Constant*	D_1	R^2	*F*
1st April-31st July	Profit	177.00* (100.55)	-43.90* (-21.36)	0.887	456.273*
1st Aug-30th Nov	Profit	143.68* (25.85)	-23.73* (-3.65)	0.187	13.377*
1st Dec-31st March	Profit	133.68* (197.99)	-7.77* (-9.86)	0.627	97.323*
Total Period	Profit	151.56* (68.74)	-25.29* (-9.82)	0.625	96.494*

Note: Figures in the parentheses indicate Students' t - ratio.
* Indicates significance at 1 per cent level.

Average Per Day Profit and Age of the Women Vendor

Based on the age of the women vender, all the women vendors are grouped into three namely young, middle and old age. Women vendors having ≤ 30 years of age are considered as young, women vendors in between 31-50 years are considered as middle aged and women having ≥ 51 years are considered as old aged.

Average Profits and Age Groups–Total Women Vendors

The Tables 8.7.1 presents the average per day profit of the women vendors during the three seasons and for the financial year according to the age group. It could be observed from the Table that the average per day profit of the women vendors are increasing as the age group increases during all the three seasons as well for the whole year. During the 1st season old age women vendors are getting highest profits (Rs. 128.75). During the 3rd season women street vendors are getting least profits (Rs. 84.42).

The results of the regression analysis presented in Table 8.7.1(a) reveal significant differences in profits derived by middle aged and old aged groups with the young age group. The coefficients of both dummy variables D1 and D2 indicate the difference between the profits of the middle age and old age vendors with that of young aged vendors. The coefficients are statistically significant at 1% level in all seasons and for the total period.

Average Profits and Age Groups–Total Women Fish Vendors

The Tables 8.7.2 presents the average per day profit of the women fish vendors during the three seasons and for the financial year according to the age groups. It could be observed from the Table that the average per day profit of the old age women fish vendors is higher than the young age women fish vendors for all the three seasons as well for the whole year for all the categories of vendors namely Fish street vendors, Fish small petty vendors, and Fish petty vendors.

The results of the regression analysis presented in Tables from 8.7.2(a) to 8.7.2(d) reveal significant differences exists in profits derived by young age vs middle aged and old aged women fish vendors. The coefficients of dummy variable indicate the difference between the profits of the young and middle aged vendors and young aged and old aged women fish vendors. In case of fish street vendors and fish small petty vendors for all the seasons and for the financial year, the differences are statistically significant at 1% level, where as in case of fish petty vendors both coefficients are significant for 2ndseason, and during the 1st and 3rd and total year only D2 is significant. This implies that, the difference in the profits earned by young and old age gish petty Vendors are statistically significant. .

Among the total fish vendors the difference in average per day profits is maximum (Rs. 41.47) in 1st season between young age and old age vendors and minimum (Rs. 12.40) in 3rd season between young age and middle age vendors. Among the Fish Street Vendors the difference in average per day profits is maximum (Rs. 33.70) in 3rd season between young age and old age vendors and minimum (Rs. 14.70) in 1st season between young age and middle age vendors.. Among the fish small petty vendors the difference in average per day profits is maximum (Rs. 24.88) in 1st season young age and old age vendors and minimum (Rs. 6.25) in 2nd season young age and middle age vendors. Among the fish petty vendors the difference in average per day profits is maximum (Rs. 55.23) in 1st season young age and old age vendors and minimum (Rs.5. 59) in 3rd season young age and middle age vendors.

It could be inferred that difference in average per day profit based on the age groups reveal that during 1st season old age fish vendors are getting more profits and during the 3rd season middle age fish vendors are getting more profits.

Table -8.7.1
Average Profits of the Women Vendors – Age-groups

(Value in Rs. Per day)

Seasons	*Total*			
	≤ *30*	*31-50*	≥*51*	*Total*
1st April-31st July	93.06	106.57	128.75	106.86
1st Aug-30th Nov	85.60	94.38	107.33	94.26
1st Dec-31st March	84.42	96.77	104.07	94.30
Total period	87.72	99.21	113.37	98.46
n	117	167	76	360

Table -8.7.1 (a)
Results of the Estimated Regression Equations (Profits Vs Age Groups)– Women Traders

(i= 1 to 360 or n=360)

Season	*Dependent Variable*	*Constant*	D_1	D_2	R^2	*F*
1st April-31st July	Profit	93.06* (27.57)	13.51* (3.07)	35.69* (6.63)	0.110	22.027*
1st Aug-30th Nov	Profit	85.59* (30.85)	8.77* (2.42)	21.73* (4.91)	0.063	12.085*
1st Dec-31st March	Profit	84.41* (36.30)	12.35* (4.07)	19.64* (5.30)	0.080	15.567*
Total Period	Profit	87.71* (33.11)	11.49* (3.32)	25.65* (6.07)	0.094	18.565*

Note: Figures in the parentheses indicate Students' t - ratio.

* Indicates significance at 1 per cent level.

Table -8.7.2
Average Profits of the Women Fish Vendors – Age-groups

(Value in Rs. Per day)

Seasons	Fish Vendors															
	Street Vendors				Small Petty Vendors				Petty Vendors				Total			
	≤ 30	31-50	≥51	Total	≤ 30	31-50	≥51	Total	≤ 30	31-50	≥51	Total	≤ 30	31-50	≥51	Total
1st April-31st July	63.10	77.18	89.42	74.93	62.48	82.20	87.36	76.50	120.65	130.65	175.88	140.13	81.75	95.01	122.93	97.19
1st Aug-30th Nov	59.60	74.64	79.83	70.67	60.90	67.16	73.43	66.43	118.05	137.57	145.29	133.25	79.21	91.22	103.63	90.12
1st Dec-31st March	59.30	76.61	93.00	74.12	64.00	82.08	79.36	75.12	120.45	126.04	130.76	125.52	80.97	93.37	103.49	91.58
Total period	60.70	76.14	87.42	73.25	62.52	77.08	80.07	72.68	119.75	131.39	150.59	132.95	80.69	93.17	110.00	92.96
n	20	28	12	60	21	25	14	60	20	23	17	60	61	76	43	180

Table -8.7.2(a)
Results of the Estimated Regression Equations (Profits Vs Age Groups)—Fish Trade

(i= 1 to 180 or n=180)

Season	*Dependent Variable*	*Constant*	D_1	D_2	R^2	*F*
1st April-31st July	Profit	81.75 (15.10)*	13.25 (1.82)	41.17 (4.89)*	0.121	12.134*
1st Aug-30th Nov	Profit	79.21 (18.97)*	12.01 (2.14)	24.41 (3.76)*	0.075	7.148*
1st Dec-31st March	Profit	80.96 (24.45)*	12.40 (2.79)**	22.52 (4.37)*	0.100	9.879*
Total Period	Profit	80.68 (19.80)*	12.48 (2.28)	29.31 (4.62)*	0.108	10.701*

Note: Figures in the parentheses indicate Students' t - ratio.
* Indicates significance at 1 per cent level.

Table 8.7.2(b)
Results of the Estimated Regression Equations (Profits Vs Age Groups)- Fish Street Vendors

(i= 1 to 60 or n =60)

Season	*Dependent Variable*	*Constant*	D_1	D_2	R^2	*F*
1st April-31st July	Profit	63.10 (1971)*	14.07 (3.35)*	26.31 (5.03)*	0.381	13.319*
1st Aug-30th Nov	Profit	59.60 (46.86)*	15.04 (9.61)*	20.23 (10.36)*	0.705	68.244*
1st Dec-31st March	Profit	59.30 (21.31)*	17.30 (4.75)*	33.70 (7.41)*	0.501	28.560*
Total Period	Profit	60.70 (27.68)*	15.44 (5.37)*	26.71 (7.46)*	0.514	30.123*

Note: Figures in the parentheses indicate Students' t - ratio.
* Indicates significance at 1 per cent level.

Table 8.7.2(c)
Results of the Estimated Regression Equations (Profits Vs Age Groups)- Fish Small Petty Vendors

(i= 1 to 60 or n =60)

Season	*Dependent Variable*	*Constant*	D_1	D_2	R^2	*F*
1st April-31st July	Profit	62.47 (23.44) *	19.72 (5.45) *	24.88 (5.90) *	0.437	22.108*
1st Aug-30th Nov	Profit	60.90 (38.55) *	6.25 (2.91) *	12.52 (5.01) *	0.310	12.788*
1st Dec-31st March	Profit	64.00 (45.45) *	18.08 (9.46) *	15.35 (6.89) *	0.631	48.749*
Total Period	Profit	62.52 (35.68)*	14.55 (6.12) *	17.54 (6.33)*	0.482	26.491*

Note: Figures in the parentheses indicate Students' t - ratio.
* Indicates significance at 1 per cent level.

Table 8.7.2(d)
Results of the Estimated Regression Equations (Profits Vs Age Groups)- Fish Petty Vendors

(i= 1 to 60 or n =60)

Season	*Dependent Variable*	*Constant*	D_1	D_2	R^2	*F*
1st April-31st July	Profit	120.65 (11.29)*	10.00 (0.68)	55.23 (3.50) *	0.194	6.873*
1st Aug-30th Nov	Profit	118.05 (29.72)*	19.51 (3.59) *	27.24 (4.64)*	0.295	11.909*
1st Dec-31st March	Profit	120.45 (76.59)*	5.59 (2.60)	10.31 (4.44)*	0.260	9.989*
Total Period	Profit	119.75 (23.41)*	11.64 (1.66)	30.83 (4.08)*	0.228	8.441*

Note: Figures in the parentheses indicate Students' t - ratio.
* Indicates significance at 1 per cent level.

Average Profits and Age Groups – Total Women Vegetable Vendors

The Tables 8.7.3 presents the average per day profit of the women vegetable vendors during the three seasons and for the financial year according to the age groups. It could be observed from the Table that the average per day profit of the old age women vegetable vendors is higher than the young age women vegetable vendors for all the three seasons as well for the whole year for all the categories of vendors namely vegetable street vendors, vegetable small petty vendors, and vegetable petty vendors.

The results of the regression analysis presented in Tables from 8.7.3(a) to 8.7.3(d) reveal significant differences exists in profits derived by young age Vs middle aged and old aged women vegetable vendors. The coefficients of dummy variable indicate the difference between the profits of the young and middle aged vendors and young aged and old aged women vegetable vendors. In case of vegetable street vendors and vegetable small petty vendors for all the seasons and for the financial year, the differences are statistically significant at 1% level, where as in case of vegetable petty vendors both coefficients are significant for 1st and 3rd and total year and for the 2nd season only D2 is significant. This implies that, the difference in the profits earned by young and old age vegetable petty vendors are statistically significant..

Among the total vegetable vendors the difference in average per day profits is maximum (Rs. 30.95) in 1st season between young age and old age vendors and minimum (Rs. 4.45) in 2nd season between young age and middle age vendors. Among the vegetable street vendors the difference in average per day profits is maximum (Rs. 20.68) in 3rd season between young age and old age vendors and minimum (Rs. 5.25) in 1st season between young age and old age vendors. Among the vegetable small petty vendors the difference in average per day profits is maximum (Rs. 43.54) in 1st season young age and old age vendors and minimum (Rs. 4.17) in 2nd season young age and middle age vendors. Among the vegetable petty vendors the difference in average per day profits is maximum (Rs. 39.76) in 1st season young age and old age vendors and minimum (Rs.3.92) in 3rd season young age and middle age vendors.

Table -8.7.3

Average Profits of the Women Vegetable Vendors – Age-wise

(Value in Rs. Per day)

Seasons	Vegetable Vendors															
	Street Vendors				Small Petty Vendors				Petty Vendors				Total			
	≤ 30	31-50	≥51	Total	≤ 30	31-50	≥51	Total	≤ 30	31-50	≥51	Total	≤ 30	31-50	≥51	Total
1st April-31st July	87.13	95.35	92.40	92.67	95.05	114.10	138.60	112.15	128.62	146.08	168.38	144.80	105.38	116.23	136.33	116.54
1st Aug-30th Nov	59.00	75.59	79.00	71.73	94.05	98.23	99.90	97.18	116.76	123.58	147.08	126.28	92.55	97.01	112.15	98.40
1st Dec-31st March	64.81	82.76	85.50	78.43	67.63	93.87	88.20	84.62	124.57	128.50	132.46	127.98	88.18	99.62	104.82	97.01
Total period	70.25	84.56	85.60	80.92	85.58	102.06	108.80	97.97	123.38	132.62	149.38	133.02	95.38	104.25	117.76	103.97
n	16	34	10	60	19	31	10	60	21	26	13	60	56	91	33	180

It could be inferred that difference in average per day profit based on the age groups reveal that during 1st season old age small petty vendors are getting more profits.

Average Per Day Profit and Experience of the Women Vendor

Based on the experience of the of the women vendor, all the women vendors are grouped into three namely categories. Women vendors having ≤ 5 years of experience, women vendors in between 6-10 years experience and women having ≥ 10 years of experience.

Average Profits and Experience – Total Women Vendors

The Table 8.8.1 presents the average per day profit of the women vendors during the three seasons and for the financial year according to the experience group. It could be observed from the Table that the average per day profit of the women vendors are increasing as the experience increases during all the three seasons as well for the whole year. During the 1st season, ≥ 10 years of experienced women vendors are getting highest profits (Rs. 143.17). During the 2nd and 3rd seasons women having ≤ 5 years of experience are getting least profits (Rs. 68.93 or Rs.68.23).

Table -8.7.3(a)

Results of the Estimated Regression Equations (Profits Vs Age Groups) Vegetable Trade

(i= 1 to 180 or n=180)

Season	*Dependent Variable*	*Constant*	D_1	D_2	R^2	*F*
1st April-31st July	Profit	105.37* (30.15)	10.85* (2.44)	30.95* (5.39)	0.141	14.559*
1st Aug-30th Nov	Profit	92.55* (26.02)	4.45 (0.98)	19.59* (3.35)	0.062	5.882*
1st Dec-31st March	Profit	88.17* (27.18)	11.43* (2.77)	16.64* (3.12)	0.063	5.938*
Total Period	Profit	95.37** (29.82)	8.87 (2.18)	22.38* (4.26)	0.093	9.096*

Note: Figures in the parentheses indicate Students' t - ratio.

* Indicates significance at 1 per cent level.

Table 8.7.3(b)

Results of the Estimated Regression Equations (Profits Vs Age Groups)- Vegetable Street Vendors (i= 1 to 60 or n =60)

Season	*Dependent Variable*	*Constant*	D_1	D_2	R^2	*F*
1st April-31st July	Profit	87.12* (66.23)	8.22* (5.15)	5.25* (2.48)	0.318	13.319*
1st Aug-30th Nov	Profit	59.00* (25.93)	16.58* (6.01)	20.00* (5.45)	0.435	21912*
1st Dec-31st March	Profit	64.81* (24.11)	17.95* (5.50)	20.68* (4.77)	0.384	17.759*
Total Period	Profit	70.25* (35.37)	14.30* (5.94)	15.35* (4.79)	0.409	19.742*

Note: Figures in the parentheses indicate Students' t - ratio.

* Indicates significance at 1 per cent level.

Table 8.7.3(c)

Results of the Estimated Regression Equations (Profits Vs Age Groups)- Vegetable Small Petty Vendors

(i= 1 to 60 or n =60)

Season	*Dependent Variable*	*Constant*	D_1	D_2	R^2	*F*
1st April-31st July	Profit	95.05* (23.82)	19.04* (3.75)	43.54* (6.40)	0.424	20.936*
1st Aug-30th Nov	Profit	94.05* (166.09)	4.17* (5.80)	5.84* (6.06)	0.458	24.105*
1st Dec-31st March	Profit	67.63* (36.54)	26.23** (11.16)	20.56* (6.52)	0.690	63.497*
Total Period	Profit	85.57* (42.52)	16.48* (6.45)	23.22* (6.77)	0.512	29.954*

Note: Figures in the parentheses indicate Students' t - ratio.

* Indicates significance at 1 per cent level.

Table 8.7.3(d)
Results of the Estimated Regression Equations (Profits Vs Age Groups)- Vegetable Petty Vendors

(i= 1 to 60 or n =60)

Season	*Dependent Variable*	*Constant*	D_1	D_2	R^2	*F*
1st April-31st July	Profit	128.61* (39.44)	17.45* (3.98)	39.76* (7.54)	0.501	28.603*
1st Aug-30th Nov	Profit	116.76* (24.33)	6.81 (1.05)	30.31* (3.90)	0.219	7.981*
1st Dec-31st March	Profit	124.57* (172.96)	3.92* (4.05)	7.89* (6.77)	0.452	23.507*
Total Period	Profit	123.38* (52.63)	9.23* (2.93)	26.00* (6.85)	0.453	23.555*

Note: Figures in the parentheses indicate Students' t - ratio.
* Indicates significance at 1 per cent level.

The results of the regression analysis presented in Table 8.8.1(a) reveal significant differences in profits derived by 6-10 years experienced and ≥ 10 years of experienced groups with the ≤ 5 years experienced group. The coefficients of both dummy variables D1 and D2 indicate the difference between the profits of these three groups. The coefficients are statistically significant at 1% level in all seasons and for the total period except the coefficient of D1 in 1st season.

Average Profits and Experience – Total Women Fish Vendors

The Tables 8.8.2 presents the average per day profit of the Women Fish Vendors during the three seasons and for the financial year according to the experience groups. It could be observed from the Table that the average per day profit of the ≥ 10 years experienced women fish vendors is higher than the ≤ 5 years experienced women fish vendors for all the three seasons as well for the whole year for all the categories of vendors namely Fish street vendors, Fish small petty vendors, and Fish petty vendors.

The results of the regression analysis presented in Tables from 8.8.2(a) to 8.8.2(d) reveal significant differences exists in profits derived by the ≤ 5 years experience Vs 6-10 years and ≥ 10 years experienced women fish vendors. The coefficients of dummy variable indicate the difference between the profits of the ≤ 5 years experience Vs 6-10 years and ≥10 years experienced women fish vendors. In case of Fish street Vendors and Fish Small Petty Vendors for all the seasons and for the financial year, the differences are statistically significant at 1% level, where as in case of Fish Petty Vendors both coefficients are significant for 2nd season, and during the 1st and 3rd and total year only D2 is significant. This implies that, the difference in the profits earned by young and old age Fish Petty Vendors are statistically significant. .

Table -8.8.1

Average Profits of the Women Vendors – Experience

(Value in Rs. Per day)

Seasons	*Total*			
	≤ 5	*6-10*	*≥10*	*Total*
1st April-31st July	89.78	101.24	122.58	106.86
1st Aug-30th Nov	74.20	94.11	102.09	94.26
1st Dec-31st March	74.87	94.01	102.12	94.30
Total period	79.56	96.44	108.95	98.46
n	45	196	119	360

In case of Total Fish Vendors the differences between the averages per day profits with respect to experience during various seasons are not at all significant. In case of Fish Street Vendors the difference in average per day profits between different experience groups are statistically significant with respect to all the seasons. In case of Fish Small Petty vendors the difference between the 1st and 3rd groups are significant.

Table -8.8.1(a)
Results of the Estimated Regression Equations
(Profits Vs Experience)– Women Traders

(i= 1 to 360 or n=360)

Season	*Dependent Variable*	*Constant*	D_1	D_2	R^2	*F*
1st April-31st July	Profit	89.77* (16.32)	11.46 (1.88)	32.80* (5.08)	0.091	17.901
1st Aug-30th Nov	Profit	74.20* (16.68)	19.90* (4.03)	27.89* (5.34)	0.074	14.276
1st Dec-31st March	Profit	74.86* (20.17)	19.14* (4.65)	27.25* (6.25)	0.099	19.594
Total Period	Profit	79.55* (18.60)	16.88* (3.56)	29.39* (5.85)	0.093	18.223

Note: Figures in the parentheses indicate Students' t - ratio.

* Indicates significance at 1 per cent level.

Average Profits and Experience – Total Women Vegetable Vendors

The Tables 8.8.3 presents the average per day profit of the women vegetable vendors during the three seasons and for the financial year according to the experience. It could be observed from the Table that the average per day profit of the 3rd group (more than 10 years) women vegetable vendors is higher than the other two groups. It could be observed from the Table that the average per day profit of the ≥ 10 years experienced women fish vendors is higher than the ≤ 5 years experienced women vegetable vendors for all the three seasons as well for the whole year for all the categories of vendors namely vegetable street vendors, vegetable small petty vendors, and vegetable petty vendors.

The results of the regression analysis presented in Tables from 8.8.3(a) to 8.8.3(d) reveal significant differences exists in profits derived by the ≤ 5 years experience Vs 6-10 years and ≥ 10 years experienced women fish vendors. The coefficients of dummy variable indicate the difference between the profits of the ≤5 years experience Vs 6-10 years and ≥ 10 years experienced women fish

Table -8.8.2
Average Profits of the Women Fish Vendors – Experience

(Value in Rs. Per day)

Seasons	Fish Vendors															
	Street Vendors				Small Petty Vendors				Petty Vendors				Total			
	≤ 5	6-10	≥10	Total	≤ 5	6-10	≥10	Total	≤ 5	6-10	≥10	Total	≤ 5	6-10	≥10	Total
1st April-31st July	55.40	69.53	86.70	74.93	53.00	63.96	87.42	76.50	120.00	124.14	186.19	140.13	89.53	89.17	109.14	97.19
1st Aug-30th Nov	50.20	67.81	79.09	70.67	52.00	61.56	71.00	66.43	114.50	123.89	163.69	133.25	84.73	87.84	94.18	90.12
1st Dec-31st March	50.20	67.69	88.26	74.12	55.50	65.60	83.52	75.12	120.00	122.56	134.94	125.52	88.13	88.37	96.46	91.58
Total period	51.80	68.38	84.70	73.25	53.50	63.72	80.64	72.68	118.13	123.50	161.63	132.95	87.40	88.46	99.93	92.96
n	5	32	23	60	2	25	33	60	8	36	16	60	15	93	72	180

vendors. The differences are significant with respect to vegetable street vendors and vegetable small petty vendors for all the seasons.

Table -8.8.2(a)

Results of the Estimated Regression Equations (Profits Vs Experience)

Fish Trade (i= 1 to 180 or n=180)

Season	*Dependent Variable*	*Constant*	D_1	D_2	R^2	*F*
1st April-31st July	Profit	89.53* (7.88)	-0.36 (-0.03)	19.60 (1.57)	0.084	4.426*
1st Aug-30th Nov	Profit	84.73* (9.73)	3.10 (0.33)	9.44 (0.98)	0.010	0.926
1st Dec-31st March	Profit	88.13* (12.65)	0.23 (0.03)	8.32 (1.08)	0.022	1.961
Total Period	Profit	87.40* (10.19)	1.06 (0.11)	12.53 (1.33)	0.029	2.651*

Note: Figures in the parentheses indicate Students' t - ratio.
 * Indicates significance at 1 per cent level.

Table -8.8.2(b)

Results of the Estimated Regression Equations (Profits Vs Experience)- Fish Street Vendors

(i= 1 to 60 or n =60)

Season	*Dependent Variable*	*Constant*	D_1	D_2	R^2	*F*
1st April-31st July	Profit	55.40* (8.87)	14.13* (2.10)	31.29* (4.54)	0.351	15.444*
1st Aug-30th Nov	Profit	50.20* (21.57)	17.61* (7.03)	28.88* (11.25)	0.721	73.59*
1st Dec-31st March	Profit	50.20* (8.99)	17.48* (2.91)	38.06* (6.17)	0.497	28.179*
Total Period	Profit	51.80* (12.12)	16.57* (3.60)	32.89* (6.98)	0.539	33.296*

Note: Figures in the parentheses indicate Students' t - ratio.
 * Indicates significance at 1 per cent level.

Table -8.8.2(c)
Results of the Estimated Regression Equations (Profits Vs Experience)- Fish Small Petty Vendors

(i= 1 to 60 or n =60)

Season	*Dependent Variable*	*Constant*	D_1	D_2	R^2	*F*
1st April-31st July	Profit	53.00* (7.23)	10.96 (1.44)	34.42* (4.56)	0.580	41.811*
1st Aug-30th Nov	Profit	52.00* (10.83)	9.56 (1.91)	19.00* (3.84)	0.393	18.419*
1st Dec-31st March	Profit	55.50* (18.10)	10.10* (3.17)	28.01* (8.87)	0.834	142.706*
Total Period	Profit	53.50* (12.02)	10.22* (2.21)	27.13* (5.93)	0.682	61.008*

Note: Figures in the parentheses indicate Students' t - ratio.
* Indicates significance at 1 per cent level.

Table -8.8.2(d)
Results of the Estimated Regression Equations (Profits Vs Experience)- Fish Petty Vendors

(i= 1 to 60 or n =60)

Season	*Dependent Variable*	*Constant*	D_1	D_2	R^2	*F*
1st April-31st July	Profit	120.00* (7.55)	4.13 (0.23)	66.18* (3.40)	0.287	11.482*
1st Aug-30th Nov	Profit	114.50* (35.63)	9.38* (2.64)	49.18* (12.49)	0.815	125.828*
1st Dec-31st March	Profit	120.00* (59.93)	2.55 (1.15)	14.93* (6.09)	0.520	30.860*
Total Period	Profit	118.12** (17.61)	5.37 (0.72)	43.50* (5.29)	0.469	25.187*

Note: Figures in the parentheses indicate Students' t - ratio.
* Indicates significance at 1 per cent level.

Table – 8.8.3

Average Profits of the Women Vegetable Vendors – Experience

(Value in Rs. Per day)

Seasons	Vegetable Vendors															
	Street Vendors				Small Petty Vendors				Petty Vendors				Total			
	≤ 5	6-10	≥10	Total	≤ 5	6-10	≥10	Total	≤ 5	6-10	≥10	Total	≤ 5	6-10	≥10	Total
1st April-31st July	87.09	95.60	98.43	92.67	90.00	100.50	133.17	112.15	122.00	133.34	175.12	144.80	89.90	112.15	143.17	116.54
1st Aug-30th Nov	59.83	76.13	92.00	71.73	90.00	96.28	100.00	97.18	121.00	119.78	142.59	126.28	68.93	99.77	114.21	98.40
1st Dec-31st March	65.04	84.10	98.14	78.43	62.00	78.69	97.78	84.62	120.50	126.02	133.59	127.98	68.23	99.11	110.79	97.01
Total period	70.61	85.27	96.14	80.92	80.60	91.78	110.35	97.97	121.00	126.34	150.53	133.02	75.63	103.64	122.77	103.97
n	23	30	7	60	5	32	23	60	2	41	17	60	30	103	47	180

Table – 8.8.3(a)

Results of the Estimated Regression Equations (Profits Vs Experience) Vegetable Trade

(i= 1 to 180 or n=180)

Season	*Dependent Variable*	*Constant*	D_1	D_2	R^2	*F*
1st April-31st July	Profit	89.90 * (22.55)	22.24 (4.91)	53.27 * (10.44)	0.402	59.372*
1st Aug-30th Nov	Profit	68.93 * (16.24)	30.83 (6.39)*	45.27 (8.33) *	0.284	35.149*
1st Dec-31st March	Profit	68.23 (17.91) *	30.87 (7.13)	42.55 (8.72) *	0.307	39.293*
Total Period	Profit	75.63 (20.67) *	28.00 (6.73)	47.13 (10.06) *	0.364	50.691*

Note: Figures in the parentheses indicate Students' t - ratio.
* Indicates significance at 1 per cent level.

Table 8.8.3(b)

Results of the Estimated Regression Equations (Profits Vs Experience)- Vegetable Street Vendors

(i= 1 to 60 or n =60)

Season	*Dependent Variable*	*Constant*	D_1	D_2	R^2	*F*
1st April-31st July	Profit	87.08 (94.69) *	8.51 (6.96) *	11.34 (5.95) *	0.521	31.015*
1st Aug-30th Nov	Profit	59.82 (53.67) *	16.30 (11.00) *	32.17 (13.94) *	0.805	117.532*
1st Dec-31st March	Profit	65.04 (43.82) *	19.05 (9.65) *	33.09 (10.77) *	0.730	77.021*
Total Period	Profit	70.60 (67.08) *	14.65 (10.47) *	25.53 (11.71) *	0.761	90.951*

Note: Figures in the parentheses indicate Students' t - ratio.
* Indicates significance at 1 per cent level.

Table 8.8.3(c)

Results of the Estimated Regression Equations (Profits Vs Experience)- Vegetable Small Petty Vendors

(i= 1 to 60 or n =60)

Season	*Dependent Variable*	*Constant*	D_1	D_2	R^2	*F*
1st April-31st July	Profit	90.00 (13.35)*	10.50 (1.44)*	43.17 (5.80)*	0.552	37.332*
1st Aug-30th Nov	Profit	90.00 (115.02)*	6.28 (7.46)*	10.00 (11.58)*	0.718	76.207*
1st Dec-31st March	Profit	62.00 (15.95)*	16.68 (3.99)*	35.78 (8.34)*	0.640	50.776*
Total Period	Profit	80.60 (26.00)*	11.18 (3.35)*	29.74 (8.69)*	0.685	65.143*

Note: Figures in the parentheses indicate Students' t - ratio.
* Indicates significance at 1 per cent level.

Table 8.8.3(d)

Results of the Estimated Regression Equations (Profits Vs Experience)- Vegetable Petty Vendors

(i= 1 to 60 or n =60)

Season	*Dependent Variable*	*Constant*	D_1	D_2	R^2	*F*
1st April-31st July	Profit	122.00 (22.18)*	11.34 (2.01) *	53.11 (9.13) *	0.865	182.194*
1st Aug-30th Nov	Profit	121.00 (7.59)*	-1.22 (-0.07)	21.56 (1.28)	0.179	6.210*
1st Dec-31st March	Profit	120.50 (70.86)*	5.52 (3.17)*	13.08 (7.28) *	0.709	69.469*
Total Period	Profit	121.00 (18.87) *	5.34 (0.81)	29.52 (4.35) *	0.610	44.583*

Note: Figures in the parentheses indicate Students' t - ratio.
* Indicates significance at 1 per cent level.

III

This Section presents the results of the multiple regression with the selected five explanatory variables. The analysis was carried out both at aggregate level and disaggregates level. Separate regression functions were estimated for the total women vendors, total fish vendors, total vegetable vendors, and also for each trade for all the three categories of vendors. The same exercise is done for all the three seasons as well as for the total period.

Multiple Regressions

Multiple regression analysis is used to identify the determinants of the profits earned by women traders by employing the following function namely,

Profits = ¦ (Literacy Level, Marital Status, Age, Experience, Working Capital)

Measurement of the variables and the expected signs of the coefficients

$$P = a + b_1 LD + b_2 MSD + b_3 AD_1 + b_4 AD_2 + b_5 ED_1 + b_6 ED_2 + b_7 WC + \epsilon \quad \text{— (2)}$$

where

LD = literacy level represented by 1 if literate, and '0' if illiterate

MSD = Marital status represented by 1 if married, and '0' if unmarried

AD1 = Age dummy represented by 1 for all those women who possess more than 30 years and less than 50 years of age, and '0' otherwise

AD2 = Age dummy represented by 1 for the age group >50 years, and '0' otherwise

ED1 = Experience dummy represented by 1 for all those who have more than 5 years but less than 10 years of experience, and '0' otherwise

ED2 = Experience dummy represented by 1 for the group >10 years of experience, and '0' otherwise

WC = Working Capital per day

Measurement of the variables and the expected signs of the coefficients

Variables considered in the profit analysis are examined below:

Profits: The profit (Rs.) from the trade is defined as the difference between total revenue and total expenses. Profit per day is considered for the analysis. This is taken as the dependent variable.

Working Capital: The 'amount of working capital' (Rs.) spent by the vendor is considered as explanatory variable, which is the first important factor determining the profit. The expected sign of the coefficient of the variable is positive. This implies that an increase in the amount of working capital increases the profits and vice versa.

Literacy: The literacy level of the woman vendor is considered as explanatory variable. Dummy variable is employed in the equation to represent this variable. The variable takes the value zero (0) for the illiterate woman vendor and one (1) for the literate woman vendor. The assumption is literacy enhances the vendor perceptions hence positive association with the profits.

Age: Another variable considered as explanatory variable is 'age of the woman vender'. It was categorized into three groups. Up to 30 years is considered as 'young age', in between 31-50 years as 'middle age' and above 50 as 'above middle age'. It is expected to be negatively correlated with the dependent variable as the young can work hard and are more devoted than the middle aged or above middle aged who have to bear household responsibilities and also for health limitations that influences negatively the level of profits of any female vendor. Two dummy variables were used to represent these three categories.

Marital Status: Marital status of the woman vendor is considered as another explanatory variable. It is represented by a dummy variable, for which value zero (0) is given for the married woman vendor and one (1) for the unmarried woman vendor. It is expected that marital status influences the profits because the earnings of the married women are necessary for the family which inturn reflects in the profits.

Experience: The experience of the woman vendor in that particular trade is also used as one explanatory variable. This variable is divided into three categories. The first category is less than 5 years (<5), in between 5 and 10 years as second category, and more than 10 years (>10) as the third category. Two dummy variables were used to represent this variable.

a) Women Vendors

The results of the estimated regression function for the total women vendors are presented in Table 8.9. The function was estimated for the three seasons and for the financial year as well.

For the financial year, the R-bar square value is 0.844, which can be treated as good fit. The coefficients of variables marital status, AD1, and ED1, and working capital are statistically significant in determining the profits.

The regression results revel that unmarried women are getting less profit compared to the married women by Rs 4.37 per day. Those women vendors who have the above 5 years and below 10 years experience also getting higher profits than others. The middle aged women vendors are getting higher profits than the others. The working capital variable is significant with the coefficient value 0.56, indicates that with the presence of the other variables also it increases the profits by 56 percent. In detail, if the working capital increases by One rupee, it yields an increase in the profits by 56 paise.

Form the 1st season regression equation; even though the R bar square value is 0.73, except working capital and ED1 dummy other variables are statistically not significant. This implies that during the 1st April -31st July the profits are influenced by working capital and experience. The other variables are not at all influencing the profits.

The results of the 2nd season regression equation show that marital status, experience and working capital are the significant variables influencing the profits of the women vendors. Along with marital status and experience working capital influences the profits of the women vendors during 1st August – 30th November. The coefficient of working capital 0.45 implies that a one rupee increase in the working capital results in 45 paise per day increase in profits. This profit will be increased if the woman is unmarried and experienced in between 6-10 years of conducting this vending.

The results of the 3rd season regression equation reveal that only working capital is significant variables influencing the profits of the women vendors during 1st December – 31st March. The coefficient of working capital 0.30 implies that a one rupee increase in the working capital results in 30 paise per day increase in profits.

b) Women Fish Vendors

The results of the estimated regression function for the women fish vendors are presented in Table 8.10.

The equation estimated for the financial year revel that the R-bar square value is 0.838, which can be treated as good fit. The coefficients of variables, literacy, AD1, ED1, ED2, and working capital are statistically significant in determining the profits. The sign of the literacy dummy is negative that literate women are getting higher profit. Those women vendors who have the above 5 years experience also getting lower profits.

Form the 1st season regression equation; the R bar square value is 0.73. The coefficients of variables, working capital, ED1 dummy and literacy are statistically significant in determining the profits of the women vendors. This implies that during the 1st April -31st July the profits are influenced by working capital, literacy and experience.

The results of the 2nd season regression equation show that experience and working capital are the significant variables influencing the profits of the women vendors. Along with experience working capital influences the profits of the women vendors during 1st August – 30th November. The coefficient of working capital 0.48 implies that a one rupee increase in the working capital results in 48 paise per day increase in profits.

The results of the 3rd season regression equation reveal that the coefficients of literacy, AD_2, ED_2, and working capital are significant variables in determining the profits of the women vendors during 1st December – 31st March. The coefficient of working capital is 0.19 implies that keeping the other things constant, a one rupee increase in the working capital results in 19 paise per day increase in profits of the fish vendors.

c) Women Fish Street Vendors

The results of the estimated regression function for the women fish street vendors are presented in Table 8.11. R-bar square value is 0.728, which can be treated as good fit. The coefficients of variables ED1, and working capital are statistically significant in determining the profits. The sign of the ED1 is positive implies that those women vendors who have the above 5 years and less than 10 years experience are getting higher profits by Rs. 8.67 per day keeping other things constant. It could be observed from the other equations that except working capital no other variable is significant during 3rd seasons. In the 1st season even the working capital is also not significant. During the 2nd season both age dummies and experience dummies are statistically significant. All are coefficients have positive signs implies that higher the age group and higher the experience profits will be high.

d) Women Small Petty Fish Vendors

The results of the estimated regression function for the women small petty fish vendors are presented in Table 8.12. The estimated regression equation for the financial year reveals that R-bar square value is 0.917, which can be treated as good fit. The coefficients of variables AD1, ED1, ED2 and working capital are statistically significant in determining the profits. The signs of the regression coefficients of all the variables are positive, implies that middle aged women small petty fish vendors are getting more profits, and if more experienced the women small petty fish vendors, higher will be the profits.

The estimated equation for the 1st season reveals that along with working capital, literacy, and ED2 are statistically significant in determining the profits in the 1st season. Literacy has a negative sign means literates are getting less profits by Rs 9. per day. If the vendor is having more than 10 years of experience, the profits will be higher by Rs. 17.64 per day.

Table – 8.9

Results of the Estimated Regression Equations – Women Vendors (N= 360)

Season	*Constant*	*Literacy*	*Marital status*	*Age* D_1	D_2	*Experience* D_1	D_2	*Working Capital*	*Adjusted* R^2	*F*
1st April-31st July	19.57	-5.82 (-1.53)	-5.22 (-2.04)	-5.63 (-1.96)	4.15 (1.17)	-12.49 (-3.51)	-4.37 (-0.94)	0.53* (26.99)	0.736	144.162*
1st Aug-30th Nov	21.52	4.12 (1.46)	-5.27* (-2.66)	-2.77 (-1.25)	-0.86 (-0.31)	5.63 (2.07)	4.19 (1.17)	0.45* (29.39)	0.754	158.072*
1st Dec-31st March	35.94	7.19 (1.98)	0.40 (0.40)	1.45 (0.50)	0.31 (0.08)	5.59 (1.56)	-0.76 (-0.16)	0.30* (12.72)	0.420	38.083*
Total Period	10.51	-3.40 (-1.52)	-4.37* (-2.86)	-3.97* (-2.32)	-2.39 (-1.12)	-4.42 (-2.07)	-3.30 (-1.19)	0.56* (38.75)	0.844	279.500*

Note: Figures in the parentheses indicate Students' t - ratio.

* Indicates significance at 1 per cent level.

The estimated equation for the 2nd season reveals that along with working capital, literacy, and ED2 are statistically significant in determining the profits during 2nd season also. In this season literacy has a positive sign means literates are getting more profits by Rs 5. per day. If the vendor is having more than 10 years of experience, the profits will be higher by Rs. 7.64 per day.

The estimated equation for the 3rd season reveals that along with working capital, AGD1, ED1 and ED2 are statistically significant in determining the profits during 3rd season. Al the coefficients have positive signs, indicate middle aged vendors are getting higher profits by Rs 5 per day, the experience of 6-10 years yields higher profits by Rs. 10 and the experience above 10 years yields Rs. 20 profits per day. The influence of working capital is very less in this season.

e) Women Petty Fish Vendors

The results of the estimated regression function for the women petty fish vendors are presented in Table 8.13. The estimated function for the financial year has R-bar square value is 0.88, which can be treated as good fit. The coefficients of variables AD1, ED1 and working capital are statistically significant in determining the profits. The coefficient of AD1 is -19.08 imply that middle age women vendors are getting lower profits by Rs. 19 per day. The coefficient value for ED1 is -17.11 imply that those women having experience between 5-10 years of experience are getting lower profits by Rs. 17 per day. The coefficient of working capital is 0.50 implies that an one rupee increase in working capital increases profits by 50 paise.

The estimated equation for the 1st season reveals that along with working capital, AD1, and ED1 are statistically significant in determining the profits in the 1st season. The ED1 has negative coefficient implies that the women vendors with experience of 6 – 10 years are getting less profits by Rs.61 per day. In the similar manner AD1 is also negative implies that the vendors in the age group of 30-55 years are getting less profits by Rs. 44 per day. The coefficient of working capital is positive and it is 0.97.

The estimated equation for the 2nd season reveals that along with working capital, literacy is statistically significant in

Table – 8.10

Results of the Estimated Regression Equations - Fish Vendors (N= 180)

Season	*Constant*	*Literacy*	*Marital status*	*Age* D_1	D_2	*Experience* D_1	D_2	*Working Capital*	*Adjusted* R^2	*F*
1st April-31st July	12.50	-14.83* (-2.28)	-0.52 (-0.11)	-12.70* (-2.39)	-1.21 (-0.20)	-17.29* (-2.52)	-5.91 (-0.68)	0.65* (18.53)	0.727	69.033*
1st Aug-30th Nov	31.22	2.37 (0.60)	-0.19 (-0.06)	0.61 (0.18)	2.60 (-0.69)	-10.29* (-2.41)	-17.19* (-13.19)	0.48* (23.75)	0.813	112.442*
1st Dec-31st March	65.08	14.27* (2.28)	-0.98 (-0.21)	10.55 (1.99)	13.30 (2.20)	-10.62 (-1.54)	-26.96* (-3.12)	0.19* (4.59)	0.252	9.622*
Total Period	14.19	-12.69* (-3.34)	-2.52 (-0.97)	-7.11* (-2.31)	-4.70 (-1.33)	-15.53* (-3.93)	-17.53* (-3.53)	0.64* (26.12)	0.838	133.278*

Note: Figures in the parentheses indicate Students' t - ratio.

* Indicates significance at 1 per cent level.

determining the profits during 2nd season also. In this season literacy has a positive sign means literates are getting more profits by Rs 15. per day. The coefficient of working capital is 0.16.

The estimated equation for the 3rd season reveals that along with working capital, AGD1, literacy and ED2 are statistically significant in determining the profits during 3rd season.

f) Women Vegetable Vendors

The results of the estimated regression function for the women vegetable vendors are presented in Table 8.14. R-bar square value is 0.944, which can be treated as good fit. The coefficients of variables marital status, AD2, ED1 and working capital are statistically significant in determining the profits. The coefficient of AD2 is -1.90 implies that above middle age women vendors are getting lower profits by Rs. 1.90 per day. The coefficient value for ED1 is -3.89 imply that those women having experience between 5-10 years of experience are getting lower profits by Rs. 3.89 per day. The coefficient of working capital is 0.56 implies that an one rupee increase in working capital increases profits by 56 paise. The coefficient of marital status is -2.54, implies that unmarried women are getting lower profits by Rs. 2.54 per day.

The estimated equation for the 1st season reveals that along with working capital, marital status, ED1 and ED2 are statistically significant in determining the profits in the 1st season. The ED1and ED2 have negative coefficient implies that the women vendors with experience of 6 – 10 years are getting less profits by Rs.19 per day and the other category by Rs. 23.69. In the similar manner marital status is also negative implies that the vendors who are married are reducing profits by Rs. 10 per day. The coefficient of working capital is positive and it is -0.96. The estimated equation for the 2nd season reveals that as in the case of 1st season the same variables are influencing this season also.

The estimated equation for the 3rd season reveals that along with working capital, marital status, AGD2, and ED2 are statistically significant in determining the profits during 3rd season.

Table – 8.11

Results of the Estimated Regression Equations - Fish street vendors (N= 60)

Season	*Constant*	*Literacy*	*Marital status*	*Age* D_1	*Age* D_2	*Experience* D_1	*Experience* D_2	*Working Capital*	*Adjusted* R^2	*F*
1st April-31st July	14.85	0.50 (0.05)	0.26 (0.05)	2.67 (0.47)	2.67 (0.92)	11.74 (1.67)	8.51 (0.79)	0.38 (1.43)	0.377	6.109*
1st Aug-30th Nov	13.47	2.41 (1.50)	1029 (1.36)	8.02* (7.87)	6.83* (4.47)	12.47* (8.87)	12.94* (6.99)	0.35* (4.82)	0.921	99.552*
1st Dec-31st March	10.98	2.69 (0.47)	-0.98 (-0.28)	-1.75 (-0.38)	4.97 (0.86)	5.25 (0.98)	-9.77 (-1.00)	0.32* (3.85)	0.685	19.358*
Total Period	-6.49	-2.20 (-0.47)	-0.90 (-0.35)	-0.23 (-0.07)	3.25 (0.77)	8.67* (2.28)	-3.69 (-0.55)	0.54* (4.41)	0.728	23.548*

Note: Figures in the parentheses indicate Students' t - ratio.

* Indicates significance at 1 per cent level.

g) Women Vegetable Street Vendors

The results of the estimated regression function for the women vegetable street vendors are presented in Table 8.15. The function was estimated for the whole financial year. R-bar square value is 0.963, which can be treated as good fit. The coefficients of variables AD2, and working capital are statistically significant in determining the profits. The coefficient of AD2 is -2.23 imply that above middle age women vendors are getting lower profits by Rs. 2.23 per day. The coefficient of working capital is 0.43 implies that an one rupee increase in working capital increases profits by 43 paise.

For the vegetable street vendors during the 1st season along with working capital, literacy AD2, ED1 and ED2 are statistically significant. In the 2nd season only one variable ie., literacy is significant. In the last season, literacy, ED1 and working capital are statistically significant in determining the profits.

h) Women Vegetable Small Petty Vendors

The results of the estimated regression function for the women vegetable small petty vendors are presented in Table 8.16. The equation for financial year, R-bar square value is 0.96, which can be treated as good fit. The coefficients of variables literacy, AD1, ED2 and working capital are statistically significant in determining the profits. The coefficient of AD1 is 3.17 imply that above middle age women vendors are getting higher profits by Rs. 3.17 per day. The coefficient of literacy is 4.02 imply that literate vegetable small petty vendors are getting more profits by Rs 4.02 per day. The coefficient of ED2 is 5.49, implies that above middle aged vegetable small vendors are getting more profits by Rs. 5.49 per day. The coefficient of working capital is 0.31 implies that an one rupee increase in working capital increases profits by 31 paise.

With respect o various seasons for the 1st season literacy, AD2, ED1, and ED2, Working capital are the determinants of profits. For the 2nd season also same variables are influencing the profits of vegetable In the third season AD1, ED1, ED2, and working capital are the important variables.

Table – 8.12

Results of the Estimated Regression Equations— Fish small petty vendors (N= 60)

Season	*Constant*	*Literacy*	*Marital status*	*Age* D_1	*Age* D_2	*Experience* D_1	*Experience* D_2	*Working Capital*	*Adjusted* R^2	*F*
1st April-31st July	15.88	-9.49 (-2.36)	0.79 (0.37)	2.78 (0.83)	3.84 (1.23)	8.66 (1.87)	17.64* (3.35)	0.34* (6.79)	0.856	51.226*
1st Aug-30th Nov	43.80	5.05* (3.75)	0.61 (0.58)	-2.00 (-1.19)	0.51 (0.01)	4.18 (1.68)	7.70* (2.73)	0.13* (7.59)	0.872	58.164*
1st Dec-31st March	44.84	2.22 (1.54)	1.96 (1.65)	5.20* (2.75)	3.69 (2.09)	10.26* (3.92)	20.44* (7.00)	0.07* (3.15)	0.891	70.154*
Total Period	31.81	-1.09 (-1.15)	1.00 (1.57)	2.29 (2.24)	1.58 (1.64)	5.93* (4.11)	12.60* (7.58)	0.23* (15.96)	0.917	287.972*

Note: Figures in the parentheses indicate Students' t - ratio.

* Indicates significance at 1 per cent level.

Table – 8.13

Results of the Estimated Regression Equations - Fish petty vendors (N= 60)

Season	Constant	Literacy	Marital status	Age D_1	Age D_2	Experience D_1	Experience D_2	Working Capital	Adjusted R^2	F
1st April-31st July	-9.74	-4.12 (-0.13)	1.33 (0.14)	-44.53* (-3.76)	-11.08 (-0.85)	-61* (-4.04)	-55.42 (-1.59)	0.97* (8.30)	0.697	20.365*
1st Aug-30th Nov	93.47	15.56* (2.56)	0.14 (0.07)	-4.22 (-1.75)	-1.14 (-0.43)	0.23 (0.08)	10.88 (1.60)	0.16* (8.00)	0.931	99.704*
1st Dec-31st March	97.85	-4.53* (-2.34)	-0.99 (-1.65)	-2.87* (-3.90)	-0.71 (-0.88)	-4.45* (-5.08)	-5.07* (-2.30)	0.18* (20.85)	0.947	152.914*
Total Period	54.31	-2.55 (-0.27)	-1.00 (-0.34)	-19.08* (-5.24)	-6.62 (-1.66)	-18.60* (-4.27)	-17.11 (-1.62)	0.50* (13.31)	0.880	62.684*

Note: Figures in the parentheses indicate Students' t - ratio.

* Indicates significance at 1 per cent level.

Table – 8.14

Results of the Estimated Regression Equations - Vegetable Vendors (N= 180)

Season	Constant	Literacy	Marital status	Age D_1	Age D_2	Experience D_1	Experience D_2	Working Capital	Adjusted R^2	F
1st April-31st July	5.99 (1.15)	-1.02 (-0.31)	-10.98 (-4.89)	1.08 (0.46)	2.90 (0.96)	-19.60 (-5.33)	-23.69 (-4.21)	-0.61 (-19.43)	0.824	120.497
1st Aug-30th Nov	21.26 (4.51)	1.10 (0.27)	-8.21 (-2.95)	-4.88 (-1.69)	2.29 (0.61)	16.55 (4.47)	20.97 (3.86)	0.41 (15.13)	0.716	65.417
1st Dec-31st March	0.49 (0.49)	-1.89 (-0.70)	9.30 (4.95)	0.53 (0.27)	-9.02 (-3.59)	0.61 (0.24)	14.75 (4.24)	0.47 (25.23)	0.848	143.838
Total Period	1.93 (0.85)	0.01 (0.00)	-2.54 (-2.24)	-0.42 (-1.24)	-1.90 (-2.64)	-3.89 (-2.36)	0.97 (0.38)	0.56 (41.30)	0.944	428.170

Note: Figures in the parentheses indicate Students' t - ratio.

* Indicates significance at 1 per cent level.

Table – 8.15

Results of the Estimated Regression Equations - Vegetable street vendors (N= 60)

Season	*Constant*	*Literacy*	*Marital status*	*Age* D_1	D_2	*Experience* D_1	D_2	*Working Capital*	*Adjusted* R^2	*F*
Season	Constant	Literacy	Marital status	Age D_1	Experience D_2	Working D_1	Capital D_2	Adjusted R^2	F	
1st April-31st July	42.79	-9.33* (-5.79)	0.20 (0.19)	-2.08 (-1.60)	-5.16* (-3.79)	-4.66* (-2.67)	-5.22* (-2.20)	0.33* (10.08)	0.830	42.037*
1st Aug-30th Nov	24.35	9.26* (5.91)	0.05 (0.04)	3.10 (1.79)	2.28 (1.25)	8.77* (4.54)	10.45* (3.31)	0.28* (4.91)	0.911	87.135*
1st Dec-31st March	16.59	9.94* (5.46)	0.13 (0.09)	-0.74 (-0.41)	-1.97 (-1.02)	5.54* (2.47)	-4.39 (-1.15)	0.39* (7.24)	0.927	107.825*
Total Period	15.90	1.79 (1.71)	0.03 (0.04)	-0.06 (-0.06)	-2.23 (-2.17)	1.10 (0.89)	-3.46 (-1.78)	0.43* (13.54)	0.963	220.705*

Note: Figures in the parentheses indicate Students' t - ratio.

* Indicates significance at 1 per cent level.

Table – 8.16

Results of the Estimated Regression Equations - Vegetable Small Petty Vendors (N= 60)

Season	*Constant*	*Literacy*	*Marital status*	*Age* D_1	*Age* D_2	*Experience* D_1	*Experience* D_2	*Working Capital*	*Adjusted* R^2	*F*
1st April-31st July	30.51	14.10* (5.08)	0.22 (0.11)	0.49 (0.24)	8.31* (3.02)	-13.56* (-3.83)	-16.90* (-3.31)	0.38* (11.32)	0.941	134.861*
1st Aug-30th Nov	76.22	1.22* (2.59)	-0.49 (-1.43)	-0.14 (-0.30)	1.60* (3.08)	3.78* (6.41)	4.08* (4.96)	0.11*(6.45)	0.916	92.843*
1st Dec-31st March	39.90	0.04 (0.01)	2.38 (1.37)	14.79 (7.93)	3.76 (1.37)	6.84* (2.74)	22.21* (6.69)	0.14* (4.56)	0.886	66.753*
Total Period	35.37	4.02* (3.19)	0.71 (0.80)	3.17 (3.29)	1.31 (0.94)	-1.68 (-1.12)	5.49* (2.94)	0.31* (12.89)	0.960	205.786*

Note: Figures in the parentheses indicate Students' t - ratio.

* Indicates significance at 1 per cent level.

Table – 8.17

Results of the Estimated Regression Equations - Vegetable Petty Vendors (N= 60)

Season	*Constant*	*Literacy*	*Marital status*	*Age*		*Experience*		*Working Capital*	*Adjusted* R^2	*F*
				D_1	D_2	D_1	D_2			
Season	Constant	Literacy	Marital status	Age	Experience	Working	Capital	Adjusted R^2	F	
				D_1	D_2	D_1	D_2			
1st April-31st July	22.70	-2.82 (-0.79)	-20.59* (-4.44)	-0.92 (-0.71)	-0.55 (-0.27)	-7.15* (-2.51)	-3.35 (-0.72)	0.56* (9.71)	0.975	334.008
1st Aug-30th Nov	-5.98	8.42 (0.36)	-2.50 (-0.08)	-4.12 (-0.43)	12.98 (1.13)	-11.68 (-0.67)	-7.52 (-0.26)	0.60 (1.20)	0.191	2.898
1st Dec-31st March	105.88	0.57 (0.24)	0.72 (0.22)	0.50 (0.45)	1.93 (1.47)	3.77* (2.15)	8.88* (3.03)	0.06 (1.38)	0.738	24.699
Total Period	-44.45	-0.25 (-0.21)	-3.20 (-0.33)	-7.77* (-2.53)	-2.36 (0.58)	-9.90 (-1.78)	-7.20 (-0.79)	0.79* (5.16)	0.778	30.548

Note: Figures in the parentheses indicate Students' t - ratio.

* Indicates significance at 1 per cent level.

i) Women Vegetable Petty Vendors

The results of the estimated regression function for the women vegetable petty vendors are presented in Table 8.17. R-bar square value is 0.778, which can be treated as good fit. The coefficients of variables AD1 and working capital are statistically significant in determining the profits. The coefficient of AD1 is -7.77 imply that above middle age women vendors are getting lower profits by Rs. 7.77 per day. The coefficient of working capital is 0.31 implies that an one rupee increase in working capital increases profits by 31 paise.

Conclusion

The results of the multiple regression coefficients reveal that working along with the working capital, unmarried women vendors are earning more profits than married women vendors. Above middle aged and 5-10 years experience are negatively influencing their profits.

In the case of fish vending, working capital and experience will decide the profits of the women vendors. Less experienced women fish vendors are getting more Profits, whereas fish street vendors, experience in between 5-10 years yields more profits. In case of small petty fish vendors, with the experience women are earning more profits. In case of fish petty vendors, young women with less than 5 years experience are getting more profits, as these two variables are significantly influencing the profits.

In case of vegetable vending it is the working capital which decides the profits of these vendors. Apart from this unmarried and young vegetable vendors are getting more profits. In case of vegetable street vendors, working capital and experience and age these three are the important determinants. Young women with less experience are getting more profits. In case of vegetable small petty vendors middle aged, married women with more than 10 years experience are getting more profits, whereas in case of vegetable petty vendors it is the working capital which is influencing more.

NOTE & REFERENCE

1. Mincer J (1974): Schooling, *Experience and Earnings*, NBER, New York

9

Women Vendors: Case Studies

This chapter presents the case studies of the women vendors for an indepth understanding of their life styles and problems. Before presenting the case studies the chapter presents the brief description of the classification of Petty Trade. Petty trade can be classified in to three main categories:

1. Street Vendors
2. Small Petty Vendors
3. Petty Vendors.

1. Street Vendors

The street vendors constitute a major category. They hawk fish or vegetables with baskets on their heads and go round the streets for selling fish or vegetables. Their trade is not regular. If the price of fish is too high or the catch is too low or when there is inclement weather most of them skip the trade on that day. There are areas and routes pre-fixed for each fisher women vendor. Other fisherwomen do not encroach into those areas just as the fisher women in the market places do not sit at some one else's allotted place. This is governed by custom and violations seldom take place. The same is the case for vegetable vending. If the prices of the vegetables are very high they buy less quantity and they reduce their volume of trade to limit the risk of getting losses.

The street vendors have regular clientele whose tastes and preferences for the variety of fish or vegetables are known to the vendor. Each street vendor carries fish worth Rs.50/- to Rs.150/- only some times. The street vendor makes good profit because the consumer does not know the prevailing market rate. A time, the Petty Trade appeals to the vendee that she is servicing the customer at her doorstep. So, she pleads that she deserves a little margin over and above the usual market price. The consumer and the seller bargain for a while finally either the bargain is settled or the product is rejected. The street vendors are in the habit of quoting a high price unlike in the market places where there are other fish stalls. Some times the Vendor leaves the customer's house in case of disagreement over the price and returns after a few minutes and sells the produce for the price offered by the consumer. The consumer may, at times, call the vendor back and pay the price suggested by the latter. The street vendors offer credit and may sometimes collect advance also. They have the advantage of going back home early and attend to their household duties. Their expenses in the trade are the minimum.

The classification street vendor, fish or vegetable trading women, suggested above, is based on pooling up of a number of important characteristics, the chief determinant being the scale of their working capital and propensity to take risks. It should, however, be made clear that these categories are not mutually exclusive. Empirical data suggest overlapping in a few dimensions. Kin structures in particular serve as an important intervening variable at several points in fostering temporary transfers of capital or eliciting cooperation of other vendors when over there is need.

2. Small Petty Vendors

They also undertake trade regularly, either in the walled markets or in the other markets. Few have storage facilities. They also trade in expensive variety of fish like Seer fish or expensive varieties of vegetables. But the scale of the daily business turnover is lower, ranging from Rs. 100/- to Rs. 250. They are effective competitors on the shore to first category of Petty trade. They use technology similar to the one used by the big Petty trade. They also engage auto-rickshaws, but usually one way, while carrying fish to the market. Three or four of them engage one auto. While returning home they usually catch a city bus. In case of vegetable vendors also they are the competitors for the Petty vendors. Generally they come by bus near by villages, or they purchase a significant quantity and varieties of vegetables from the whole sealer and try to sell them by the evening.

Less than a quarter of them have storage spaces in the market. As the quantity of fish or vegetables they put up for sale is limited they do not normally require any storage space. In case they are left with a surplus by the time of closure of business they carry the fish to home either for conversion in to dry fish or to store it until the next morning if storage facility is available. In case of vegetables they sell them even at losses if they are perishable, otherwise they carry them to their homes. They make an extra trip to the market the next morning only when they are lift with a surplus of unsold fish stock the previous night. Cooperation, especially among kinfolk, in such respects is very high. Again, it is based in reciprocity. The small Petty Trader who receives this kind of help would reciprocate such help some other time. When some one else sells the fish in her absence, the collection is returned to the owner later. There is complete trust a larger range and variety of fish including small fish and small prawns at the fishing harbour. On buying the fish at the harbour they rush to their respective markets, choosing mostly less expensive means of transport.

Since they don't have storage facility at the markets they carry their where withal (knives fixed to wooden planks, old cloth and a rubber or polythene sheet) with them daily. As the quantity of fish purchased by them is not high they are seldom left with a surplus. They also resort to distress sale in case a little quantity is left over towards the closing time. The case of Ravamma provides a good illustration. On one evening she brought from the harbor point Rs,15/- worth of small fish. She paid Rs.2/- for the cycle-rickshaw. She could not, however, reach the market on time. With great difficulty she was able to sell fish worth Rs.10/-. Half of the merchandise was still there by 7 p.m. many of the fisherwomen closed their stalls. Ravamma was looking around for customers desperately. One well-dressed person came and looked at the piece of small fish and walked over to the next stall where big fish are sold. At this point Ravamma divided the fish in to four lots. An old woman parsied around Ravamma's stall and asked for the price of two lots. Ravamma pouted Rs.6/- the customer offered Rs.3/-. The

Petty Trade scaled down her offer to Rs.5/-. Then the customer walked off to another stall. Another customer, a young girl, came to Ravamma's stall, had a feel of fish with her hands, smelt them and walked off. By this time, there was only one other Petty Trade in the market. One middle-aged woman turned up and asked for the price of two lots. Ravamma said, 'take it, pay me what ever you intend to". The customer offered Rs.2/- and lifted two lots. The time was 7.30 pm. Ravamma was alone in the market and still left with two lots of fish. With a pathetic face she collected the fish in her basket, saying that it is not possible to dry this variety of fish. She ended up with a loss of Rs.5/-.

Most of the small petty vendors return home in groups by foot, taking short- cut routes. A few catch the city bus, if it is available, up to some point, and walk home from there they do not offer any credit to consumers. The occasional small petty trader does not have an allotted place in the markets like the regular small petty vendor. They usually steal a corner or sit in the road side to sell their produce. Some of them request their kins- women to allow them to sit behind them to sell the produce. For such services one rupee is paid to the patron.

A few fisherwomen(less than 5percent) are reported to be in trade for other than economic purposes. They seem to enjoy selling fish and the opportunity of going outside the village. Going to market provides them an opportunity to escape, at least temporarily, from the daily routine of household work. For much trade livelihood does not depend on profits from market trade, nor are they highly motivated to build up domestic assets. In such cases, social and personal motives tend to predominate over economic motives.

3. Petty Vendors

They trade in expensive, in large quantities and varieties of fish or vegetables. They sell mostly in the walled markets with stall or storage facilities in the markets. These petty trades regularly invest large amounts of cash and the daily turnover of business of each of them ranges anywhere between Rs. 251/- and Rs.400/- depending upon the fish catch in a particular day. Necessarily, the scale of their enterprise is high. They have complete independence in their husbands. Three of them supply fish to the five – star hotels in Visakhapatnam and to the Navy and other large institutions.[12] They sell the best variety of Seer fish known locally as Konam at Rs.18/- to Rs.20/- per kg. in the average season. They also sell prawns (shrimp) at Rs.100/- to Rs.150/-per kg. As these Petty trades accumulate enough capital they aspire to become petty trade i.e., the highest category in the economic strata of the fishermen community. Indeed, three of them are simultaneously acting as petty trade in retail or whole sale business they also offer their merchandise on credit to the consumers, without charging any interest.

Their infrastructure for the trade is based on low levels of technology. They use big baskets and a lot of ice. Wooden boxes are used for storage inside the market. They use sharp knives for cutting the fish and wooden planks for sitting. These items are kept in the market place itself. The people who sleep in the market yard act as watchmen. One of them is paid a rupee per night for keeping a watch in the fish baskets. Despite this, occasionally fish are stolen at night. Once or twice in a year, they loose the entire stock or a part of it.

These petty vendors also employ casual labour to carry the big baskets from the shore to their houses and from there to the main roads, a stretch of about half – a - kilometer. The labourers are underemployed fisherwomen who get paid Rs.10/- to Rs.15/-, per month. These petty vendors invariably use auto-rickshaws (motorized three wheelers) both ways to go to the market and to return home. The fare they pay for each one-way trip ranges from Rs.10/- to Rs.15/-, depending upon the number traveling and the weight of the merchandise. Since these petty traders carry two big baskets to the market each auto is engaged by two only. Ice is brought to Jalaripeta by blocks of ice, weighing 20 to 30 kgs, are broken in to pieces of two rupees worth and retailed to the fisherwomen.

The vegetables vendors also engage auto rickshaws to bring the vegetable from wholesale market to the market place where they have the stall. They employ some times casual labour or other family members will help them in that task. Generally they have a regular, trusted customer base for their varieties. Some times they specialize in certain varieties, so that they can hold their customers.

1. Case Study - Fish Street Vendor

Ganta Achi (22), wife of Mr. Tata Rao is a native of Kakinada which is about 100 km away from Visakhapatnam. They have a four year old daughter. Fishing is their traditional profession. A year ago, on his usual chores Tata Rao went off into the sea for fishing, but unfortunately he died because of the shipwreck. After the death of her husband, Achi returned to her parents at Pedajalaripeta in Visakhapatnam as she could not find any source of income for the livelihood of the family.

Even though she is young, it is their custom not to give a widow in marriage. It is acceptable in their social community if the widow goes with a person with her own interest, as explained by her mother Volisettor Ammuramma. Hence, she is staying with her parents in the thatched house at the Pedajalaripeta beach.

Since then, following their traditional profession, she took up fish business with financial support from her mother. She purchases fish from the fishermen in auction on the beach near her residence. She keeps the fish in a basket and goes along the streets until the last fish is sold. Generally she gets the fish early in the morning and returns home at 11 A.M. after selling the days lot. The left over fish or prawns will be dried and marketed thereafter.

She invests Rs.400/- to Rs.600/- depending on the variety of the fish and season of the market. During the Hindu festival days, she finds hard times to vend the fish. On an average, she earns Rs.60/- to Rs.90/- per day.

2. Case Study – Vegetable Vending

Mrs. Koppala Chinnammalu, a 45 year old woman is a native of Visakhapatnam city. Her husband Mr. Apparao, aged 50 is working as a watchman in a private firm. He became a drunkard and his income is not sufficient for a minimum level of living. In addition to this, they had two children to share the insufficient meal. To overcome the financial crisis, Mrs. Chinnammalu took up vegetable vending.

Chinnammalu started her business with twenty rupees only. She buys vegetables at a wholesale dealer near Poornamarket. She goes along the streets of the city to sell all the kinds of vegetables. She keeps the wooden basket over her head with all varieties of vegetables like onions, bitter guard, angular guard, ladies-finger, pumpkin, curry-leaves, coriander etc. At present, she invests 200/ - to 300/- rupees and earns a margin of fifty rupees a day.

She is living in her own house with an asbestos roof. Her two children Appalakonda (daughter) and Srinivas (son) are married. But, her son is also a drunkard and a wayward because of which, the whole burden of the family rests on her shoulder.

3. Case Study: Street Vegetable Vendor

Mr. Satyavathi Kambala, 50 year old mala (scheduled caste) woman was a native of Devarajpalli Village in Visakhapatnam Dist. She came to Visakhapatnam for livelihood. She was given shelter by a riskchaw puller named Byragi. They fell in love with each other and got married. He belongs to Vodabalija social community. They had three children, two daughters named Adilaxmi and Danamma, and a son named Ramana. As days rolled on, it became difficult (they were given five thousand rupees as an incentive for inter-caste marriage by the government) for her husband to meet the family expenditure with his meager earnings. Satyavathi decided to join her hand by taking up vegetable vending. She started her business with just twenty rupees. She buys vegetables at the countryside market and hawks in the streets of Visakhapatnam city.

She found vegetable vending prosperous. Now, she earns Rs.50 - Rs.60 per day as margin after investing Rs.200 on purchasing vegetables. Her two daughters and son were married and they live independently. Recently, her husband died of some ailment. Vegetable vending gives her good company and comfort in her solitary life. She is given two hundred rupees under widow pension.

4. Case Study: Vegetable Vending (Migrant)

Mrs. Boddu Seethamma, age 36, belongs to Vadabalija social community. She is a native of Arasavilli village in Srikakulam district. She is an illiterate. She was given in marriage to Laxmayya, now 40, a daily wage worker and an addict to liquor. As he found no sufficient work to sustain their living, they migrated to Visakhapatnam in search of work. They got shelter at Kobbarithota near M.V.P. Colony. Her husband earned money required for his family maintenance but he spent it in consuming alcohol and luxuries. They have three children, one daughter and two sons. As she spent days with starvation, she decided to do something for the survival of her children and herself. She preferred vegetable vending which requires little intelligence and working capital.

She purchases vegetables from the wholesale dealer on cash payment in the previous evening. She goes to market then the streets of Visakhapatnam city in the early morning covering Maddilapalem areas. She returns home at 12:00 noon. If some vegetables are left over, she goes to hawk again in the afternoon at 4:00 P.M. She invests Rs.200/- to Rs.250/- daily and earns at least Rs.50/- to 60/- margin. Since vegetables are perishable goods, they are prone to damage or decay if they are not sold in one or two days. Such damages will affect her earnings.

Even though Seethampeta is an illiterate, circumstances made her an independent woman who can support and guide her family. By her own earnings, she procured a house for the family. Her daughter Konda (13) is studying in 8th class, sons Pydiraju (12) is studying 7th class. Her husband failed to perform his responsibilities for the family. She shoulders the major burden and almost the entire family depends on her income. She spends major part of her income on the needs of their children and family while her husband does not hesitate to spend on his personal needs such as liquor and tobacco.

5. Case Study: Vegetable Vending

Boorula Aruna , a 37 years old Settibalija woman, is at present, engaged in vegetable vending at Poorna market in Visakhapatnam. Circumstances forced her to take up the present vending business.

About 15 years ago, she fell in love with Satya Narayana, Peddakapu by caste. Her parents who run a small tea stall with a meager income at Ananda Puram near Tagarapuvalasa in Visakhapatnam district, accepted to give her in marriage. The couple started their family at Kanelarapalem. Her husband used to sell flowers for their livelihood. She gave birth to their children but they died. In the forth time, a healthy male child Yarna ,Kermar was born. In the meanwhile, her husband became a drunkard. Since his meager income is not sufficient to fulfill his alcoholic desire, he started selling all valuable household things in their family, including his wife's mangalasutra. He developed an illicit relation with a girl. He neglected his wife and child and spent most of the time with that girl. When his sister came to know that they are not living together, she rushed to him and took him to her home. Instead of giving him good counseling, she advised him to desert his wife and child simply because his wife is not from their caste. Without giving divorce to his wife he married his sister's daughter, when his son was five. Aruna suffered silently but did not make any complaint against her husband to the police.

In helplessness, she came to her parents along with her son. She lived nearly two years with her parents. It became hard for their parents to provide them everything. They were bankrupted for nearly Rs.10000/-. She realised the situation and tried to find ways to live her life independently and to provide good literacy to her son. At this crucial point of time, her elder sister advised her to start vegetable business. She encouraged her by giving Rs.500/- as intial working capital.

Even though she is illiterate, she runs the vegetable business and her family successfully. She gets all varieties of vegetables from a wholesale dealer in the market itself worth Rs.500/- a day. She avoids transport charges and she gets at least Rs.50/- a day excluding the tax for the place.

6. Case Study: Vegetable Vending

A 28 year old Scheduled Caste woman, Vaddadi Asha is swimming against the currents to feed her four children and her younger brother and sister by vending vegetables at Poorna Market,Visakhapatnam. She is a very daring and intelligent woman and she looks after her whole family when her husband left her to fate.

Asha has only primary literacy. Her parents Kadavala Babji and Maramma used to run vegetable business at Poorna Market. Her parents arranged her marriage with Ramu, a painting worker in Visakhapatnam. They were happy and everything was going well. She gave birth to two boys (twins) Kiran and Isiah. In the second delivery also, twins were born one boy, Suraj and one girl Keerthi. Problems started in their life after the second delivery. Her husband Ramu had no bad habits, as Aruna explains, like drinking alcohol, smoking etc., but he started suspecting her character. She looks beautiful and whenever she dressed up well, he could not digest it. He felt as if she got ready for some body else. She bore all that mental torture patiently for the sake of her children. As he was misguided by his sister, he thought she had an extramarital affair with some other person. The relationship of wife and husband gradually deteriorated. She came to her parents with her four children and after one year, her husband came to her arranging everything for his second marriage, to take away with him the youngest male child Suraj. But she rejected his proposal. He married another girl without taking divorce from her wife.

Soon, Asha joined with her parents in vending vegetables at Poorna Market. She took a separate stall after gaining some experience in business. She runs business by commission. The wholesale seller provides her all vegetables. She sells the vegetables on par with others in the market. Generally, she adds 20 to 30 percent margin earning Rs.60/- to 80/- per day excluding market tax. Both her parents Kadavla Babji (father) and Maramma (mother) died within a year gap. The burden of the whole family shifted to her shoulders since she was the eldest. Her younger brother, age about 24, is jobless and a wanderer. Her elder sister is about 20, who does household work at home. It is her responsibility to settle them in life.

Asha is living in her parents own house, just a street nearby Poorna market. She provided all money for all their needs, and household things like colour T.V., Dressing Table, Double Cot, Steel Vessels, Gas Stove, Crockery with her own earnings. She kept Rs.18000/- in her savings account for her sister's marriage. She took Rs.7000/- from ICICI Bank. She pays Rs.38/-every day except on Sunday. She gave Rs.5000/- to a middleman to employ her brother in a watchman post in private company. But her brother did not join in that post. Her four children Kiran (12) and Lakshmi (12) are studying 7th class and Keerthi (10) and Suraj (10) are in 5th class in Muncipal School.

When the circumstances forced Asha to make her own livelihood, she relied on vegetable business. She says it is the single source of income for the whole family.

7. Case Study: Fish Vending

Mrs.Chintapalli Satyavathi, a 32 year old illiterate fisherwoman, is a native of Jalaripeta. She is living with her husband and three children. Their two boys – Ellaji (14) and Rajesh (10) and a girl Ratna (12) are studying 7th, 6th and 3rd class respectively. She was married at the age of 18. She came into fish vending, which is their traditional business only after their second son was born. Soon her husband's earning was very meager to feed four members of the family. She joined her husband for economical support of the family.

Her husband Pothu Raju goes to open sea for fishing by his country boat. The fish caught by him are being sold by his wife at the Poorna Market. He goes to sea in the night at 10.00 pm along with neighbour fishermen in a group. He generally returns in the early hours of the next day if the weather is clear. She brings the fish to the market at 6.00 A.M. She places them in heaps on a thatch tray by size and variety. There is no fixed price for fish, since it depends on the supply in the market. If the catch is plenty, the rate automatically falls down. The vending will be over by 12 noon. Again she returns to the market at 3.00 p.m. If the unsold fish are kept on ice, on an average she earns about Rs. 90/- to 110/- per day in which her husband's labour is included.

Numerous problems are found in fish vending. She may not get fish all the days. 'Fishing Holidays' are declared restricting fishing in the sea during the period of fish breeding in summer. Some times, she incurs loss as unsold fish perish soon. She has to give up sales during the Hindu festival season as Hindus do not consume fish. Such marketability constraints in fish vending erode her family's economic background.

8. Case Study: Fish Vending

55 year old Chintapalli Kunchamma belongs to Jalaripet, near Fishing Harbour, Visakhapatnam. She is an illiterate. She is living with her husband Magnli Surya Prakasa Rao, who belongs to Telaga Community. He is a retired worker in NAD, Visakhapatnam. She has four children, three sons and one daughter. All of they had secondary school education and married. They are living separately (nuclear families) by doing them traditional fish business.

Circumstances forced her to continue her traditional business after 8 her of their marriage. When her husband's monthly income was not sufficient to meet the family expenses, she decided to do fish business with his consent. She started her business at Poorna market, Visakhapatnam. All her establishment for prawns vending is a big and a small water container. At that time her working capital was only Rs. 50/-. She buys fish auction at Harbour by 6.00 A.M. in the early morning. She comes to Poorna Market on foot which takes 15 minutes time to reach. She vends fish on the basis of size and weight. Big size prawns will be sold for Rs.120/- to 150/- per kg. based on the demand-supply conditions. She closes the business at 10.00 A.M. The remaining unsold prawns will be kept in the carrier with ice cubes.

Again she comes to market at 3.00 P.M. with the unsold or fresh prawns auctioned at the harbor. It presents she invests Rs.400/- to Rs 500/- on prawns everyday and gets benefit of Rs. 200/- to 300/-. The benefit depends on market fluctuations.

10

Summary and Conclusion

Women in any nation constitute half of its country's population. But their contribution to the economic development throughout the world is meager they were kept away from the mainstream of the economic development. Women's contribution played a vital role in the economies at family and society level. Employment and income earning opportunities in urban centers attract migrants from the nearby rural areas. This coincides with increase in the population pressure on agricultural land and mechanized agriculture. The women workforce engage in traditional sector in the rural areas is now slowly shifting to the urban areas. Consequent to this trend, a large majority of women are employed in various categories of work in the unorganized sector and it is more so in the urban areas.

Petty trading has been one of the most rapidly growing economic activities in Indian urban economy during the last two decades. Petty trader consists of many activities like fruit vending, vegetable vending, fish vending, sweet shops, pan shops, kirana shops, laundries, hair cutting saloons, plastic ware shops etc. This petty trade also includes pavement vendors, street hawkers, allied services etc. Until very recent times, there was no information about the women petty trade with respect to its origin and its problem. In petty trade also variations in level of trade exists based on the volume of trade and mode of operation of the trade. Some traders will have fixed space with proper shelter for conducting their trade which in turn allows them to invest more. Some traders will conduct the trade at a fixed space but without proper shelter. Some others will carry their activity moving around the streets either carrying head-loads or by using a push cart. Therefore, based on the nature of their activity the petty traders can be categorized as 'Street Vendors', 'Small Petty Vendors', and 'Petty Vendors'. The present study aims at analyzing women petty traders belong to these three categories in two different types namely 'Fish Vending', and 'Vegetable Vending', in Visakhapatnam city .

Objectives

The main objective of the present study is to analyze the profits earned by women vendors with respect to seasonal variations and the determining factors with reference to fish and vegetable vendors. The specific objectives of the study are:

(1) To examine the socioeconomic conditions of women fish and vegetable traders in the unorganized sector in Visakhapatnam city.

(2) To analyze the impact of migration on the women fish and vegetable traders in the unorganized sector of Visakhapatnam city.

(3) To evaluate the seasonal variations in the profits of women fish and vegetable traders.

(4) To study the determinants of profits of the women fish and vegetable traders in the unorganized sector of Visakhapatnam city.

(5) To analyse the working conditions of these women traders.

(6) To suggest the policy implications arising out of the study.

Conclusion

The following conclusions emerge from the foregoing study:

1. Majority of the vendors are Hindus (73.73%), followed by Christians (23.61%), Muslims (2.22%) and the others constitute only 0.85 percent. Among the fish vendors 72.78% are Hindus, 27.22% are Christians. Among vegetable vendors 73.89% are Hindus, 20.00% are Christians and 4.44% are Muslims and 1.68% are others.

2. Majority of the women vendors are from Backward Classes (46.94%), then by the OC category (33.61%), and Scheduled Castes (19.44%). Among all the castes of 3 social groups, it is the Vadabalija, Jalari, Relli castes which are traditionally involved in the vegetable and fish vending activity.
3. The average monthly income of the sample women vendor households is Rs. 4686; sample fish vendor households is Rs. 4421 and sample vegetable vendor households is Rs. 4951.
4. Among the sample fish vending households, the percentage of earners is 38 and the dependency ratio is 1.61, while the percentage of earners in the vegetable vendor's households is 43 and the dependency ratio is 1.29.
5. Majority of the vendors fall in the category of 31-45 years age group followed by 56 and above and then by 26-30 age group. In case of fish vendors majority fall under the category of 26-30 followed by 56 and above category. In case of vegetable vendors majority are in the age group of 31-45 and almost equal percentage are there in the three age group (26-30, 46-55, 56 and above) nearly 25 percent of the women vendors, both fish and vegetable categories are unmarried. 75 % were illiterates.
6. Generally five languages are spoken by them. They are Telugu, Hindi, English, Oriya, Relli. The percentage of vendors below 5 years of experience accounts for 12.5 % in total vendors, 8.33 in fish vendors and 16.66 in vegetable vendors. It could said that vegetable vending is the trade where the new entrants were seen than in the fish vending. In fish vending activity they traditionally involve in that and gain more than 10 years of experience.
7. 45% of the total vendors, 43.34% of fish vendors, and 41.12% of vegetable vendors are originated because of the caste based nature. The next majority is inheritance. 43% of total vendors, 42, 24% of fish vendors, 45% of vegetable vendors engaged in that because of inheritance. The rest are new entrants.
8. Majority of the vendors (26.11%) are spending 8-10 hours. In case of Fish vendors 47.22% are spending 5-7 hours. In case of vegetable vending 36.11% are spending 5-7 hours.

9. In the total women vendors, 49.44 percent constitute migrants. About 20 percent were floating vendors. Majority of the migrants are basically vegetable vendors, followed by non-agricultural labour. In the case of fish vendors, the migration with respect to the same occupation is more.

10. Out of the total vendors 64.04 percent were migrated from rural areas to the urban areas. In case of fish vendors as well as vegetable vendors, highest percentage (81.82 & 61.12 respectively) could be observed among petty vendors. On the whole, whatever may be the category of vendor, migration from the rural areas is more in fish vendors. Majority of the vendors are migrating from 'surrounding the districts' and 'within the district' (37.66 percent and 30.89 percent respectively). A significant percent i.e., 14.60 percent is migrated from other states. In case of vegetable vendors the migration from other states is higher than the corresponding fish vendors. In case of vegetable vendors, migration 'within the District' is higher among street vendors, whereas in case of fish vendors migration from 'Surrounding the District' is the highest.

11. Distance of floating of the women vendors. Only street vendors, both fish and vegetable, float from a distance of above 55 kilometers. In case of fish petty vendors 66 percent of vendors are floating from 35-45 kilometers. But, in case of vegetable petty vendors 42.85 percent were floating from a distance between 25-35 kilometers. Among the total vendors, 63.39 percent travel by train and 28.16 percent travel by bus. In case of fish vendors, 52.82 percent travel by train and 32.35 percent travel by bus, whereas in case of vegetable vendors, 67.57 percent travel by train and 24.32 percent travel by bus.

12. The variation in the average per day profits during 1st and 2nd seasons is same for all the categories of vendors, whereas the variation increases with the level of vending (starting from Street Vendors the ladder goes up towards Petty Vendors). Petty Vendors can reap more profits during the favourable season than street vendors.

13. No significant seasonal variations in the average per day profits of the fish vendors. But, the analysis at the disaggregate level fish small petty vendors have significant seasonal variations.
14. It could also be concluded that there exists noticeable variation in the profits with respect to seasons. With respect to the seasonal variation in profits of fish vendors, street vendors are getting low profits during the 2nd season whereas petty vendors are getting low profits during 3rd seasons. In case of vegetable vendors, for all the categories of vendors profits are declining from 1st season to 3rd season. But these variations in the profits are pertinent in case of vegetable vendors than in case of fish vendors.
15. The inter-category differences in profits are significant and Petty Vendors are earning more profits compared to the other two categories when all the vendors are taken together. Intra-group differences in profits also significant and during the 1st season (1st April – 31st July) generally vendors are earning more profits and per day profits are low during the 3rd season (1st Dec – 31st March).
16. When fish vendors are considered the intra-category differences are not significant. But Inter-group differences are significant; particularly in case of fish petty vendors.
17. There exists intra-category and inter-category difference in the average per day working capital for both fish and vegetable vendors. But, in comparison with the fish vendors, vegetable vendors are putting less working capital. In case of fish vendors the average working capital is low during 2nd season compared to the other two seasons. Even in fish small petty vendors category the low average working could be observed during 2nd season.
18. The average working capital of the vegetable vendors is higher than the average working capital of the fish vendors. In all the categories of vendors the same thing could be observed. During the 2nd season the working capital is low. The working capital turned out to be a significant variable in the regression analysis, implies that the influence of the working capital is more in determining the profits. With respect to the Fish

vendors, working capital yields about 30 paise per day for one rupee increase in working capital. Inter category analysis reveals that maximum profits are for the fish petty vendors. With respect to the various categories of vegetable vendors, working capital yields highest profits for the vegetable petty vendors and lowest in the case of vegetable small petty vendors. With respect to the seasons the working capital yields maximum profits per day during the 1st season.

19. It could be inferred that literate women vendors able to reap higher profits during 1st season. It could be inferred that literacy level influences the average per day profits of the fish vendors in general and highly influences the average per day profits of the fish petty vendors in particular. It could be inferred that literacy level influences the average per day profits of the vegetable vendors in general and highly influences the average per day profits of the vegetable small petty vendors and vegetable petty vendors in particular during 1st season.

20. It could be inferred that married women vendors able to reap higher profits during 3rd season. It could be inferred that influence of the marital status on the average per day profits of the fish vendors in general is not very significant, but in case of fish street vendors and fish small petty vendors the differences in average per day profits are significant.

21. It could be inferred that difference in average per day profit based on the age groups reveal that during 1st season old age vendors are getting more profits and during the 3rd season middle age vendors are getting more profits. It could be inferred that difference in average per day profit based on the age groups reveal that during 1st season old age small petty vendors are getting more profits.

22. In case of total fish vendors the differences between the averages per day profits with respect to experience during various seasons are not at all significant. In case of fish street vendors the difference in average per day profits between different experience groups are statistically significant with respect to all the seasons. In case of fish small petty vendors the difference between the 1st and 3rd groups are significant.

The differences are significant with respect to vegetable street vendors and vegetable small petty vendors for all the seasons.

23. The results of the multiple regression coefficients reveal that working along with the working capital, unmarried women vendors are earning more profits than married women vendors. Above middle aged and 5-10 years experience are negatively influencing their profits.

24. In case of fish vending, working capital and experience will decide the profits of the women vendors. Less experienced women fish vendors are getting more profits, whereas fish street vendors, experience in between 5-10 years yields more profits. In case of small petty fish vendors, with the experience women are earning more profits.

25. In case of fish petty vendors, young women with less than 5 years experience are getting more profits, as these two variables are significantly influencing the profits.

26. In case of vegetable vending it is the working capital which decides the profits of these vendors. Apart from this unmarried and young vegetable vendors are getting more profits. In case of vegetable street vendors, working capital and experience and age these three are the important determinants. Young women with less experience are getting more profits. In case of vegetable small petty vendors middle aged, married women with more than 10 years experience are getting more profits, whereas in case of vegetable petty vendors it is the working capital which is influencing more.

Policy Implications

The study enables to suggest the following broad policy implications:

1. This study clearly brought out the importance of working capital in providing the profits to the vendors. Therefore, government look into policy to provide access to credit facilities to these women vendors. Lack of proper security or space also a major problem faced by women vendors, which in turn limits their profitability. Policies should make provisions for these women vendors to provide sufficient place in the market yard

by constructing and reserving certain share for women vendors.

2. The success story of SHG, and the role of NGOs in promoting and strengthening the SHG, the importance given by the Government, NABARD, can be adopted separately for women vendors to meet the working capital needs.
3. Along with the urban growth, the informal sector grows and the petty trade or petty business or petty vendors are not only inevitable, but also necessity for the society as well as their livelihood. Therefore, proper assessment about the magnitude and their presence needs attention. The government should come forward to make arrangement by conducting various surveys, in order to have proper estimation of the magnitude and growth of this segment of the urban informal sector.
4. Whatever insurance or social security measure aimed at poor, particularly for self-employed in the urban areas, special provisions should be made for women vendors under such type of schemes.
5. The Draft National Policy on Street Vendors by the Government of India is a welcomes action to help the street vendors or hawkers. But this should be extended to cover all sorts of petty vending activities.

As majority of these vendors are illiterate, lack of awareness about various programme and policies which are intended for the betterment of these people is the main drawback. Therefore, NGO should play a major role to develop participatory mechanism for bringing them into a representative level to open their voice for expressing their needs and requirements.

Bibliography

Andhiappan, P. (1978): "Public Police and Sex Discrimination Employment in India", *Indian Journal of Industrial relation*, October.

Anjaria, Jonathan Shapiro (2006):"Street Hawkers and Public Space in Mumbai" *Review of Labour*, VOL 41 No. 21 May 27- June 02.

Anuradha, G.K. Eswar Prasad, K.V. Syed Kumar (1984): "Women Bedi Workers in Vallore", *Social Action*, January-December.

Aziz, Abdul (1983): *Urban Poor and Urban Informal Sector*.

Banerjee, Nirmala (1997): "The National Accounts Statistics Methods of Assessing: The Unorganised Sector", *Margin* special Issue, Vol.30, No.1.

Been, C. and B. Sushma (2003): "Women Entreprenuers Managing a Petty Business: A study from Motivational Perspective", *Southern Economist,* May 15, pp. 5-8

Bellagio International Declaration of Street Vendors drafted by founding members from 11 countries of the international alliance of street vendors, StreetNet, at a meeting in Bellagio, Italy, 1995.

Bhadareria, Mridula (1997): *Women in India: Some Issues*, A.P.H. Publishing corporation, New Delhi, pp.113-116.

Bhatia, D.P. (1981): *Raising wage rate gap between organized and Unorganized Sector,* Indian Association of Social Science Institution. First National Conference Social Science, New Delhi, January, pp. 6-7.

Biswas, Margrate (1983): "Women work and Struggle", *Economic and political weakly,* 17th December.

Blood, R.O. and Wolfe, R.I (1958): "The Effects of wife's employment on the family power structure", *Social Forces,* 36.

Breman, J. (1976): "A Dualistic Economy", *Economic and Political Weekly.*

Census of India. *Migration* Tables, 1981.

Chowdhury, Mohd. Hedayat Ullah (2007): "Development in the Presence of Informal Sector: A Three-Sector General Equilibrium Approach", *Indian Journal of Economics,* No. 348, Vol. LXXXVIII, July, pp.115-142.

Chowdhury, Supriya Rao (2005): "Labour Activism and Women in the Unorganised Sector: Garment Export Industry in Bangalore", *Economic and Political Weekly,* Vol. XL, Nos. 22 and 23.

Connal, John and Biplab Das Gupta (1976): *Migration from Rural Areas,* Oxford University Press, Delhi, pp.38-53.

Cross, John C. Informal Politics: *Street Vendors and the State in Mexico City* (Stanford, California, Stanford University Press, 1998)

Demko, George J. and Ronald J Jueks (1980): "Population Redistribution: Problems and Policies", *Populi,* Vol. 7, No. 4.

Devi, Lalitha (1982): *Status, Employment of women in India,* B.R. Publishing Company, Delhi, p.8

Eapen, Mridul (2001): "Women in Informal Sector in Kerala-Need for Re-examination", *Economic and Political Weekly,* Vol. XXXVI, No. 26, pp. 2390-2392.

Encyclopedia Americana, America Corporation, New York, Vol. 19, 1968, p. 48.

Enmerji, Louis (1974): "A New look at some strategies for increasing productive employment in Africa", *International Labour Review,* Vol.110, No.3, September, p.202.

Frifin, K. (1974): *Land Concentration and Rural Poverty,* London, Mcmillan.

Ganguli, B.N.(1973): *Population and Development*, S. Chand and Co. Pvt. Ltd., New Delhi.

Geretz, Clifford (1963): *Peddlers and Princes: Social Change and Economic Modernization in two Indonesian Towns*, Chapter-3, Chicago and London, University of Chicago Press.

GOI (1976): *National Employment Services: Area Level Survey, Visakhapatnam*, Ministry of Labour, Directorate General of Employment and Training, New Delhi.

GOI (1995): *Economic and Social Status of Women Working India*, Labour Bureau, Ministry of Labour, Publication No.5, New Delhi.

GOI (2002): *Final Population Totals* Census 2001 paper, Register general of India.

GOI (2006): *Economic Survey* 2005-06.

Gulati, Leela (1981): *Profile in female poverty, a study of five poor working Women in Kerala*, Hindusthan publishing corporation, NewDelhi.

Gupta, O.P. (1972): "Volume, Factors and Characteristics of Migration to Urban Delhi", Indian Census Centenary Seminar, Vol.1, Office of the Registarar General of India, Ministry of Home Affairs, New Delhi, p. 69.

Handbook of Statistics, Visakhapatnam District 2000-2001, Chief Planning Officer, Visakhapatnam

Heather and Joshi (1976): *Surplus Labour and the City – A Study of Bombay*, p. 1.

Heather and Joshi (1980): "The Informal Urban Economic and its Boundaries," *Economic and Political Weekly*, 29th March.

Heather and Vijaya Joshi (1976): "Prospects case study for Employment of women in Indian cities," *Economic and Political Weekly*, Special number August.

Helen, Safa I and Vrian M Dutoit (1975): *Migration and Development*, Mouton Publishers, The Hague.

http://timesofindia.indiatimes.com/articleshow/2481744.cms

http://www.nasvinet.org/articles/articles_1.htm

ILO / UNDP (1997): Employment Mission Report on Kenya-referred to in S.V.Sethuraman's article.

ILO/ UNDP (1977): *Employment Problem in the Rural and Informal sector in Ghana*, Report of Mission Addis Ababa.

International Council on Social Welfare (): *The Urban Dead End?*, Somaiya Publications, Pvt. Ltd.

International Encyclopedia of the Social Sciences, Macmillan and Free, Press, Vol. 10, 1968.

International Labour Organization (1972): *Employment, Income and Equality, A Strategy for Increasing Productive Unemployment in Kenya*, Geneva.

Ivan, Nye I and Hoffmen 1 M (1963): *The Employed Mother in America Chicago,* Rand Mcnally and Company.

Jansen, C J. (): *"Some Sociological Aspects of Migration"*, in JA Jackson. (ed.).

Jeemol, Unni (2005): *Urban Informal Sector: Size and Income Generation Processes in Gujarat: Parts I and II* (National Council of Applied Economic Research, Reports # 2 and 3, Delhi.

Jhabvala, Renana (1997): "Policies Affecting the Unorganised Sector" *Margin* special Issue, Vol.30, No.1 (Oct-Dec. 1997).

Jhabvala, Renana and Shalini Sinha (2002): "Liberalisation and the Women Worker", *Economic and Political Weekly*, Vol. XXXVII, No. 21, pp. 2390-2392.

Kalhan, Anuradha (2007): "Shopping Malls: Social and Economic Issues, *Economic and Political Weekly*, VOL 42 No. 22 June 02 - June 08.

Kamal Nath, (1968): "Women in the working force in India", *Economic and Political Weekly,* Aug 3.

Keith, Hart J (1973): "Informal Income Opportunities and Urban Employment in Ghana", *Journal of Modern African Studies*, London.

King, Kenneth (1974): "Keny's Informal Machine Markets: A study of small scale industry in Keny's employment Artisan Society", *World Development*, March, p.30.

Kingsley, Danis (1950): *The Population of India and Pakistan*, Princeton, New Jersey.

Kusuma (1991): "Atrocities Against women", *Yojana*, Vol.35, No.22, December.

Lal Das D.K. (1985): "Sex discrimination against female workers in unorganized sector", *Indian Journal of Industrial Relations*, October.

Lee, E.S. (1975): "A Theory of Migration" in CW Kamme, Kenneth (eds), *Population Studies*, Ronald MC Nally College Pub, Co., Chicago, p.191.

Lee, Everetts (1975): *Theory of Migration*, Keneth, U.K. Kamneyer (ed.).

Lewis, W.A. (1954): "Economic Development with unlimited supply of Labour", *Manchester School of Economics and Social Studies*, May, Vol. 22, pp.139-191.

Lubell, Harold (1974): *Urban Development and Employment, The Prospects for Calcutta*, Geneva, ILO.

Lund, Francie (1998): *Women Street Traders in Urban South Africa: A Synthesis of Selected Research Findings*, Centre for Social and Development Studies, Research Report No. 15.

Mazumdar, Dipak (1975): *The Urban Informal Sector*, World Bank Staff Working Paper, No. 211, Washington.

Mazumdar, Dipak (1975): *The Urban Informal Sector*, World Bank Staff Working Paper No. 211, July, p. 59.

Mishra, Srudar (1952): "Urban Employment and Migration of Agricultural Labour in U.P.", *Rural India*, Vol.3, March.

Monohar, Murali.K (1983): "*Socio-Economic Status of Indian Women*", ALWC, Seema, Delhi.

Muzumdar, D.N. (1960): *Social Contours of an Industrial City*, Asia Publishing House, Bombay.

Muzumdar, Vina (1975): *Women in the Unorganised Sector*, paper presented at the seminar on optimum utilization of women power for development, New Delhi.

Nirpendra. K. Mishra and Ravi. S. Srivastava (2002): "Labour and Employment in the Informal Textile Industry in Knapur", *Labour and Development*, Vol. 8, No.1&2.

NSSO (1998): *Unorganized Manufacturing in India's its size, Employment and some key estimates,* Report No. 443.

Panigrahi, N.P (1989): "Gender in quality in India", *Yojana*, Vol-33, No.12, July 15.

Papola, T.S (1976): "Wage determination in the unorganized sector in urban areas a frame work for Analysis", Gujarat Economic conference paper, Gujarat Economic Association, Ahmedabad.

Papola, T.S. (1980): "Informal sector: Concept and Policy", *Economic and Political Weekly,* 3rd May.

Paulo R Souza and victor E Tokman (1976): "The Informal Urban Section in Latin America", *International Labour Review,* Vol.114, Nov-Dec, p.356.

Prof. B. SarveswaraRao and others (1970): *"A study on commercial Industrial Entrepreneurship in coastal Region Andhra Pradesh",* Andhra University, Visakhapatnam.

Pushpangadan, K. and Shanta, N. (2004): "Growth and Efficiency of the Informal Sector in India: A Non- parametric Analysis", *Labour and Development*, Vol. 10, No.1.

Ramana,K.V. and Krishna, K.S. *Structure and Working of Unorganised Sector in the Visakhapatnam City",*

Volume-I, Department of Economics, Andhra University, Visakhapatnam.

Ranade, S.N. and Ramamohanchandra (1970): *Women and Employment, Report of pilot studies conducted in Delhi and Bombay,* TATA Institute of social science, Bombay.

Ratan Khasnabis, Pranab Nag (2001): "Labour Process in the Informal Sector: A Handloom Industry in Nadia District",

Economic and Political Weekly, Vol. XXXVI, No. 52, December 29, pp. 4836 – 4845.

Rathakrishnan, L. and Sellammalle, B. (2001): "Micro-Women Entrepreneurs and Socio-Economic Empowerment: A Study", *Southern Economist,* Vol. 40, No. 8, pp. 14-16

Ratna Kumari, B. (1994): *Self employed Women in the Unorganised Sector in Visakhapatnam City,* Project Report, Centre for Women Studies, Andhra University, Visakhapatnam.

Sen Gupta, Padmini (1960): *Women Workers of India,* Asia Publishing House, Delhi.

Sen Gupta, Padmini, (1960): *Women Workers in India,* Asia publishing house, Bombay.

Sethuraman, S.V. (1976): "The Urban Informal Sector: Concept Measurement and Policy", *International Labour Review,* July- Dec, p. 69-76.

Sethuraman, S.V. (1976): The Urban Informal Sector: Concept, Measurement and Policy, *International Labour Review,* Vol. 114, No.1, July - August.

Sharan, Rekha (1980): "Working condition and job satisfaction among industrial women workers a case study of Kanpur", *Indian Journal of Industrial Relations,* April.

Sharit, K Bhowmik (2003): "National Policy for street Vendors", *Economic Political weekly,* Vol. XXXVIII, No. 16, April 19-25, pp.1543-1546.

Sharit, K Bhowmik(2005): "Street Vendors in Asia: A Review", *Review Of Labour,* VOL 40, No. 22 and 23, May 28 - June 04.

Shetty, S.L. (1997): "Inadequacy of Domestic Saving and Other Macro-economic Issues: The Unorganised Sector", *Margin* special Issue, Vol. 30, No.1, pp. 69-76.

Shram Shakti (1984): Report on work shop on the unorganized sector, Ahmedabad, *SEW.*

Standing, G. and Skdeo, F. (): Labour Migration and Development in Gayana, *International Labour Review*, Nov-Dec., Vol. 116, No.3.

Standing, Guy (1974): *A Dichotomy Model of Urban Labour Markets*, paper presented at the Research Conference on Urban Labour Markets, Geneva, September, International Institute for Labour Studies- Doc No. ULM/DP/12.

Sudha Kumari (1989) "Women workers in Unorganized Sector in India", *Yojana*, July 1-15,1989

Tapan, Neeta (1995) : "Women Labour in Unorganized Sector : Needs Reappraisal of Labour Laws", *Southern Economist* Vol. 34, No. 12, Oct. 15.

Tara Kumari. P. (1999): *Women in Urban India*, Chugh Publications, Allahabad.

Thorner, Alice and Daniel (1961): "Occupation Classification of Women Workers", *Economic and Political Weekly*.

Todaro, M.P. (1976): *International Migration in Developing Countries,* International Labour Organisation, Geneva.

United Nations Organisation (1956): *Multilingual Demographic Dictionary,* ST/SOA/SER, Population Studies, No. 29, New York.

Upreti, D.H.C. (1981): *Social Organization of Migration Group,* Himalaya Publishing House, Bombay.

Vignara, Ponna (1990): "*Women Poverty and Resources"*, Sage Publications, New Delhi.

Vinod, Anand (2004): "Informal Sector: Connotations, Characteristics and Potentials", *Indian Journal of Economics*, part-2, Vol. LXXXV.

Waite, Louise (2001): "Kerala's Informal Labour Market Interventions: from Work to Well-Being?", *Economic and Political Weekly,* Vol. XXXVI, No. 26, June 30.

Week, John (1975): "Politics for expending informal urban sector of developing Economy", *International labour Review,* Vol.111, No.1, January.

Women in India at 50 (1997): *Facts, Figures and Analysis (1947-1997) - A Comprehensive Reference Volume*, Express Publications, Modhurai Ltd, Chennai.

Women in the Urban Informal Sector, Research Study Series, 1991.

Zachariah, K.C. (1961) *A Historical Study of Internal Migration in the Indian Subcontinent* 1901-31.

Index

❑❑❑